Philosophy
for Understanding
Theology

Diogenes Allen

John Knox Press
ATLANTA

Library of Congress Cataloging in Publication Data

Allen, Diogenes.
    Philosophy for understanding theology.

    Bibliography: p.
    Includes index.
    1. Philosophical theology.   2. Philosophy–History.
3. Christianity–Philosophy.   I. Title.
BT40.A44   1985   230'.01   84-48510
ISBN 0-8042-0688-0 (pbk.)

© copyright John Knox Press 1985
10 9 8 7 6 5 4 3 2 1
Published simultaneously by SCM Press Ltd, in Great Britain
and by John Knox Press in the United States of America, 1985
Printed in the United States of America
John Knox Press
Atlanta, Georgia 30365

Preface

A New Approach

Everyone needs to know some philosophy in order to understand the major doctrines of Christianity or to read a great theologian intelligently. But how is a person to learn the philosophy needed to understand theology?

The usual college or seminary course in philosophy and the usual book that surveys the history of philosophy do not give nearly enough help. The material is selected on the basis of what is important for *philosophy*, not what is important for *theology*. Some of the material selected on that basis is indeed relevant for theological understanding, but it usually takes *several* courses and a number of books on philosophy before a person is exposed to enough philosophical material that is directly relevant and essential for theology.

Even then its theological relevance is often not made explicit, so that it remains buried in and unrecognized amongst material of little direct significance for theology. Not even a course in the philosophy of religion, which among all the subdivisions of philosophy comes closest to theology, provides what one needs. The proofs of God's existence, the problem of evil, and the nature of religious language— the most frequently discussed topics in philosophy of religion—are only of limited value because they do not supply a sufficient range of basic philosophical concepts and distinctions which the beginner in theology needs. Even an experienced theologian finds connections with the philosophy of religion only at the periphery of theology.

Some seminaries recognize that their students need to know some philosophy. But in their efforts to meet the need, they run up against the hard fact that the discipline of philosophy today, especially in the English-speaking world, is so remote from theology that it takes prolonged study of philosophy before one's theological understanding is enhanced to a significant degree. In most seminaries the many demands on faculty and resources simply preclude provision for an extensive study of philosophy in its normal format by very many, if any, of their students. Few seminary students take more than one course of philosophy in seminary or in their college days, and most take none. Thus it is not surprising that students so often are frustrated when they begin their study of theology. They lack one of the essential prerequisites. Many of them, when they begin to realize that they need some philosophy, turn to the only available resource: a course on philosophy or a book on the history of philosophy which has not been designed to meet their needs. No wonder Tertullian's well-known rhetorical question, "What has Athens to do with Jerusalem?" is so popular with students. They have not been shown that philosophical knowledge enables one to appreciate more deeply the meaning of virtually every major doctrinal formulation and every major theologian. They feel they have tried philosophy and found it of little help; so they go their way, forfeiting the opportunity for a more fruitful engagement with theology.

This book aims to give a person the philosophy needed to understand Christian theology better because often the lack of knowledge of some key philosophic term or concept impedes significant understanding of a vital issue. It may appear pretentious to have such a high aim, but the goal is realistic because the approach used in the design of this book is precisely the opposite of the prevalent one. Instead of a brief presentation of philosophical thought which has been selected on the basis of what is important for the development of the subject of philosophy and on the basis of what philosophers themselves find important and interesting, I have made my selection from the mass of philosophical material by first looking at *theologians*. I have determined from a study of their works what philosophy influenced them and what philosophical concepts and terms they use. It is what theologians do that determines what I present and how I present it.

This means that not only can much of what the usual histories of philosophy include be omitted, but the theological relevance of the philosophical material selected can be made explicit and evident.

This allows for economy in presentation and gives the reader precisely what is needed. It also permits me to emphasize and highlight some things in philosophy, such as Plato's *Timaeus*, which are either ignored or treated slightly, except in advanced courses in philosophy, because they do not speak to contemporary philosophical interests. All too often such material is of fundamental importance for the understanding of Christian doctrine and theology. By making the principle of selection what matters for theology rather than what matters for philosophy, I aim to put the reader in a position to gain a large return for the time and effort expended.

This book is not a conventional history of philosophy from Plato to the present, not only because my approach is different as I have explained, but also because in making my selection my eye has been on what a philosopher has said which has significantly influenced Christian theology on *a few major doctrines*. For the most part it has been for their influence on a Christian understanding of God, Christ, and human beings—their nature, destiny, and power of reason. This results in treating, for example, Plato's *Timaeus* not only with more emphasis than normal surveys but also treating it first in my presentation of Plato, even though it is among his later dialogues. I also depart from strict philosophical sequence in the interest of theology by not treating Aristotle until I come to the medieval theologians (except for one work on logic), even though Aristotle is an ancient philosopher. Likewise I treat process thought in conjunction with the medievals and Aristotle even though it is a twentieth century movement. This is because Aristotle had very little influence on theology until the Middle Ages, and process thought insofar as it is a philosophy needed to understand theology is most easily understood in relation to Aristotle and medieval theologians.

From time to time I illustrate the way in which a knowledge of the philosophy I have covered enables one to understand a particular theologian or doctrine. For example, I note how a knowledge of Aristotle's *Categories* enables us to see how Gregory of Nyssa in writing on the Trinity rose above the philosophical conceptuality of his day. A person cannot recognize that achievement without a knowledge of Aristotle's *Categories*. I hope that by putting some of the philosophical material covered into action in this way that the reader will not only gain a better grasp of it but will realize its value for theology as well.

I do not, of course, pretend that this book will give a person the depth and mastery which can only come from prolonged study of primary and secondary sources in philosophy. But I do claim that given the very serious constraints on today's curriculum and staffing, it can give a student a sound foundation on which to build and can also significantly reduce the frustration now so widely felt by those who begin the study of theology without the prerequisite understanding of philosophy needed to appreciate it.

As a seminary teacher for nearly twenty years and as one who was rigorously trained as a purist in philosophy, I have tried many different ways to overcome this educational problem. The approach used in this book has in my experience proven to be the most economical and fruitful way to deal with it.

In a few places I have not sought to use inclusive language because I preferred to keep the examples used by the authors whose ideas I was explaining. I hope this does not prove an obstacle to anyone.

Numbers in parentheses after quotations refer to the pagination to be found on the margins of most texts of Plato, Aristotle, and Kant. This will enable one to find quoted passages easily even should one's editions of texts be different from those I have used.

For James I. McCord
Chancellor, Center of Theological Inquiry
Princeton, NJ

Acknowledgments

I am deeply grateful for the many helpful suggestions made by Jesse de Boer, professor emeritus, University of Kentucky, my first philosophy teacher, who read virtually the entire text, to David Burrell, C.S.C., University of Notre Dame, for his careful reading of chapter six on Thomas Aquinas, and to my colleague E. David Willis, Hodge Professor of Systematic Theology, Princeton Theological Seminary, for reading the text and for his encouragement. None is, of course, to be held responsible for what appears in this book.

Other books by Diogenes Allen:

The Reasonableness of Faith

Finding Our Father

Between Two Worlds

Traces of God in a Frequently Hostile World

Three Outsiders: Pascal, Kierkegaard, and Simone Weil

Mechanical Explanations and the Ultimate Origin of the Universe According to Leibniz

Leibniz's Theodicy (edited and abridged)

Contents

Introduction

The Foundation of
Christian Theology:
The World Was Created

The two main sources of Christian theology are the Bible and hellenic culture, especially Greek philosophy. The biblical view of creation is so familiar to us that its role as the foundation of all Christian theology may not be apparent. It differs in crucial respects from the views of all the ancient philosophers. The Genesis stories of creation make it clear that the world has a *beginning*. Because it has a beginning, it is not eternal. This means it is not ultimate. God, its Maker, who is without beginning or end, is ultimate.

This is utterly different from Aristotle's view. For him the universe had no beginning. It has always existed and always will exist. Aristotle's first cause or prime mover (which he also called the unmoved mover) is the most excellent and exalted being in the universe, but it is indeed just that, a being which is in, or a part of, the universe. Its existence is inferred from the motions we observe on earth and in the heavens. We see here two fundamental ways in which Aristotle differs from the apparently simple story of Genesis: *ontologically* and *epistemologically*. To show the extent of these differences, let me explain the meaning of these two philosophical terms.

First, look at a person; then, think about a fictional person. The two differ from each other ontologically. Their status in reality differs. The relationship between such things as actual persons and fictional persons is part of the academic discipline of ontology (from the Greek word *ontos*, or being). Whenever we assume or judge that a thing is a particular kind of reality—for example, that what we see floating on a pond is a decoy duck rather than a real duck, but nonetheless a decoy duck and not a hallucination—we are making ontological distinctions. Real ducks and decoy ducks are different kinds of reality, but even decoy ducks though not real ducks are nonetheless more real than hallucinations. Or consider the ontological difference between colors and tables. Tables are the sort of thing which may be colored, but colors are not the sort of thing which may be "tabled." Colors are properties of such things as tables, but tables are not properties at all, and so they are not properties of colors. The distinction between tables and colors is also an ontological distinction. To make or to assume ontological distinctions does not mean that we are thereby engaged in the *discipline* of ontology. Rather it is the other way around. The discipline presupposes that we make ontological distinctions.

Likewise in Genesis where it is said that in the beginning God made the heavens and the earth, an ontological distinction is made between God and the universe, even though the writer of Genesis is not a practitioner of the discipline of ontology. The cosmos (an ordered world) is said to have a beginning, not to be eternal, and hence not to be ultimate. God is distinguished from the universe. God has no beginning but is everlasting. As Creator of the universe, God is not part of the universe nor is it a part of God. Creation depends on God for its existence. The ontological status of the universe (the kind of reality it is) is distinguished from the ontological status of God. These ontological distinctions do not mean that Genesis (and the rest of Scripture whose meaning we have assumed in our interpretation of Genesis) is engaged in the practice of the discipline of ontology. We shall now see this by showing that the *epistemological* basis of its claim differs from the epistemological basis of the claims of Aristotle, who does practice the discipline of ontology.

Every claim we make has some basis or ground (unless it is groundless, and we tend to dismiss groundless claims). The ground of a claim may be something we see or hear. The discipline which makes a study of the kinds of grounds on which we make claims and which studies the relationship between different kinds of grounds is called epistemology (from the Greek *episteme*, knowledge), or theory of knowledge.

The bases of the claims Genesis and Aristotle make are radically different. Aristotle is concerned to account for the order of the world we perceive. Nothing is asserted or postulated which is not needed to account for its order. It never occurred to Aristotle, one of the greatest minds in history, to raise the question of why we have a world at all rather than nothing. He takes the world's existence for granted. For him its existence is in no way problematic. Accordingly, what concerned him was to discover the principles of the world's operation. This involved an investigation of the various kinds of beings in the universe (hence the practice of the discipline of ontology), and it led him to infer that there is a first unmoved mover as the highest and most exalted kind of being. The grounds for the claim that there is an unmoved mover are a series of intricate distinctions and arguments, but finally all the reasoning rests on the epistemological principle: we assert only what must be asserted to account for the operations of the world. A search for the principles of the world's operations is what *motivates* Aristotle. What *validates* the claims he makes is their success in explaining its operations. Priestly oracles and poetry allegedly written under divine inspiration are dismissed as a basis for making claims about the world's operations.

In contrast to Aristotle, the claims made by Genesis and the rest of the Scriptures of ancient Israel do not spring from a desire to discover the principles of nature's operation, nor even to account for the existence of the universe. Belief in a Creator is not affirmed by the ancient Israelites because they desire to explain the world's existence and order. Its existence and order do not form the grounds for their belief in God. On the contrary, they believed in God because they believed God's self-revelation, first to Abraham, the founder of their race, and then to other patriarchs, such as Isaac and Jacob, and to the prophets. Their belief in the divine is a *response* to God's initiative, rather than the result of their investigations of nature's order and origin. Thus not only is the unmoved mover of Aristotle *part* of the world, its top story, so to speak, and thus ontologically of a radically different status than the Jewish Maker of the universe, but the *grounds* for his claim that there is an unmoved mover is *epistemologically* different from the grounds for the Jewish claim that there is a Creator.

From what we have said so far, there would seem to be ample justification for Tertullian's dismissive remark, "What has Athens to do with Jerusalem?" But this is not so. However much the ancient Israelites may have been lacking in curiosity concerning the principles of nature in comparison to the ancient Greek philosophers, Christian theology is nonetheless inherently hellenic. I use the word "hellenic" instead of "Greek" to refer to the spread of Greek culture and ways of thinking to non-Greek peoples, an influence which received powerful impetus from the conquests of Alexander the Great and Rome. Christian theology is inherently hellenic because it could not exist as a *discipline* without the kind of intellectual curiosity which was unique to ancient Greece. The ancient Egyptians said that the Greeks were like children because they were always asking "Why?" It is not that other ancient peoples including the Israelites, did not ask for the whys and wherefores of many things. It is rather that in ancient Greece the practice became a matter of principle. The Greeks did not think of every significant question that has ever been raised, but they asked questions persistently and systematically as a deliberate program until they developed the very idea of disciplines—areas of *theoretical* knowledge defined by principles and investigated by appropriate methods of inquiry. A practical question, such as the need to determine the boundaries of a piece of property may start an investigation, but the various rules of thumb concerning the relation of lines to angles were not allowed to remain just rules of thumb even though they were perfectly satisfactory for all practical purposes. They were pushed until the theoretical science of geometry was created, a discipline that continues to yield new knowledge today. As a result of this particular attitude, which led to the very notion of a "discipline," the ancient Greeks became the founders of many of our traditional disciplines, including theology itself. Let me explain.

In the Old Testament we find many instances of persistent questioning and inquiry, such as, Why do the righteous suffer and the wicked prosper? This arises out of the Israelites' practical concern for the justice of God, and their desire for deliverance from oppression. It does not lead to a theoretical discipline. In addition, the range of their questions is much more limited than that of the ancient Greek philosophers, who sometimes became tiresome to the average Greek because of their predilection for theoretical questions and disputes.

This systematic search for reasons, or for the *logos* for anything and everything, is something we today take for granted. It is part of our mental make-up. We do it automatically. We share with the ancient Greeks a desire to push back the domain of the unknown and to unveil all mysteries, and we share with them the concept of *disciplines*, which have their distinctive principles and methods of inquiry. Likewise it was part of the mental make-up of the early Church Fathers of Christianity who fashioned Christian doctrines in a decisive way in the first centuries.

The early Church Fathers, as we shall see, sought to retain a proper sense of mystery, but they too were persistent in asking of the revealed truth, "How is that so?" Their minds were hellenic to that extent, and because they were hellenic, they created the *discipline* of theology. It was thus much more than the use of particular Greek philosophical concepts that constitutes the hellenic influence on Christianity. An essential part is a mental make-up, an attitude of mind, an outlook that prizes coherence, that presses as a matter of principle the questions, "Why and how is that so?" that searches for principles to organize diverse things, and that seeks to discover the basis or ground for every claim that is made. There would have been no such discipline as Christian theology without the Bible and without a believing community. But likewise we would not have the discipline of theology without the hellenic attitude in Christians that leads them to press questions about the Bible and the relations of the Bible to other knowledge. Thus when people call for purging Greek philosophy from Christian theology, unless they are referring to specific ideas or concepts, they are really calling for the end of the discipline of theology itself, though they may not realize it.

We ourselves are, of course, concerned here largely to explain the philosophical concepts and ideas which influenced Christian theology and which we need in order to study and understand theology better. But we shall also have to come to terms with the mental attitude which created the discipline of theology. For a mind that has the attitude which is constitutive of the very being of theology as a discipline must be tempered with another fact. It must recognize that however much it may want complete comprehension, the ontological status of deity is such that God exceeds our comprehension.

This brings us to a major and controversial issue in theology, the possibility of natural theology. Here we can see the effect of the ontological status of God on epistemology, that is, the effect of the *kind* of being we are dealing with in theology on what we can hope to understand and on the nature of the ground or basis of the claims we make.

We have pointed out that the ancient Israelites claimed that their knowledge of God was the result of God's initiative. They knew God because of God's self-revelation to them. This raises the question, "Could God ever have been known apart from such divine initiative? Had God not chosen self-revelation to Israel, would Israel or anyone else ever have realized that deity existed?" Or let us put it another way, "Is there anything about the created universe, its order and its very existence, which gives us a basis to claim that it has a Creator?"

This question forms the basis for the subdivision in theology called natural theology. It is a major place where philosophy of religion intersects theology. Philosophies of religion examine what the sheer existence of the universe entails, that is, what it forces us to conclude, and likewise what its order entails. Some theologians do the same. In other words, the two disciplines examine the traditional proofs for God's existence to see whether from the bare existence of the world or from its order we can know that there is a God.

Philosophers of religion are concerned to determined the validity of the traditional proofs (does the conclusion "God exists" logically follow from the premises?) and the truth of the premises from which the conclusion is said to follow. This has generated a substantial body of literature, and it takes about half a semester of a college course to survey its high points. Protestant theologians have often objected to natural theology. Even should some of the proofs of God's existence be sound, they claim that the "god" whose existence is demonstrated is not the Christian God. That god is just the top story of the universe (Aristotle's unmoved mover) or some part of the universe. Whether natural theology is to be dismissed and why is a major area of investigation in Christian theology. Roman Catholic theologians who defend natural theology are more than ready to agree that there are significant differences between what we can know of God by means of natural theology and what we know of God by revelation. How what we know by each of these two ways is to be related is also a major area of investigation in theology.

Many Protestant and Roman Catholic theologians, however, do not consider the various proofs of God's existence from the order and existence of the world as *rigorous* demonstrations, or proofs in the technical sense. They believe that the mind can nonetheless in some fashion apprehend God apart from special revelation, as the biblical witness is called. General revelation is possible because the created world bears some marks of its dependence on God for its existence and order. Such apprehension is not limited to what we can gain from the sheer existence and order of nature. Human nature as part of the creation also bears marks of its dependence on God.

This position raises several questions. If the created world bears marks of its dependence on God, are those marks sufficient to give a person who recognizes them salvation, or a "saving knowledge" as it is called, or do they simply give knowledge of God's existence in the same way as we have knowledge of anything else which exists, a sheer fact without any power to redeem us and regenerate our will? There is also much discussion about what value such knowledge has as a preparation for receiving special revelation or as confirming it. Granted that the created world bears marks of its dependence on God, a major issue in this discussion is how clear and persuasive the marks are. Are they so strong that it would be irrational not to believe that there is a God? Are they merely such that they give a person who *already* believes in God because of special revelation, additional grounds?

Another issue which leads to division among theologians, and even denominations, is the issue of the effects of sin on us. Luther and Calvin believe that original sin has so perverted our reason as well as our will that without the grace of God we cannot respond with faith to special revelation, and without that response we are unable to see the marks of God on creation. With such a view it does not matter how clear and strong the marks are; apart from special revelation they are inoperative.

In today's crowded seminary curriculum, natural theology tends to be identified by many students and clergy with the rigorous proofs of God's existence. But it should be clear from what we have just seen that to dismiss the traditional proofs because they fail to be rigorous demonstrations is not to have dismissed the issue of general revelation. The issue of what marks the universe bears of its Maker's hand and our ability to recognize them is part of natural theology too. It is not settled by pointing out that the biblical God is neither the top story of the universe, nor some philosophical abstraction, the end product of the traditional proofs of God's existence from the order and the existence of the world.

Another confusion frequently occurs among students and clergy. Natural theology, either in the sense of rigorous proofs or in the sense of traces of God in the universe, is not to be identified with all of philosophy. Nearly all Protestant students and clergy have heard that Karl Barth rejected natural theology. They then mistakenly think that they have his support for their own rejection of all philosophy as having no theological significance. But in fact Barth did not reject philosophy wholesale with his rejection of natural theology. Not only was Barth very sophisticated philosophically, but he employed reinterpreted philosophical concepts in his theological work very much as did the early Church Fathers. He and they were guided by and rooted in theological convictions, and frequently used reshaped philosophical terminology and views for their own theological purposes. In an essay written to honor his brother Heinrich, who was a philosopher, Barth explicitly distinguished between natural theology and philosophy. He recognized the necessity and value of philosophy, even though it is of limited value, he argued, from the perspective of a Christian believer. It is, he argued, "the wisdom of this world"; it is of this world in the biblical sense, but nonetheless it is wisdom. Hard-pressed students and clergy, confused by the many subjects and disciplines they must study today, are only too glad to jettison philosophy in order to lighten their burden. But they cannot do so with the blessing of Karl Barth. He does not spare them the need to wrestle with philosophy.

So far we have examined only one major aspect of the issue of our knowledge of God as it arises from the theological belief that the world is created, and hence that God as Creator is not a part of the universe. The other aspect is that we do not know what God is in essence. That essence, God's very being, is unknowable. This follows from the Christian conception of creation and is much more profound and far-reaching than what we have so far indicated. God the Creator is ontologically not part of the world, nor is the world part of God. There is a distinction between God and the world which is more fundamental than any distinction between any two things which are both part of the world. However great the ontological difference may be between things that are part of the world, it is dwarfed in comparison to the ontological difference that exists between the Creator and creatures.

The difference between Creator and creature is sometimes expressed in terms of the distinction between necessary and contingent beings. The Genesis story of creation says that the world began. Things which are contingent begin and end; a necessary being is everlasting. Particular beings, such as leaves and trees, which start and end in the created universe may be contrasted to matter and energy which, according to our science, are conserved in all transformations. But the contrast between existing things in the universe, such as leaves and trees on the one hand, and matter and energy on the other, is not as fundamental as that between God and the universe. Matter and energy, like leaves and trees, are contingent. Even though they are conserved in all transformations of various things within the universe, they and indeed the entire universe *began*, and they and it may end, should God so will. Only God is everlasting, and is so by divine nature. Matter and energy depend on God for their creation and continued existence.

The ontological difference between God, who is inherently everlasting, and all else, which is contingent, is more fully expressed by the notion that God, who created the universe, created it *freely*. God did not have to create the universe. God felt no external or internal compulsion to create. On the one hand, since God is the source of everything, nothing would be external to God prior to creation to compel God to create. There would be an internal compulsion were God inherently unstable so that a creation might result from a pressure of forces within which compel God to create, a belief held as we shall see, by Plotinus. There could also be internal compulsion if God were in want or lacking completeness. God then might create a world so that God could be enriched with what is not divine. But the God of the Bible acts *freely* and thus is inherently stable and inherently full, complete, or perfect. The act of creation is thus an act of sheer generosity.

God's freedom in creation is the reason we view creation as an act of sheer generosity and also the reason God is unknowable in essence or being. Since the world *began* and since God made it *freely*, God can exist without a world. The *relation* between God and the world (the relation of Creator and creature) is less basic than one of the terms of the relation, namely God. In other words, God is more fundamental than the relation between God and the world. The Godhead in itself—in its very being or essence—is without a relation to the world, i.e., to anything outside itself. God fully establishes a relation by the act of creation itself. So God is not more with a world than without a world. God is not incomplete without a world. A God who creates freely is full, complete, and perfect, and so is not made more by creating nor less by not creating. The world plus God is not more than God alone. God less the world is not less than God alone. However paradoxical this may appear at first sight, it follows directly from the claim that the world began and that God created it freely. However harsh it may appear to say that God does not need a world, it is only because God does not need a world that we can say that the existence of the world is the result of an act of sheer generosity or grace. So it does not mean that God is not concerned about us, but quite the contrary.

A being who is complete in essence, who is inexhaustibly rich, lacking nothing, is beyond our comprehension. The world consists of beings which we classify according to their likenesses and differences into various kinds of beings. But God is not a being within the world. Deity is not one among other beings but the source of all other beings. Thus concepts by which we understand various kinds of things within the world do not enable us to comprehend God because God does not fall under any classification or genus within which we place the various beings of which the world consists. Nonetheless, we have some understanding of God. Because the world begins and God does not, and because God makes the world freely, God is rich and full. Divine perfection is not according to some notion of perfection which we gain by comparing created beings with each other. Rather we understand *that* God is perfect (complete and full) because God created the world freely, and we can understand that even though we do not *comprehend* the perfection of divine being. It is divine action that establishes a relation in which we have some knowledge of God. We know that God is full and complete from the act of creation. But we do not comprehend that fullness or completeness, that is, what God is in essence, apart from the act whereby God establishes a relation. We know God, therefore, not in essence but only in relation to us. It is because God makes a world and relates to us in other ways that we gain some understanding of deity.

God is related to us in two major ways. God is related to the world as Creator and as one self-revealed to the people of ancient Israel and to the new Israel, the Christian church. Whether God can be known from the existence and order of the world, i.e., apart from divine initiative, does not affect the fact that God is related to the universe as Creator. However much theologians differ over natural theology, they all agree that God is the Creator and that the existence and order of the universe show that God is generous. Without being able to comprehend divine being, we know from the act of creation *that* God is generous, and we know something of the immensity of divine generosity from the nature of the world. That gift does not, however, exhaust the extent of God's generosity. We learn this from the second way God is related to us, namely through the call of the people of Israel to a specific mission and through the incarnation. In creation God gave the physical universe its nature, and to human beings God gave their kind of life. But with the acts of calling Israel and becoming incarnate for our sakes, we learn that God created us in order to have a life with God, indeed that we are ultimately to share the divine life, which is beyond our mode of existence. Divine generosity is thus greater than we could realize simply from God's being related to us as Creator. Only in seeing

God as Redeemer, indeed as Redeemer in Christ do we realize the even greater depths of divine generosity.

However immense the generosity expressed by God as Creator and incarnate Redeemer, the inexhaustible source from which that generosity springs is beyond our comprehension. We may become aware *that* God is generous and know a good deal about the nature of that generosity from God's relations to us as Creator and incarnate Redeemer, but this is not to comprehend God as an inexhaustible source of generosity. Those relations to us do not and cannot reveal the divine essence to us; for creation is an *effect* of God's. The incarnation and our reception of the new life which comes from it, are also results of God's action. All these effects of God do not exhaust the magnitude of their source. An effect, however great, cannot reveal the full extent or nature of an inexhaustible source. So even in the acts of creation and redemption, God's essential nature or being is unknowable. Even though that essential nature is present, as it is uniquely in the incarnation, we cannot fully comprehend it. God's actions never exhaust the divine nature, and we know God only as God acts or relates to us.

This essential unknowability of God is not a reason to lament. It is rather a reason to rejoice that what we are in contact with is inexhaustibly great, rich, and full. Were we able to get formulations about God which were fully comprehensible, then we would know that they were incorrect. The essential unknowability of God thus springs from God's inherent nature—its inexhaustible fullness—and not simply from the *specific* limitations of our faculties. All creatures, however exalted in being, are unable to comprehend God. Only God, who is infinite, can comprehend God's own inexhaustible being.

Let us pursue a little further the epistemological implications which arise from the radical ontological difference between God and creation. As we have seen, it implies that the reality with which we deal transcends our intellectual ability to comprehend it fully. This should prepare us to recognize as we examine the philosophical concepts employed by theologians, that they themselves recognized the essential mystery of God. For them the mystery of God is not just one theological doctrine to be set alongside others. Rather mystery penetrates and is part of *every* doctrine about God. This implies, for one thing, that our language about God can never be reduced to the discourse we employ to talk about created realities. It also means that we frequently will be able to understand *that* we are to say certain things about God, for example, that God is triune, without being able fully to comprehend the nature of that unity. That is, we are able to see *that* Father, Son, and Holy Spirit are one God without being able to understand *how* they are one God. Likewise we shall be able to understand why it is true to say *that* Jesus is both God and human without being able to comprehend fully *how* he is God and human. As we have said, should God indeed be the Creator, and have created freely, a formula which we do comprehend fully is a sure indication that it is inadequate. We shall see when we come to the philosophical language employed in the statement of the crucial doctrines of the Trinity and the person of Christ, how important it is to remember that the God of whom we are speaking is the Creator, whose full nature is beyond our comprehension so that even when God is self-revealed, we still do not and cannot comprehend God fully. This conviction that the Creator is ontologically distinct from all creatures prevented philosophical concepts from determining the theological formulations of the early church. This is not to say the early Fathers were not influenced by philosophical concepts in their formulations of doctrine or that philosophical concepts have not shaped these formulations.

One need not feel threatened by the necessary limitations in our knowledge of God. It does not mean that we are totally in the dark. For even with created things, we can understand a great deal without having full comprehension of them. We can see quite a lot by means of light and know many of its properties without being able fully to comprehend *what* light is. It has both particle and wave properties, and yet nothing can be both a wave and a particle. And so we do not know precisely what it is, and yet we are not without reliable knowledge about some of its paradoxical properties. So too with God, who is in principle beyond a creature's full comprehension. We may see by the "light" God has given us and have quite reliable knowledge about God, without a full comprehension of the divine nature. A sound understanding of what God has shown us of God's nature enables us to recognize and practice theology as reflection on the mystery of God made manifest in creation and revelation.

This Introduction is thus an introduction in two senses. It not only stands at the start of the book to lead the reader into a study of the philosophical concepts which are needed for a better understanding of theology, but it is also intended as a companion which is to accompany the reader as I present various philosophical concepts and their use by theologians. It is to remind the reader that the explorations and formulations of theologians who know their business are always conducted in the light of the biblical conviction that there is a fundamental distinction between God and creatures. God's ontological uniqueness limits our understanding of God, and the essential hiddenness of the divine permeates all our theological reflection and formulations of doctrine.

1

Plato:
The World Is the Handiwork of a Mind

For Plato as well as for Christians, the world had a beginning. This may seem astounding after the Introduction in which I said that the Christian view of creation is the foundation of Christian theology. But Plato also astounded the Apologists and the early Church Fathers. When they encountered Plato's creation story in the *Timaeus,* they said that Plato either had read Moses (whom they supposed had written Genesis) or he had received his knowledge by divine revelation. They did not feel threatened by Plato, as contemporary Protestants are when they encounter parallels to the Bible in non-Christian writers. On the contrary the early Christian thinkers were delighted to find a witness to Christian truth among the Greeks. In their defense of Christianity against the attacks of pagan writers, the Apologists and early Church Fathers often cited the correspondence between Christian teaching and Plato as a reason why pagans should give credence to Christian claims.

They were, of course, well aware of the differences between Plato's creation story and Genesis, and indeed aware of many discrepancies between other parts of his philosophy and Christianity. Nonetheless, they deeply respected the merits of the *Timaeus* and were significantly influenced by it. And so, let us look at the main elements of Plato's story of the creation of the world, and then we shall point out its far-reaching influence on Christian theology. We shall see that his story of the beginning of the visible world is probably not really a story of a beginning at all, and that in other crucial respects it differs from the Christian story of creation.

The *Timaeus* was a very mature dialogue, written some years after he wrote the *Republic,* but it opens as though the discussion which made up the *Republic* had taken place only the day before. After Socrates has summarized roughly the first half of the *Republic* for his companions, Critias says that such an ideal city as Socrates had described once actually existed. Its history was still known among the priests of Egypt. Critias proposes that before he tells them the story, Timaeus, an astronomer, describe for them the generation of the natural world, going down to the generation of human beings. Then with this setting, he, Critias, will take the city Socrates described in the *Republic* as an ideal and show it in actual operation, as recorded by the Egyptian priests.

Critias' introduction of Timaeus' long, virtually uninterrupted discourse on the creation of the visible world, reflects Plato's desire to link the morality of the *Republic* with the order of the natural world. In the *Republic* the main virtues of an individual person—courage, temperance, wisdom, and justice—are defined by means of an analogy to the virtues of a rationally organized city-state. On the grounds that the society is larger than the individual and thus the detection of the virtues easier in what is larger than in what is smaller, Socrates constructed an ideal city-state before proceeding to define the virtues of the individual. The order of the ideal city-state provided the pattern for determining the proper order of virtues of the individual person. Now in the *Timaeus* the organization of the physical universe is described as also rationally organized, so that the rationally organized city-state and its virtuous citizen have the rational order of the natural world for their foundation. True morality is thus not the product of convention or arbitrary enactment of human will, but the virtuous individual is a counterpart in miniature of the order and harmony of the cosmos. The properly ordered individual soul is thus a miniature of the properly ordered city-state, and both of these are images or reflections of the order of nature. This hierarchical pattern of organizations at different levels has a still higher level, the world of eternal Forms on which the physical universe is modeled, as we shall see in the *Timaeus.*

This conviction of a hierarchy with each level analogous to every other level, in one form or another, became the basis of natural law—of living in accord with nature—and has deeply influenced Christian conceptions of morality, society, and politics. It is the rejection of a hierarchy of value by modern science in the seventeenth century which led to the need to find new foundations for society, the state, and morality in the modern period. We shall go into this later, but I wanted to point out this conviction of a hierarchy's presence in the opening of the *Timaeus* because, unlike nearly all of Aristotle, this dialogue is known by theologians throughout the early centuries of the Christian era and right through the Dark Ages.

After this important preliminary, the floor is given to Timaeus who proceeds to describe the creation of the visible world. He asks rhetorically, "What is that which always is and has no becoming?" (28).* The contrast between what is unchanging or "being" on the one hand and "becoming" on the other is fundamental to Greek philosophy. It is a contrast between what is fundamental, primary, or ultimate and what is dependent and derivative. Timaeus' question is thus a request for what is ultimate.

What we perceive by our senses cannot be described as always being with no becoming. Since the world as a whole is visible and tangible, that is, perceived by the senses, it cannot be fundamental. But what is its cause? Here Timaeus makes a cryptic remark which reverberated powerfully in the Christian reader's ear. "The father and maker of all this universe is past finding out, and even if we found him, to tell of him to all men would be impossible" (28c). Timaeus does not pursue this any further, and he develops another line of thought. An idea or concept never changes. It comes into people's minds at times and at other times is not thought about, but the idea or concept itself is not born nor does it decay. The number two, for example, is not born, nor made, and it will not die or rot. It is always the same. The only thing that is unchanging is what is graspable by the intellect. The physical universe by contrast is always changing. Nonetheless it is marvelously organized and stable in its motions. It must therefore be the result of intelligence and

---

* Most quotations are from *The Collected Dialogues of Plato,* ed. by Edith Hamilton and Huntington Coerns, Bollingen Series LXX (Princeton, N.J.: Princeton University Press, 1961).

goodness, and its order and stability the result of being a copy of something which is unchanging, an ideal pattern which is graspable by the intellect. This pattern is Plato's famous world of Forms. So although the father of all things is beyond us, the world's order is such that it must have a cause. Its order must be the result of some intelligence. We may also say that this cause must be good and free of jealousy because the world is so harmoniously ordered. The motive in making the universe must have been to make it as orderly as possible, both as a whole and in every detail (33), so that it is a series of suborders fitting into larger and larger wholes. Timaeus then proceeds to give in great and, to us today, boring detail the structure of the world and its inhabitants, on the basis of a combination of mathematical ratios and geometric shapes, down to the very bones, skin, hair, and nails of the human body.

It is clear that in this creation story there is no creation *ex nihilo*. It is a story of order being brought to preexisting material. Genesis 1 itself may also be a story of order being brought out of chaos. But taken in conjunction with the rest of the Old Testament and the New Testament, it is clear that the world—matter, space, and time—are creatures of God. The early church was immediately aware of this difference between Plato and the Bible.

In Plato's account, matter places limitations on the demiurge or craftsman who brings order out of chaos—that is, on that which tries to copy the world of Forms as nearly as possible. In a famous passage Plato writes, "Mind, the ruling power, persuaded necessity to bring the greater part of created things to perfection. ... But if a person will truly tell of the way in which the work was accomplished, he must include the variable cause as well, and explain its influence" (48a).

There is inherent in matter itself its own motions, which are irrational ("variable"). This necessity in matter is also referred to by Plato as "chance" or "irrationality" because it is purposeless. Plato says that "mind persuades necessity" by the imposition of order on its motions. Order is brought about by introducing "limits" on its motions, directing them purposively. This is what turns chaos into a cosmos, or chaos into orderly (predictable) motion. But reason or mind (the craftsman) can never fully reduce matter to perfect order.

The "variable cause"—matter's inherent irrationality—cannot be completely overcome. The sensible world is forever inferior to the ideal because it is in motion; furthermore its orderly motion is only an image of the unchangeable reality and its unruly motion is not fully reducible to order. The visible world is the best possible, but not the perfect, image of the world of Forms.

Clearly, for Plato this world is good, even though it is not perfect. (This is true of the Bible as well: the universe is good, indeed very good, but even before the Fall, it is not said to be perfect.) But equally clearly, the disorderly element of blind necessity is never completely mastered by the mind which designed the world, and the world soul which governs its motions in the heavens. So the evils and imperfections of the physical world are the result of matter. (The Bible, on the other hand, affirms the goodness of the *material* world.) That matter is evil does not take on really serious proportions, however, until we introduce Plato's understanding of the nature and destiny of the soul. The soul has fallen into a sensible world, and it must return to the supersensible world if it is to attain its proper destiny. The sensible world with its capacity to gratify our sensuous desires must be shunned, or the soul will be diverted from its destiny. But as far as the physical universe itself is concerned, matter's resistance to being reduced to perfect order does not prevent the world from being fair and beautiful (29 and 30). The physical universe in its proper place and station is good and indeed glorious. Plato's view is by no means that of Genesis, but it is not the total rejection of the world by the Gnostics and Manichaeans. We should not confuse Plato's attitude to the physical universe, however much he stresses the need to transcend it and the body, with views which totally reject it, as superficial Christian writers so often do. Nor should we contrast "the Greeks" to "the Hebrews," identifying Plato with all Greek thought, and saying the Greeks reject the body and the Hebrews affirm it. After all, the ancient Greeks have given us sculptures of the human body which have yet to be surpassed.

The Platonic story of the origin of the cosmos differs from the Christian view not only because it takes matter as given, but because there is a pattern from which the cosmos is copied. Plato's view of Forms is one of the most difficult parts of his philosophy to understand, but for the moment let us only deal with one widespread but erroneous view. Plato's Forms are not *duplicates* of sensible things. The Form of beds is not itself a bed which is of no particular size or shape or material. It would be a pretty absurd perfect bed if one could not sleep on it! It is not at all clear that there is a Form for every class of things. Plato never tells us that there is a Form corresponding to every general idea which we can think of, such as bed, toenail, or mud, even though he raises the question himself in his dialogue, *Parmenides* (130). It is far nearer the mark to think of a mathematical ratio than to think of nonsensible duplicates as Forms. For example, take the displacement of water caused by placing a body in a vessel. The loss of body weight is proportionate to the displacement of water. The height to which the water rises on the sides of the vessel is expressible as a mathematical ratio to the decrease in the body's weight. That ratio is not itself material; it cannot be tasted or weighed. It is neither a particular nor a universal. Although we can see the body put into the water and see the water move up the sides of the vessel, it is by our intellect that we grasp the notion of a proportion or a ratio, and the rule or generalization about the displacement of liquids by bodies. A Form is analogous to a mathematical ratio or function. It is not tangible or visible but something grasped by the intellect. It is itself not a particular but applies to many particulars; particulars "participate" in it although it is not physically present in them or they in it. It does not change, so it is timeless, though what it applies to does change. All these things can be said both of a mathematical function and a Platonic Form.

But Plato does not say that the Forms are mathematical ratios or functions or numbers. At the end of his life he did think of them as being capable of being expressed by a mathematical formula or number, the highest principle of all being the Form of the Good, or One. But he does not equate them with numbers or "mathematicals," as the circles and triangles of pure mathematics that are treated in the *Republic* are called. Mathematicals are a class of entities *between* sensibles and the Forms. Nonetheless, we are nearer the mark using a mathematical function as an analogue for the Forms than in thinking of them as immaterial duplicates of every class of thing we perceive.

Plato is quite definite, however, that it is Forms which give reality to the sensible world. It is only because sensibles "participate" in a Form that they can be said "to be" at all. This again makes sense if we think of a chaos, and think of ratios as "limits" placed on the motions present in chaos, so that an order—a regularity or permanence in relations—is established.

Plato is also quite definite in his belief that the Forms exist by themselves apart from a sensible world and in his belief that they can be grasped by the intellect. How the sensible world "participates" in them is a question which he addressed in several ways, including the approach he used in the *Timaeus*. As we have seen, in the *Timaeus* he has a craftsman or demiurge make the visible universe by using the world of Forms as the pattern or blueprint. The Forms are thus not *in* the sensible universe. Their relation is that of copied to copy, so that Plato calls the sensible world an image or reflection of the Forms.

The bridge between the world of Forms and the world of sense perception is the craftsman and intelligent souls. Soul for Plato is the source of motion. The craftsman fashions a world soul which fills the entire universe. This *anima mundi* is an intelligent living creature, with the visible world as its body. The stars and planets have orderly motion, so Plato thinks that they have intelligent souls. Because they do not perish, he calls them gods. The human soul is fashioned by the craftsman in the same ratio as is the world soul, so it is intelligent, but the craftsman entrusts the celestial gods with organizing the mortal parts of the human soul and body. Human souls and the world soul thus belong to both worlds—the unchanging inasmuch as they have intelligent souls, and to the changing world inasmuch as they live and change. Matter is organized into four basic kinds—earth, air, fire, and water—and they consist of various proportions of geometric shapes. Thus they and all that arises from them are perfectly proportioned or rational. The entire sensible universe is directed toward good, that is, each part is structurally organized as perfectly as possible and moves to perform a function, thus contributing to the on-going harmony and beauty of the universe insofar as matter will allow.

In Plato space or "the receptacle" is just a given, but time—in the sense of countable units of motion—comes to be with the visible universe (*Timaeus*, 37e–38b). Until heavenly bodies move (with regular, periodic motions) there are no days and nights or years. The heavenly bodies are a copy of the eternal nature of the world of Forms, which do not change. The heavenly bodies *do* change but they resemble the world of Forms inasmuch as "the created heaven has been and is and will be in all time" (38c). There is never *a time*—past, present, future—when they are not because without them there is no time. So Plato says that they are "a moving image of eternity" (37d). It appears from these remarks on time that Plato did not believe that the visible world began. We shall see shortly an even stronger reason than this to believe that Plato did not think that the world had a beginning in spite of his story about it being made by a craftsman.

Plotinus (A.D. 205–70), whom we shall consider more fully later, was puzzled by Plato's view of time as an image of eternity. He rejected the Aristotelian notion of time as the measure of the everlasting circular motion of the everlasting universe. He said that we indeed use the motions of the heavenly bodies to measure the passage of time, but the motions of bodies are motions *in* time and are not the same thing as time.

For Plotinus motion is the product of Soul. Soul is the lowest of Plotinus' intelligible hierarchy of three great hypostases (or substances) from which the sensible world emanates. The Intelligent Soul cannot grasp the contents of the world of Forms all at once. So it receives them one by one, and so engenders time (and subsequently the sensible world). Time is thus the life of Soul, having a continuous series of thoughts. This is Plotinus' interpretation of Plato's notion of time as a moving image of eternity.

Augustine was influenced by both Plato's view that time is created with the universe and by Plotinus' notion that time is a *mental* phenomenon instead of it being primarily the motion of bodies. But because of the Christian doctrine of creation, his views depart from both of them in significant ways. Some of the most important remarks Augustine makes about time and eternity are in his *Confessions*, Book 11. The occasion is the attack on the Christian doctrine of creation by the Manichaeans, a religious group to which Augustine once belonged. The Manichaeans asked, "If God created the world and created it out of nothing, why did God create it at the time God did and not sooner or later? What was God doing before the world was created?"

Augustine points out that it is true to say that the universe *began*, as Genesis reveals, but the universe did not begin *in time*. Time is created *with* the creation of all things. So there is no time before the universe began. The Manichaeans' questions can be raised only because of an erroneous notion of time.

Augustine recognizes that behind the Manichaeans' question lies the serious and difficult matter of the relation of time and eternity. So Book 11 of the *Confessions* is much more than a reply to their charges. He explains that God is eternal in contrast to all creatures. God is complete and full; nothing passes away from the divine life and nothing is added to it. In contrast to this, all creatures vary and change. There are things which were once true of us but are no longer true of us, and things which are not yet true of us.

The motions of the sun, stars, and planets do not constitute time. For if there were no heavens, the turning of a potter's wheel or even our talking would involve the passage of time. So time is not identical with the motions of the heavens. Nor does time exist on its own, independently. For when time is past, it is no more; when it is future, it is not yet. It exists only as present. But the present vanishes to an unextended point when examined closely. Augustine seems to give up trying to define time and instead describes what it is to be a time-conscious or historical being. For us there is a present, past, and future. What is present, flows through human consciousness and becomes past; and the future comes into our consciousness and becomes present and then past. But once the future has passed through us and become past, it is no more, just as when it was future, it was not yet. The past then exists as memory; the future exists as expectation; and the present exists as attention. For us to exist as temporal beings, then, is to act *now*, with memory and anticipation.

For God all things are present. In God there is nothing which passes away or comes to be. God's word of creation does not pass away; for if it did, all created things would pass away too. That word abides forever; it is spoken eternally. It is not subject to time.

The world indeed began, as Genesis teaches, but not because it is preceded by time. It is created with time by God who is eternal. There is an *absolute* beginning of time and the universe because all things depend on God who is ever the same.

Because God is eternal, we cannot comprehend the divine in its essence. We may make true statements about God's relation to time (as Creator; as the One who called Israel; and the like) and we can make correct statements about God's eternity, but full comprehension is beyond us. Temporal categories are foreign to the divine nature. In addition our very thinking is subject to a temporal order of before and after, which makes it impossible for us to reach a point at which God is circumscribed or contained. The object of our thought is not subject to the limitations which hold for all our thought. Intuition or vision is much more adequate than discursive thought and concepts.

These views of Augustine on time enable him to break with the theory of time as the circular motion of the everlasting universe. No longer is time cyclical, with things repeating themselves. This paves the way for Augustine to develop a Christian view of history, in which events such as creation, the call of Israel, and the incarnation give direction and purpose to human history.

Let us now return to the view that the sensible universe is a copy. The existence of a pattern to be copied implies a subtle but far-reaching difference between the Genesis account and Plato. It means, to start with, that Plato does not really have a *creation* story. This is obvious to the extent that Plato has preexisting matter, so that his is a story about the origins of the order of the sensible universe and not about why we have anything at all rather than nothing. Genesis itself is perhaps a story about God giving order to a chaos as well, with other biblical convictions needed to yield a view of creation *ex nihilo*. But the *Timaeus* story is also not a creation story because there is no *creative* element in it. The Forms are not exemplars which a creative mind considers individually, and then from those unordered or unrelated Forms conceives an order, and then takes that order it has conceived, and executes it as a sensible universe. In Plato, the world of Forms exists *already* as an ordered whole independently of being considered by the craftsman or anybody else. The craftsman is indeed just a craftsman, not a designer. A designer is creative. Even though materials are given, the designer creates the design. But the craftsman only *copies* the world of Forms, follows a ready-made blueprint. This work is thus not creative but rather it is imitative. In contrast to this, the Genesis account is about a creative, inventive act. There is nothing ready made to be imitated.

Plato's *Timaeus* was adapted for Christian use by the identification of the Forms with the divine mind. This was first done by the Middle Platonists in the first century B.C. Many Christian theologians followed their lead in this matter. Just as preexistent matter was taken care of by the Christian view of creation *ex nihilo*, Plato's other independent existent, the world of Forms, was accommodated to the Christian view by making it part of the divine mind. The consequences of this identification of the Forms with the divine mind for theology and indeed for the development of modern science were immense. It led to a very different view of God and of God's relation to the world, as we shall see when we cover the Middle Ages and the modern period.

The identification had immense attractions, for it meant that the universe, with an apparently very slight change, could become a reflection of the mind of God instead of a reflection of the world of Forms. On the one hand this suggests the possibility that considerable understanding about God can be gained from a study of the created universe, and on the other hand, the integrity of natural things is provided for because although they reflect the mind of God they are not part of it.

The Christian theologians who made Plato's Forms part of the divine mind fail to do justice to Plato himself. For Plato, the mind, whether it be the human mind or that of the craftsman, is essentially receptive. It recognizes its objects; it does not create them. Objects are not the acts of mind. Let us see why it is that Plato views the world of Forms as independent of mind.

Tables and chairs exist because there are functions for them to fulfill or perform. They serve purposes. Our minds do not create these functions or purposes. Tables and chairs also exist because human minds can grasp these functions or purposes and then make things to fulfill them. That is, we can make tables and chairs. Natural things also have purposes or fulfill functions in contributing to the maintenance of an orderly world. But the maximum rational order is prior to the existence of the specific things in nature which serve to maintain the order of the physical universe. Natural things exist because there is a mind to make natural things to serve that order. Just as there are human minds to grasp functions and make things to serve those functions the natural world is a result of intelligence or mind. Forms do not come from the matter of the universe. For the physical world owes its existence as a cosmos to principles (Forms) which are ordering principles. Matter is chaotic; it is not self-ordering. It cannot produce ordering principles. So the Forms are not the product of mind or of matter. They are graspable by mind—they are the objects the mind attends to—and they are used by a mind to order matter, but they are independent of both mind and matter. The world soul made by the craftsman moves matter in an orderly way; it does so because it is a mind moving all things in imitation of the Forms, but they are not part of the divine craftsman's mind or its own mind.

The independence of the world of Forms implies that the mind is passive. To shift their locale into God's mind does not deal with the implications of the conceptuality which conceived of mind as passive. It does not face the essential uncreativeness this implies for the mind of God. What the Forms are thought to be—and this varies greatly among philosophers and theologians who speak of ideas as part of the mind of God—affects what the divine mind is. It also affects what natural things are thought to be because they are copies of the Forms. To make objects primary, so that mind is a passive recipient of them, deeply affects the way we conceive of the agency of God. We shall have to look at this more closely when we come to the Middle Ages since Aristotle greatly influenced what the Forms were considered to be.

But even to think of the world as a copy instead of the result of a creative mind fails to appreciate the radical difference between the *Timaeus* and Genesis. For the *Timaeus* is not to be interpreted to mean that the world literally began. As we have said, it is Plato's way to deal with the problem of the connection of the Forms to the sensible world. Plato is convinced that the sensible world exhibits the marks of intelligence. He writes, for example, in the *Sophist* (265c,e):

> Does nature bring forth [animals, plants, and lifeless substances] from self-acting causes without creative intelligence; or are they from reason and divine knowledge? . . . I will only lay it down [not argue for it] that the products of nature, as they are called, are works of divine art, as things made out of them by man are works of human art.

The world is not simply the way it is, but the way an agent *wants* it to be, a conviction also expressed explicitly in the *Laws* (886e, 889b–e) and in the *Philebus* (26e). But the Forms are not agents. Plato has to introduce an agent and since the father of all things is beyond us, Plato has recourse to what he calls a "likely story." He uses a craftsman as an agent because the things of nature, which fit into a rational order resemble the things a craftsman makes which fulfill functions. Our agency is used as an analogue to account for the way things in nature fit together into a harmonious, stable order. The craftsman makes a world soul, and that world soul is the ordering principle in the visible universe. Thus the gap between the world of Forms and sensible reality is bridged.

This story of the craftsman is probably not to be taken to imply that the cosmos has a *beginning*, not because of Plato's impressive reasoning which shows that time is made *with* the cosmos, but because the issue for Plato is whether intelligence and mind are primary or whether things just are the way they are blindly. He wants to affirm that the visible universe operates rationally, that is similarly to the human mind, in the production of natural things. It has that similarity for him because things do fulfill functions that keep the order stable and, as we have seen, ordering principles are not a function of matter but of intelligence. The fact that the visible universe began does not imply the likeness of the visible universe's operations to the intelligence shown in human handiwork. So the assertion that the cosmos began does not in itself assert the likeness of the visible world's operation to the intelligence shown by human handiwork. But in Genesis it is the primacy of God that is affirmed;

and this is affirmed by saying that only God did *not* begin in contrast to all else that did begin.

But Plato does not know *how* ordering principles (the Forms) can be related to natural things which by fulfilling their functions, maintain the world as an on-going, harmonious, good, and beautiful system. For this Plato gives a story which, according to his own distinction, is *mythos* not *logos*. Roughly, this distinction in his writings means that he tells a story which contains his firm convictions but those firmly held beliefs are not expressed in ordinary reasoned arguments. In this instance, the story exhibits the conviction that natural things are the way things are intended to be–orderly, rational, good, and beautiful as a whole and in every part–and not the way they simply happen to be by chance or necessity. The conviction is expressed in terms of the human making of things–the way a craftsman makes things. That the account is mythical does not mean it is not intended seriously. For there is indeed a radical difference between viewing the world as something which simply is as it is–a fact–and as something whose order reveals intention or purpose.

To see that this difference represents a fundamental cleavage, we need to recall the philosophy Plato inherited. The ancient Greeks were fascinated by the way things fit together. They wondered why things are as they are and how they happen to act as they do. The first persistent investigation of the natural world motivated by a desire simply to know this for its own sake arose among the Ionian Greeks. They lived on the coast of western Turkey and on nearby islands, the richest and most advanced part of the Greek world in the sixth century B.C. The early Ionian philosophers–Thales, Anaximander, and Anaximenes–were all from Miletus; hence they are collectively called the Milesians. They posed for the first time one of the most important problems in the history of philosophy: the problem of the One and Many. We are all aware of immense diversity in the universe, yet all things are thought to be somehow connected, and thus somehow to have a unity. The Milesians shared the traditional Greek religious assumption that the universe was not *made* but was *born*–that is, the basic analogy was that of giving birth, rather than that of human construction, on the lines of a craftsman.

The Greek word for "origins" is *genesis*, meaning birth. They differed radically however, from the old Greek myths about the origins of the gods and the sensible world, as found for example in Hesiod's *Theogony* with its genealogy of the gods, in at least one major way. There is no anthropomorphism in their account. No purpose or intention is suggested. Instead of the vague personifications of the old myths, we have a description of the basic material stuff out of which the diversity that we observe is produced. The process is conceived impersonally and in terms of natural forces and necessary movements. They are not antireligious but simply nonreligious. They ignore the stories handed down from earlier times or as told by allegedly inspired poets about the origins of gods, earth, and people. Instead of tradition, they report *their own views* on the ground that they are the most reasonable interpretations of the operations of nature and its unity, relying on observation and reason. Their accounts of the principal stuff from which all else develops by its inherent nature are crude. Thales called it "moisture" since water is the principle of life according to primitive observation. Anaximander's principle is the *apeiron* (the unbounded or indefinite) and suggests that the world's diversity came from some process of specification or the introduction of limits to the unbounded. Anaximenes' basic principle is vapor. The details here do not matter; it is the fundamental turn to a rational account of the processes of nature by which diversity emerges from a source that gives unity to all the multiplicity of nature, and does this without anthropomorphic personification, or any other implication of purpose or intention.

These early thinkers were followed in the next century by two men of great stature who developed quite opposite views and introduced a second major problem in philosophy: the relation of change and permanence. Around 500 B.C. Heraclitus, an Ionian from Ephesus, passionately put forward the view that *nothing* is permanent, but that all is in perpetual flux. One of his most famous remarks was that one cannot step into the same river twice. We have often been told in theology that the Greeks had a prejudice for permanence. This is indeed in Greek thought, but Heraclitus is as Greek as anyone and he argued powerfully for the view that nowhere is there to be found anything which is unchanging. Not only is there perpetual change but also perpetual conflict. Hot, wet, and good are the necessary complements of cold, dry, and evil. Their opposing tension results in harmony. There is thus no preference expressed for either member of the opposing pairs in the cosmic process. Each member of the pair is necessary, and opposition is natural. The order of nature can only exist with opposition.

The balance between opposites is maintained by an immanent principle that maintains a ratio or proportion between opposites. The common Greek word *logos* has a host of meanings. Heraclitus uses it in a technical sense for the first time to refer to this principle of balance. *Logos* also gives unity to the multiplicity of the universe as it runs through all opposition, maintaining the degree of balance or ratio of tension of each of the opposing pairs. The world process is not one of unmoving balance, however. It is a constant process of dissolution and reconstitution as the ratio of tension constantly varies, and the entire universe goes through a cycle of chaos and order. The *logos* is called fire by Heraclitus, presumably by analogy with the way fire can fuse or break the bond between things, but it is of course not our ordinary fire. He says that *logos* is the principle of life and intelligence for human beings, as it must be presumably because the ratio or balance is the source of everything. This notion of *logos* as the principle of nature and of human intelligence as well has immense implication when Christ is identified as the *Logos*, as we shall see.

Parmenides, a younger contemporary of Heraclitus, lived in the Greek city of Elea, in southern Italy. In his reflections on the problem of the One and Many, he accepts the idea that the world is derived from a single everlasting something, and in this sense the world is one. But by logical arguments he claims to show that reality is one, without multiplicity and change. His basic proposition is, "That which is *is*, and it is impossible for it not to be." The common sense view that change takes place is rejected as an appearance, and so we get a radical opposition between *reality*, achieved by logical reasoning, and *appearances*, given by our sense experience. For Parmenides "to be" means to exist fully and completely, now and always. The primal One is as it is forever unchanged. It cannot increase or decrease, nor can anything come out of it. This is what is ontologically real, and the only thing which is ontologically real. All that is changing does not have being; it is forever *becoming*. Thus arises the famous contrast in Greek philosophy between "being" and "becoming."

Parmenides' position was strengthened by his disciple Zeno of Elea, who developed paradoxes such as Achilles and the Tortoise, to show that the consequences which arise from the assumption of motion or change are more absurd than the consequences that arise from Parmenides' assumption that motion was a delusion of the senses. (Parmenides and his disciples are referred to as the Eleatics).

The radical distinction between reality and appearances, being and becoming, was so well-argued that in spite of its clash with common sense experience, no subsequent philosopher could ignore the issue of what it is "to be." It becomes a central ontological question.

Plato sought to accommodate Parmenides' insistence that what is ultimate must *be*—and that to be is to be fully actual or complete, and hence unchanging. He agreed with Heraclitus to the extent that he said that all sensible things are in flux, but Plato said that there are nonsensible things, the Forms, which are unchanging. As we have seen, he also gave some degree of reality to sensible things by relating them to the world of Forms, as copies of the Forms.

All these philosophers, then, influenced Plato. He had to face the question of what gives unity to, or accounts for, all else. He had to face the question of "what is," of "what gives being." He was convinced by Heraclitus and his own reasoning that what gives unity and has being could not be found among those things which are perceived by the senses. His notion of "Forms" was the fundamental reality and the proper or true object of knowledge. We must now turn to the Pythagoreans, whose stress on mathematics as the place to find what gives unity to multiplicity, influenced Plato's development and his theory of Forms.

Pythagoras himself predates Heraclitus and Parmenides, but his followers continue throughout the course of hellenic civilization. Pythagoras, an Ionian, went to south Italy about 530 B.C. His concern, unlike that of his fellow Ionian philosophers, was fundamentally religious. Some major beliefs from Orphism, a religion that appeared in Greece about 600 B.C., were held by the Pythagorean brotherhood. The soul is not an unsubstantial, shadowlike something, far less real than a living person, but instead it is a divine or immortal being which has fallen into the world and been imprisoned in the body. It is doomed to reincarnation unless it can purify itself and return to the divine world. Pythagoras himself apparently thinks that what makes the soul divine is the intellect, the power to know the true, unchanging reality. This is the order, proportion, and harmony in the universe evident to reason and the senses. The fixed proportions of the musical scale, which give harmony, are an image of the harmony to be observed in the heavenly bodies, and to be sought in the rest of sensible things. As Greek mathematics is geometric, that is, a study of the ratios between various lengths and areas and angles, rather than numerical, so ratio or proportion is the basic conception of rationality and order for the Pythagoreans and later for Plato. The Pythagorean doctrine that "things are number" is not wholly alien to Heraclitus' *logos* as establishing various proportions of the opposing pairs of things making up the universe, but it is much closer to Plato's notion in the *Timaeus* of the Forms as expressible by numbers in the four traditional elements—fire, air, earth, and water—and in the numerical proportions that are present in the world soul which moves the heavens according to number.

These thinkers, the pre-Socratics, all influenced Plato, but to a much lesser extent than Socrates did. It is Socrates who gives a distinctive meaning to the problems of pre-Socratic thought with which Plato wrestles. We can get a sound, if not extensive, understanding of the revolutionary turn Socrates gave to philosophy by considering his autobiographical remarks in Plato's *Phaedo*. It is to be remembered, of course, that Socrates' own views, like Jesus', depend wholly on the reports of others because neither Socrates nor Jesus wrote anything. In the *Phaedo* Socrates describes his excitement upon hearing that Anaxagoras, an older contemporary, had written a book in which he claimed that the moving principle in nature is *nous* or mind. Socrates says that when he read Anaxagoras, however, he was deeply disappointed because the moving principle was not really mindlike at all. The materials of the universe which are combined and separated in order to account for all the changes or movement in nature did not act for any purpose. It is as if someone were to claim to have explained why he, Socrates, remained in prison awaiting execution by giving an account in terms of the bones and sinews of his legs instead of his *reasons* for refusing to escape. To show that the mind is the cause of change in the universe requires one to give reasons for its actions and how it has ordered all things for the best. For a mind that is reasonable acts purposively, and it seeks to achieve the best results. Anaxagoras by referring to the cause of the universe as mind thus led Socrates to expect that he would give an account which was different from that of the Milesians, who eschewed anthropomorphic notions and spoke only of impersonal causes in their accounts of how the diversity of the cosmos originates from some source.

Socrates did not want to return to the archaic cosmogonies (accounts of the generation of the cosmos) with their crude personification, especially since the gods in these tales are frequently described as acting immorally and irrationally. He wanted descriptions of *natural* processes which cause the operations of nature. But unlike the accounts of the Milesians and Anaxagoras, his account of such natural processes would also give the *reason* for those processes. He did not consider nature or human life to be explained when the accounts only tell us that they simply are the way they are, instead of showing us that they are the way they are because that way is rational and good. So Socrates goes against the entire drift of philosophy before him, except perhaps for the Pythagoreans.

Socrates in the *Phaedo* said that he himself lacked the aptitude for cosmology (the study of the principles of nature), so he decided early in life to devote himself to discovering what was good for human life, or what was good for the soul. Philosophy was decisively turned in this direction by Socrates, the direction further explored by his pupil, Plato, who treated all the philosophical issues he inherited from the perspective and in the context of the search for the good life. The *Timaeus* represents Plato's foray into cosmology, doing there what Socrates wanted, but felt unable to do, by arguing that the world is the handiwork of mind, and it is as it is because a mind intended it to be so.

The Genesis story of creation and the rest of the Bible appear at first sight to be anthropomorphic, similar in their naivete to the cosmogonies written before the pre-Socratic philosophers. But early Christian theologians such as Clement of Alexandria were quick to point out that the Bible, just as Plato, stresses that the source is ineffable. Clement cites the passage from the *Timaeus* which says "The father and maker of all this universe is past finding out, and even if we found him, to tell of him to all men would be impossible" (28c). Scripture, these theologians argue, is no more anthropomorphic than is Plato; both recognize the ineffability of God. The language of Scripture is an accommodation to our limited capacities. Accounts of nature's operations by natural causes are not *rivals* to scriptural accounts insofar as natural causes are given for natural processes. But natural causes must themselves be understood. Natural operations cannot be said to be "just the way things are," but instead we must say that they are the way they are because they are creatures of God and express God's will. For example, Augustine in facing the question of the relation between the natural activity of things and the activity of God, adapts a Stoic precedent. The formative principle of the individual things in nature are "seeds" or seminal *logoi* (or *rationes seminales* to use Augustine's Latin terminology). God created everything in the beginning, Augustine says, but allowed some creatures to remain latent, waiting for the right time and environment for their actual appearances. They are created as "seeds" and come into fullness later. This enabled Augustine to safeguard the natural, causal efficacy of things and the temporal unfolding of causal sequences, and yet to keep them within the scope of God's creative activity. (Augustine's natural science does not have to be correct for him to be correct about the distinction and relation between the operation of natural causes and God.)

The question raised by Plato in the *Sophist* (265c)—"Does nature bring forth [animals, plants, and lifeless substances] from self-acting causes without creative intelligence; or are they from reason and divine knowledge?"—thus indicates a major division in the way the universe can be understood. The shift from *birth* to *making* ("the products of nature. . . are works of divine art, as things made out of them by men are works of human art"—*Sophist* 265e) is an indication of the cleavage. Birth suggests blind reproduction, whereas "human making" out of the things of nature suggests intelligence and purpose. Plato was thus seen to be on the "right" side of that division by Christian thinkers. For Plato the inadequacy of natural causes as explanations of nature's operations is that they neglect the beauty and goodness of the visible world order as a whole and in every detail. And Plato's ground for the conviction that the world is a handiwork of intelligence is largely that he thinks nature's order resembles the activity of human intelligence. We shall see the significance of this shortly.

Once nature is understood by Plato to exhibit intelligence on the model of the intelligence present in the human making of things, the relation of humanity and nature is reversed. Now, instead of seeing the world as the handiwork of mind (because it resembles the products of human intelligence), we see nature's order as a foundation for the conviction that human nature has a purpose, and that there is thus a proper way for human life to be ordered, politically and morally, in order to fulfill its nature. The reasoning is not a vicious circle. The issue is whether nature is indeed similar to the products of human labor which are made in order to serve various purposes. If nature is similar to human handiwork, then nature can be used as a support for seeking the best order for society, the state, and the individual, for humanity, like everything else, has a place in the general order. The issue of the similarity of nature's operations to the products of human labor is a major one in the latter part of the seventeenth and the eighteenth centuries. We shall see the significance of that debate for Christian theology when we come to the modern period. The issue is still with us today as can be seen in Fred Hoyle's recent work in cosmology. He has said that in order to account for the origins of life we must postulate that some intelligence was operative.

In the case of Plato himself, Aristotle shows how one may retain the notion that the universe operates in a purposive way, or teleologically, and yet have no beginning. Plato's world of Forms is utterly independent of the world of the senses. By the agency of a craftsman, who makes a copy of the world of Forms, the world's movement is caused by means of the world soul. Thus the gap between the Forms and the sensible world is bridged. But Aristotle did not believe that the Forms exist by themselves, independent of matter. They are always present in matter. They can be apprehended by means of a process of abstraction from their presence in sensible things. Since the Forms do not exist by themselves, there is no gap to be bridged between the Forms and the visible world. The world is not a copy of anything.

The world does, however, operate in a manner similar to the operations of human intelligence because every natural thing has a function or role in the world order, so that the world as a whole and in each part is teleologically ordered. But such purposive operations do not imply that nature is the way *someone intended it to be*. Aristotle shows a way to think of purposive activity or goals being achieved throughout nature, and for human beings to have an end to be achieved, without seeing the world as being the way someone intended it to be.

The ease with which Plato's story of the mind making a visible world can be rendered superfluous by an alternative account of the order of nature shows how different Genesis is from the *Timaeus*. The context of Plato's creation story is that of a search for a rational explanation of nature's workings. His problem is posed by such questions as the relation of the One and the Many and the relation of permanence and change. Reasoned arguments to understand phenomena may lead in the direction of a *Timaeus*-like creation story, in which nature is to be regarded as being the way it is because it is mindlike in its operations. But reasoned arguments may lead to such a story being rendered useless by an account such as Aristotle's, which indeed recognizes nature as operating in a mindlike way but as not being intended to be the way it is by an intelligent being. For Aristotle there is no craftsman looking to a model and no father who is beyond all finding out.

The Christian belief in God the Creator does not arise out of an attempt to deal with the problems with which Plato and Aristotle wrestled. Its conviction does not arise from a perception that nature operates in a mindlike way. It rests on a belief in God's initiative in calling a people and in God's continuing dealings with them. Awareness of divine sovereignty over all things and God's independence from all things led and leads to an awareness of the dependence of all things on God. The search for a rational account of nature's operations is not the origin or the ultimate basis for the Christian belief in the Maker of heaven and earth.

On the other hand, the creation, as we mentioned in the Introduction, bears marks of its origin from the hand of God. The reflections of great philosophers, such as Plato and Aristotle, on the order of nature are instructive. They supply us with valuable data as we try to form an estimate of the *extent* of these marks and *how well* the mind can discern them. Philosophical reflection on the order of the universe is thus of interest to theology.

2
Plato:
This World
Is Not
Our Home

For Plato, as for Christianity, this world is not our home. We have a destiny which cannot be fully achieved here, and human life is a journey from this world to ultimate reality. Plato and Christianity differ on the nature of this world, on what our true home is, and on how we get there. But their common insistence that the sensible world depends on a nonsensible reality and that our happiness or well-being is to be found there makes them allies. Plato provided great support for Christianity against materialist views in the ancient world. Augustine in his *Confessions* describes the assistance he received from the Platonists. He said that they enabled him to overcome in his journey to Christianity the hindrance caused by his own inability to conceive any reality that was not sensible. We shall examine Plato's account of the nature of the soul and how it makes its journey to its true home.

The very word "soul" is a puzzle to us today. The Greek word *psyche* which we translate as "soul" meant to the average Greek the breath of life or what is needed in order to be alive. Anything alive had a soul. Should the soul survive death, apart from the body, its existence was miserable. Homer describes the abode of the dead in the *Iliad* as a shadowy sort of life. Achilles says that he would rather be the servant of a poor man on earth than king of the dead. Not even the Orphics and Pythagoreans who considered the soul to be "divine" (or immortal) and imprisoned in the body, considered it to be the intellectual and morally responsible aspect of a human being. It was Socrates who first treats soul not only as the source of motion but also as the intelligence or mind of a person. (See, for example, *Republic* Book 1, 353d.)

When Socrates turned his attention away from a study of the physical world after his disappointment with the failure of Anaxagoras to explain the order of the world in terms of the achievement of good ends, he began his search for the good for human life. What is its purpose? What is truly beneficial to our souls? He tells us in his defense at his trial (Plato's *Apology*) that instead of introducing strange gods and corrupting the youth of the city, as he had been charged with doing, he had been of service to his fellow citizens. The oracle of Delphi had said that he, Socrates, was the wisest man in Athens. He found this impossible to believe until he began to question his fellow citizens concerning the nature of virtue (*arete*, which is better translated "human excellence"). Under his questioning, they fell into contradictions, and so it became clear that they did not know. Thus the oracle of Delphi was correct. He was the wisest man in Athens, for he knew that he knew nothing, whereas his fellow citizens thought that they knew but they did not. In obedience to the gods, he accepted the task of making his fellow citizens aware of their ignorance of the proper way for a human being to live, that is of how to find a life that is truly beneficial, and of helping them to realize that the care of the soul is the most important task. Thanks to Socrates, "care of the soul" became a major pursuit and concern in the hellenic world. This was of tremendous assistance to Christianity in the early centuries.

Socrates was distressed by the Sophists, who claimed to be able to teach people how to live successfully. The Sophists were by and large teachers of rhetoric. It was particularly important in ancient Greece for a freeman to be able to speak well in the assembly and law courts since all freemen took part in the assemblies of their city-states and, since there were no lawyers, they had to plead their own cases and defend themselves against charges. The Sophists claimed to be able to teach people the art of persuasion without reference to the truth or falsity, justice or injustice of any matter at issue in the assembly or courts. They were not interested in a profound examination of moral issues or the nature of the moral life, but accepted the mores of their time and place and showed a person how to live successfully in his own milieu.

In the dialogues named after two great Sophists, *Protagoras* and *Gorgias*, Socrates presses the importance of belief in genuine goodness over against the Sophists who viewed morals as a matter of custom and convention. Just to have the power of persuasion conferred on one by possessing the art of rhetoric might actually do one harm unless one knows what is beneficial or good for human beings. Socrates claimed not only that it was necessary to know what was good or beneficial, but that virtue was a kind of knowledge. It cannot be conferred on one person by another person. Instead it must be achieved by an active search. Socrates seeks to goad people into making a search—to become concerned about the good of their souls—by convincing them of their ignorance, and persuading them not to be led astray by the success that the Sophists promise. When, for example, in the *Republic*, a companion quotes a poet as an answer to a question concerning the nature of justice, Socrates leads him by means of questions into giving contradictory answers. Socrates' point is not that what the poet said is necessarily incorrect, but that the person whose education consisted of learning what others have said, does not necessarily arrive at knowledge.

Socrates' method of teaching by questions and answers leads to puzzlement (*aporia*). In Plato's early dialogues, Socrates himself does not resolve the puzzlement by telling people what is beneficial to human life. The various virtues are left undefined. People must acquire knowledge of virtue for themselves, for it is a kind of knowledge which changes a person in the very acquisition of it. Thus it cannot just be given to one person by another, but each person must himself or herself search for what is good. Socrates compares this kind of teaching to the midwife's art. The midwife puts nothing into a mother but helps her deliver what is within her. By his questions Socrates stimulates another person to discover what is within and finally to deliver the right answer.

Plato is assisted in his understanding of that knowledge which benefits the soul by his familiarity with Pythagorean teaching. The soul, according to the Pythagoreans and to Orphism, is a fallen god

imprisoned in the body. It is preexistent and undying, and by purification can escape reincarnation and return to its proper place. Plato
shared with Socrates the conviction that the sensible world is the
result of benevolent intelligence long before he wrote the *Timaeus* in
which he tries to describe it. The rational principles used to give
order to nature do not arise out of matter. Rather it is these rational
principles that make the physical universe orderly. Human reason is
akin to the rational principles we see in the order of nature, for we
grasp the ordering principles by our intellects, not our senses. Thus
Plato does not simply adopt uncritically Orphic or Pythagorean
notions, but he has his own reasons for treating the human soul as
distinct from the sensible world.

For Plato perfect happiness is to know the supreme pattern upon
which the world is modeled. His tales of the soul's preexistence,
survival of bodily death, and the need to avoid reincarnation by a
good life on earth and a desire for the nonsensible world, are all told
in mythical form, often using Orphic and Pythagorean material. But
it is clear that he regards the soul as immortal, and knowledge of the
world of Forms as our blessedness because the present goodness of
the world which attracts us powerfully is only a reflection of the truly
good on which it is patterned. Thus it is imperative for us to turn
from the sensible world, literally a change in our inner being (*meta-
noia*), and to search for knowledge of the supersensible reality on
which this world depends. Philosophy for Plato, as for Socrates, is
thus a way of life. It is to live a life which seeks the true good and
which knows that this is beyond this world although this world
reflects it.

How is the soul to make this journey? How are we to find what is
truly our good? Love is our great assistant. Plato devotes two major
dialogues, the *Symposium* and the *Phaedrus*, and an early one, *Lysis*,
to the subject of love. The *Phaedrus* is the simplest to describe, and it
introduces several themes we need to consider for our purposes, so
we shall examine it. In the *Phaedrus* Plato describes the preexistence
of the soul in myth. He uses the image of the soul as a charioteer
drawn by two horses, a white and a black one. The soul is considered
to have three distinct aspects: intelligence which guides a person,
honorable desires and appetites, and dishonorable ones. The chario-

teer represents the intelligence, the white horse honorable appetites, and the black horse dishonorable and unruly ones. The horses have wings so they draw the charioteer through the sky and thus can rise through the opening in the dome which envelops the heavens, or at least rise high enough to get a glimpse through the opening in the dome to the supersensible reality that is outside the dome of the heavens. But since the two horses have contrary desires, it is difficult for the charioteer to manage to get high enough to get a glimpse through the hole in the dome. When it once proved impossible to get them to go high enough, the soul failed to get the nourishment provided by a glimpse of genuine reality beyond the dome. Without this nourishment, the feathers of the horses' wings molt, and they cannot fly, so the soul falls to earth–or becomes incarnate.

It is able to return to its proper home, however, because it retains a memory of the Forms it used to catch glimpses of. The memory is latent, however. It can be awakened by the sight of beauty, in the *Phaedrus* by the beauty of a boy. The person does not realize or understand why the beauty of the boy so powerfully moves him with desire. It is actually because of the latent knowledge of the true beauty of the world of Forms that he is stirred by the boy's beauty which resembles it. Both desire for the world of Forms and sexual desire for the boy move the man. This is portrayed in the image of the soul as a conflict between its different parts: the black horse is passionately aroused by the boy and lunges forward seeking sexual gratification; the white horse which has been honorably trained, tries to hold back and to obey the charioteer, who out of reverence and awe for beauty, tries to restrain the desire for sexual gratification, as personified by the black horse. This picture is a great image of the conflicts we feel with many other kinds of desires for sensual gratification. It is far more realistic than the view expressed by Socrates in the early dialogues. In them Socrates claimed that we always seek good, and we only do evil out of ignorance. It would be well to keep in mind the image of the soul in the *Phaedrus* to have a more balanced understanding of Plato's views concerning human action.

If the charioteer is able to control the black horse, then the person may become a seeker after that nonsensory world which he now passionately desires as a lover, and which had been latent until it was awakened by the sight of a beautiful boy. If a person persists faithfully in pursuit of knowledge of what is beyond the world of senses, eventually he or she will return there and not be reincarnated. For Plato, everyone gets what one loves or desires the most: sensual life in the world again and again (and with punishment between each reincarnation) or continuous knowledge of the true reality which gives never-ending joy.

The tripartite structure of the soul is also present in the *Republic* where the ascent to knowledge of the world of Forms is most fully described. Love which assists us is capable of being employed by any part of the soul. The lowest part of the soul is the appetites which can be gratified by bodily things, such as water, food, sex. Frequently the desire or love for wealth stems from a desire to be able to gratify the sensuous appetites. If the lowest part of the soul becomes dominant, one becomes a slave to one's appetites. We are like leaky vessels (*Gorgias* 493 a–d); we keep seeking to fill ourselves but we never fill up. So we are forever seeking for more and different gratifications, more driven by our appetites the more we seek to satisfy them. Our appetites also conflict with each other, so if all we ever seek to do is to gratify our appetites, our lives become disorderly and miserable. We are like a city torn apart by a civil war. Plato's extensive descriptions of how the gratification of our appetites can enslave us and prevent us from returning to our proper home are a major reason why strictures directed toward concupiscence are so prominent in early and medieval theological writing. According to Plato, the lower part of the soul must be guided by intelligence if we are to avoid being dominated by sensuous pleasures.

The middle part of the soul is described as the concern for honor or social prestige, and evinces some of the higher emotions such as anger. The desire for social approval is described by Plato as the pleasure we gain from applause. This part of the soul is a very useful ally against the lower passions, for if we are trained to love honor and abhor anything base, it can help us to control our appetites and gratify them moderately and in honorable ways. On the other hand, the desire for prestige can be highly destructive. For we may so care for prestige that we seek it in dishonorable ways. Instead of prestige being based on true merit, we will practice hypocrisy or seek social approval from those who have no discrimination or who admire power and wealth above all. The middle part of the soul, called the spirited part in the *Republic*, thus also needs to be guided by the mind. To give guidance, however, the mind which is the highest part of the soul, must *know* what is good for the soul as a whole, and how this good is to be sought, and how to apply this knowledge to all the exigencies of life.

In the *Republic* the soul is seen as analogous to a city-state. There are three major tasks which must be performed in a state: production of goods to meet the material needs of the people, protection from injury from both internal attack and external enemies, and leadership to govern and guide the city's life. People differ in their abilities. In an ideal city-state people are to be assigned to whichever of those three tasks for which they are most suited: production, for example farming or shoemaking; military service; or governing. There is social mobility because children of any of the three classes are given those tasks which they are most suited to perform and women are just as eligible to enter the military and ruling classes as men. Thus, Plato's conception of the ideal state is quite radical.

The virtues or excellences of the individual correspond to the virtues of the city so that the individual soul is like a miniature city. The productive function of the state provides the goods which meet our bodily needs and desires, and in the individual this corresponds to the lower appetites of the soul. The protectors of the state are noble and correspond to the middle part of the soul which is disciplined and so resists the inordinate demands of the appetites. The rulers have the knowledge needed to guide the state and correspond to the mind of the individual which has knowledge to guide the soul. Intelligence or wisdom—in the city and in the individual soul—allows each part to function properly, stay within its bounds, and so give health to the city and the soul. The good of the whole depends on each part doing what it is most suited to do by nature and by a proper education. A proper education is determined by what is needed to develop each part of the soul to perform its natural function within the individual and to develop each individual's natural capacity so that each person can perform his or her function well in the state.

The virtues are then defined in terms of the parts of the soul and their relations. Wisdom is the virtue or excellence of the mind and of the rulers. Courage is the virtue of the spirited or honor-seeking part of the soul and of the soldiers. Temperance is the virtue of controlled appetites and of the producers of goods who do not try to rule the state. Justice is the virtue (or excellence) of every part of the soul and every part of the state performing the function it is best suited to perform, and not overstepping its boundaries by trying to perform another function.

Although the *Republic* is supposed to be concerned with defining justice, Socrates says that there is something beyond justice: the Good which is the source of all the virtues, and gives human and physical nature their goodness and unity. It is possible for only a very few people to gain a knowledge of the Form of the Good. It is very advanced education for which few people are suited. Only the very best of those people in the ruling class who have proven their worth to the city by performing their duties well are given this education. It is beyond that education given to all the protectors and rulers as children and young adults. This distinction between two levels and kinds of education—one is largely training, the other is called dialectic—suggests that the virtues exhibited by people are largely the result of training and not the result of knowledge of the basis and foundation of virtue. This also represents a departure from the Socrates of the early dialogues who said that everyone should concern himself or herself with the care of the soul by seeking to learn what is truly beneficial for it. But in the *Republic* only a very few people are able to go beyond the training in virtue to a knowledge of the ultimate foundation of virtue which is beyond justice or beyond the value a properly ordered state and society have for the health or good of the soul of the individual. It also means that the proper conduct of life in this world, although it can result in a good life, is not the highest good for the soul. Christianity agrees with this conviction. It does not, however, believe that knowledge or the highest good for the soul is restricted to those few who have the intellectual capacity to achieve it. For example, Justin Martyr, a trained philosopher of the second century who became a Christian Apologist, said that such knowledge is not possible for anyone using only one's natural capacities. It is only by faith in God's revelation by the incarnate Word that such intimate knowledge of God is possible, and such faith is not restricted to those of superior intelligence.

For Plato, knowledge of the Form of the Good is very difficult to achieve and only in the *Republic* does he express confidence that a few people have the capacity to gain a vision or knowledge of it. Even so, Plato gives us only *likenesses* of the Form of the Good. In three famous images—the sun, the divided line, and the cave—he gives us his basic ontological and epistemological conviction. So it is only by means of analogies that Plato will speak of the Form of the Good.

Fundamental to Plato's ontology and epistemology is the division between what is sensible and what can be grasped by the intellect only, between the world of the senses and the world of Forms. The three images of the sun, the divided line, and the cave describe by analogies the relation of the Form of the Good to the intelligible world of Forms on the one hand, and on the other hand to the world of the senses. Let us examine these three images in turn.

In order to see things we must have a capacity to see, or eyes, and objects to be seen. We also need light, or the sun. The sun makes objects visible and also enters the eyes so that they can see. When we look at colored things by moonlight, the colors are dim and the eyes seem to be almost blind; but when we look at the same things by sunlight, not only are the colors vivid but the eyes see them distinctly, and so, Plato says, it is clear that the eyes are not blind but have the power of vision. The Form of the Good in the world of Forms plays the same role as the sun in the world of the senses. The Form of the Good gives the objects of the intellect their truth and, to the person who grasps their truth, the power of knowing. This is the essential nature of Goodness. It is the cause of truth and of knowledge of the truth. That is, it is the ontological basis of truth and the epistemological basis of the knowledge of truth. The Form of the Good, Plato says, is thus not identical with truth or knowledge of truth, any more than light and vision are identical with the sun. This gives us Plato's famous trinity: the True, the Good, and the Beautiful. Good is necessary for truth; it is what gives objects their truth. Good also gives the power of vision to the intellect, and the knowledge of the truth fills us with beauty. There is thus a *likeness* between the truth of objects, knowledge of the truth, and the Good, but they are not identical.

The sun is also analogous to the Good because it gives things their nourishment and causes them to grow. It gives them their power of "becoming." The Good then not only enables things to be known by lighting them up and enables the intellect to operate, it also gives things their very being. This leads to a very cryptic remark: "the good itself is not essence but still transcends essence in dignity and surpassing power" (509b). Plato does not explain this in any of his extant writings. We know that he gave a lecture in the Academy on the Good, but our only information about it is the statement, "The Good is One."

These two cryptic remarks about the Good were richly developed by Plotinus almost six hundred years later so as to yield a vastly populated and integrated *spiritual* universe that emanates from the One or the Good, and continues down to our material universe. This Platonism played a major role in Christian thought, as we shall see. But we can see now the ease with which Platonism could be adapted for specifically Christian purposes. God is the Good from which everything derives its being. There is a universe of nonsensible beings between incarnate beings and God. The notion that the Good gives vision to our intellect as the sun gives sight to our eyes is the germ of Augustine's view that knowledge of eternal things requires divine illumination. Plato's doctrine of recollection, whereby the soul recalls the Forms it knew before it became incarnate, is abandoned by Augustine and other theologians (except Origen) because they reject the preexistence and the reincarnation of the soul. In its place Augustine holds the view that God illumines the mind so that it is able to achieve some knowledge of external truths from sensible things since what is nonsensible cannot otherwise be known by the senses. A major division among theologians in the medieval period is between those who follow Augustine's lead and those who develop an Aristotelian line of thought. According to the latter we attain such measure of knowledge of God as is possible for us in connection with sensible things. Thus we know God by divine effects. For

Augustinians we rise to knowledge of God only insofar as God illumines the intellect.

Another feature of the Augustinians will become clearer when we come to the allegory of the cave. It describes the ascent of the soul from sense perception (the cave) to the vision of the Good. Moral improvement or purification of the soul is achieved with increasing knowledge of reality. Thus in theology we have the notion that the increase in knowledge of God goes hand in hand with moral improvement and vice versa. There is no intimate knowledge of God without such a moral change in the knower. This Platonic-Augustinian epistemological tradition goes along with the likeness between knowledge and vision, and the belief that such vision is higher than the knowledge which can be gained discursively with concepts.

This tradition can easily be illustrated by some of the main features of Descartes' *Discourse on Method*. According to Descartes, everyone's intellect is by nature adequate to perceive truth. Ignorance and error are caused primarily by prejudice produced by custom and sense experience that impede our vision. If one methodically clears them away, the intellect is able to "see" or intuit the truth, just as the eye can see. Plato is the source of such metaphors in epistemology as the "natural light" of reason, "clarity," "obscurity," "brightness," and "dimness." To overcome impediments is to enable the reason to intuit the truth, to "see" it, and so the highest level of knowledge is vision, and often the search for knowledge ends in contemplation. To treat knowledge in terms of vision, however, presumes that knowledge is always about objects or things. But to know that a statement is true or false is not to know an object or thing. Only very late (in the *Theaetetus* and *Sophist*) does Plato recognize that knowledge is expressed by use of sentences, but he never integrates this with his earlier remarks about vision.

Plato's second analogy, that of the divided line, describes both the relation between the world of sense and the world of Forms, and the dialectical method of reasoning by which one comes to a knowledge of the relationships between the Forms. A line is first divided into two unequal parts to represent the visible world and the intelligible world. Then each segment is subdivided in the same proportion as the main division. (These proportions are not represented in the chart.) These proportions represent degrees of comparative clarity or obscurity. They are labeled, starting from the visible end, A through D, which approaches the world of Forms. A stands for "images," that is shadows and reflections of material objects we can see in water or on shiny surfaces. B stands for material objects. The degree of reality and truth of shadows and reflections in comparison to the reality and truth of material things is the ratio of the lengths of the line segments A and B. These images and material objects are both in turn "images" of the intelligible world. As A is to B in terms of reality and truth, so is the entire sensible world (A and B together) to the entire intelligible world (C and D together). The entire sensible world is like a shadow or reflection in water in terms of its reality and truth compared to the intelligible world. In terms of what it is (ontologically considered) and in terms of the truth that can be known from it (epistemologically considered) the sensible world is like a shadow or reflection of the intelligible world. Plato thus calls the visible world the world of "appearances" (*phenomena*) and the amount of truth we gain by reliance on it "opinion" (*doxa*). (See chart on next page.)

This very strong denigration of the reality of the sensible world and Plato's views about what we can know by the senses are considerably modified in the *Theaetetus* and the *Timaeus*. These dialogues were written some time after the *Republic*, and they represent Plato's most extended work on sensible knowledge and cosmology respectively. In the *Republic* Plato treats the senses in utter isolation from the mind so that all we have is a flow of sense data (*gignomena*, "becomings") which are utterly transient in the strongest possible sense, and the visible world is then nothing but the world as our eyes alone present it. But in the *Theaetetus* and *Timaeus* he notes that clearly, insofar as sensible things are "images" of intelligible things, and insofar as they are made with the intelligibles as their pattern (so that they are the best possible copy as the *Timaeus* emphasizes), we cannot properly estimate their ontological status by comparing them to shadows or reflections in a pool of water.

Plato does not concern himself, as we have since the rise of empiricism and modern science, with whether we can be certain of empirical facts. But he would never call such certainty "knowledge"

ANALOGY OF THE DIVIDED LINE

visible world (opinion)		*intelligible world* (knowledge)	
A	**B**	**C**	**D**
shadows and reflections	sensible objects	reasoning from unexamined assumptions (the only examples Plato gives are from mathematics)	reasoning from assumptions up to what they depend on (using only Forms)

Frequently commentators contrast the visible and the intelligible worlds by calling one "appearances" and the other "reality." This is misleading because for Plato there are *degrees* or *grades* of reality. The visible world, even though it is a world of appearances, is nonetheless real. One might say that it is a "dimmer" reality than the intelligible world, which in contrast is perfectly real.

(*episteme*). This does not mean that his position excludes certainty of empirical facts. Degrees of clarity of objects are correlated with their ontological status, so that epistemology and ontology are coordinated. Among intelligibles (C), those which are lower in the scale of being are said to be knowable (*episteme* is used of them). Even though they are *not* the highest reality ontologically (for they depend on higher Forms, and ultimately all the Forms depend on what is even higher, the Good), we can know them. So if "knowledge" is used of what is not the highest ontological reality, the use of "certainty" for empirical fact is not necessarily excluded by Plato's ontology of Forms.

The other important aspect of Plato's discussion of the divided line is the description he gives of dialectic, the kind of reasoning by which we achieve a vision of the Good. The part of the line which stands for the intelligible world is divided into two sections, C and D. With C, the mind uses material objects in its reasoning and, by making some assumptions, it is able to reach sound conclusions. The reasoning is not upward to a principle, but downward to a conclusion. Plato illustrates what he means by the practice of mathematicians. They use drawings of figures in their reasoning, and by assuming the truth of their axioms and definitions, they demonstrate their conclusions. Their reasoning and conclusions are not about the particular sensible figures they use but are about mathematical realities which are not sensible.

Section D of the line refers to what the intellect is able to apprehend when it treats the assumptions upon which reasoning to various conclusions is based. They are no longer treated as assumptions from which one may reach conclusions, but their bases are found by an examination of the relationships between the Forms. This is done by dialectical reasoning which gathers various Forms under a more inclusive Form. Then it determines the precise relation of these Forms to each other. This is done by a process of dividing and subdividing the more inclusive Form, finding, as Plato puts it in the *Sophist*, the joints in its structure. The mind thus arrives at a clear conception of the order and relationship of the less universal Forms which are included under a higher one. This practice yields a precise definition of the particular Form, whose definition was sought. The more general a Form, the richer its content, or the greater its reality. Thus the Form of the Good, which presides over all the Forms and brings them to their final unity, contains in itself all the kinds of good that there can possibly be.

Plato's dialectic is very different from Aristotle's logic. Aristotle is concerned with the form of a *proposition*, in a very different sense of "form." His form is an abstraction, devoid of particular content. The form of a universal proposition is "All A is B." This form can stand for many very different things. Aristotle studied the relationship between the forms of propositions. Plato, however, is not concerned with propositions at all, but with nonmaterial realities that exist apart from our minds.

What Plato is saying can be put this way: If you had only reflections of material objects in water, you would be able to learn something about them, but not nearly as much as you could if you were able to examine material objects themselves. Likewise, you would know far more if you understood the principles which give material objects their properties and characteristics. You would know still more if you knew how the principles themselves were connected and interrelated to each other. And finally the highest knowledge would be knowledge of the organizing principle on which they all depend. So having mounted up to the highest principle, you could reverse your direction and go from the highest (the Good) down to all the principles organized under it and connected to it and to each other.

The third image, the allegory of the cave, concerns the education of the soul, or how it must be altered in order to gain a knowledge of the Good. This is the journey of the soul from illusion to reality which purifies it so it may gain knowledge. By such knowledge the soul finds a degree of fullness in this life, though this is only complete when it ceases to be reincarnated and permanently dwells in its proper home, the world of Forms. This journey from illusion to reality is Plato's account of the way of salvation.

Plato conceives of ordinary life as though we were all deep in a cave, with a long passage way leading to the light outside. We are chained so that we can only look in front of us toward a wall. Behind us statues of living things are pushed in front of a fire so that their shadows are cast on the wall we are facing. We may mistake these shadows for reality. Then, one of the prisoners is released and made to see the fire and the statues. He is dazzled by the sudden light and thinks that the statues are less real than the shadows he had seen before because the shadows were more easily and more clearly seen. He would therefore have to be *forced* along the passageway up toward the cave entrance. When taken outside into the daylight, at first he would not be able to see anything at all because of the brightness. In time his eyes would adjust to the light, and he would see objects as they really are, and even be able to look at the sun. He would come to realize that the sun causes the seasons and the growth of all things. Now he would pity his fellows who are still in the cave, bound fast. He would no longer respect those who are honored as wise among them because of their ability to detect patterns in the shadows. Everyone has the capacity to learn, just as everyone has eyes with which to see. What is needed is to be turned in the right direction, so that one is pointed away from the shadows toward the light. Then just as the eye can see, so too the intellect can understand.

What we need then is *conversion*. We need to be turned from sensible objects, which are not true objects of knowledge, to what can be grasped by the mind. In earlier parts of the *Republic* and in his other dialogues, conversion has to do with renunciation of the objects of the lower and middle parts of the soul: gratification of the senses. These satisfactions do not lead one toward reality, toward the Good. Our desires are conflicting and never ending (we are like leaky vessels). They can enslave us. They, just like the desire for applause or prestige, drive us to seek wealth and power. Plato sought to get people to recognize this and so turn from these pursuits because it is in their own best interest. Knowledge is the food of the highest part of the soul. We are satisfied only by a knowledge of genuine reality, which is permeated by the true Good, the source of the good which various good things have.

To a person who has not yet turned or who has only just turned, conversion seems totally destructive, for it is to renounce sensuous delights and social position as the ways to happiness. Thus, in the *Phaedo*, Plato describes philosophy, the love of wisdom, as the practice of dying. One is progressively to renounce the delights of this world, to be "dead" to their allure. Renunciation of sensual pleasure and social status is a preparation for finding reality and truth, and thus for finding our true fulfillment and happiness. As far as it goes, it is very much in line with Christianity and reminds one of some of Jesus' sayings, such as "What does it profit a man, to gain the whole world and forfeit his life?" (Mark 8:36).

It is in connection with the ascent of the soul that this world gets painted as corrupting and full of illusion. As an image of reality the visible world is good, as we saw in discussing the *Timaeus*. But in relation to our need to return to our true home, it is a tissue of illusions, for it cannot give us what we seek. But Plato tells us that the person who has turned toward what is unseen is able to gratify the lower two parts of the soul in such a way that they do not get out of control, and that this results in a balanced or healthy soul. An informed mind directs the wants and emotions of the soul so that we may attain our chief end, and in doing so, enjoy this world better than those who ignore their chief end and seek to find their happiness in the things of this world.

We need to say more about the soul in Plato. In the *Sophist* Plato describes the soul as both changing and unchanging, and explicitly rejects Parmenides' identification of the unchanging with real being and his denial that what changes can be real being (248–249d). The soul knows the Forms, Plato points out, and therefore, he asks rhetorically "are we really to be so easily convinced that change, life, soul, understanding have no place in that which is perfectly real— that it has neither life nor thought, but stands immutable in solemn aloofness, devoid of intelligence?" (249a). So the soul for Plato is fully real even though it changes.

But it is not clear what the soul is essentially. We have described it in this chapter as tripartite, following the *Republic* and the *Phaedrus*. But is the soul essentially intelligence (*nous*), or are the middle and lower parts of the soul, though less important than *nous*, nonetheless *soul*, and so part of our person, as we have been treating them?

From the *Phaedo* it would seem that the former is true. In that dialogue Plato contrasts the soul with the body and even uses the Pythagorean expression "The body is the prison house of the soul." Socrates argues in the *Phaedo* that the soul survives separation from the body. The emotions and appetites, if they belong to the body, do not survive death. They are felt only because the soul is for a time connected to a body. The soul is thus treated as simple, not tripartite, and identified with *nous*. We must discount this dialogue to some extent however, because its setting is the last hours of Socrates' life before his execution, and he has been asked by his friends for the reasons he believes the soul survives separation from the body. In addition, in the *Phaedrus* we have the three activities of the soul (intelligence, emotion, and appetite) both before and after it falls into the body.

The difficulties of harmonizing Plato's accounts of the soul seem to be mitigated somewhat when he distinguishes between the immortal soul and the mortal soul in the *Timaeus*. (This distinction is exploited in a very significant way by Plotinus as a contrast between a higher and lower soul.) Plato gives these two souls different origins.

But this cannot be harmonized with the *Phaedrus* where soul as such is eternal (or divine in the Greek sense of being undying). In the *Laws* (897a) emotions and appetites are attributed to the discarnate world soul.

There seem to be intractable problems with any attempt to harmonize the different things Plato says about the soul. He seems to be able to talk about what we are only in allegories and imaginative descriptions and these do not cohere. This is not due to his lack of ability, but because of the difficulties in determining what we are, and his own honesty in highlighting important things about us without trying to gloss over the difficulties.

If one, however, takes the *Phaedo* as definitive of Plato's view of the soul, then it seems to make the emotions and desires not only subordinate but also nonessential to the nature of a human being. We are essentially reason or intelligence alone. We feel because we are in contact with something that is not essential to us, but our nature is that of a spiritual substance. This picture of Plato is quite common in Christian circles. It makes Plato seem simple at the price of gross misrepresentation and also makes him seem much more gnostic in his attitude toward the body than can be justified, if we give any weight at all to what he says about the soul in the *Republic* and the *Phaedrus*. In these works the soul (or person) is not only reason or *nous*. Emotions and appetites or desires have a rightful function in a person's life. They are clearly to be under the guidance of reason and are to be subordinated in the task of attaining our ultimate destiny. But neither the dogmatic asceticism of Diogenes the Cynic, who looked to Socrates for inspiration, nor "shame over having a body," an attitude exhibited by Plotinus, nor hatred of the body as evil are justifiable from Plato's views of the soul.

Plato's various views on the nature of the soul caused Augustine and other Christian Platonists difficulties. They are actually more immediately in contact with the Platonic revival and especially with Plotinus than with Plato himself. These Platonists opposed the materialism of the Stoics, who considered the soul to be simply a more rarefied kind of matter. Stoics could thus conceive of only two types of union: mere juxtaposition and a mixture. Juxtaposition is no union at all, and a mixture implies an alteration in the substances mixed so that the soul and body by their union are transformed into a new, third substance. The Platonists' view of the relation of the soul and body is neither of these. The relation is much too close to be mere juxtaposition, yet there cannot be a mixture. Nor will Aristotle's view of the soul as form of the body do since soul cannot then exist unembodied. So they developed the notion of a "union without confusion." The phrase is to be found in Porphyry, an important disciple of Plotinus, but Plotinus himself definitely has the same idea. The soul is united to a body, but the soul is not altered in any way by the union.

The relation of the soul (mind) and body is a continuing philosphical problem, and the relation of the human and divine natures of Christ is a mystery, as we shall see in the next chapter. But the Platonic tradition which deeply influenced many theologians led them to think of the human soul as a spiritual substance which could exist disembodied. So the problems of the relation of the soul (mind) and body in a human being, and the problem of the relation of the human and divine natures in Christ were set up for Augustine and others in a Platonist philosophical framework. The Platonists' formula—union without confusion—is present in the definition of the union of two natures in one person which was issued by the Council of Chalcedon (451).

It should be noted that one of Plato's fundamental reasons for his conviction that the soul does not die with the body is a moral one. He believed that the consequences of the evil we do are not avoided if we manage to escape punishment in this life. We cannot escape the punishment we deserve by simply dying before we are detected. Justice is fundamental for Plato, and so the soul will have to face judgment after death. We shall be rewarded or punished on the basis of how we have lived. To Plato it would be morally outrageous for good and evil not to receive their deserts. This moral conviction is worked up into an explicit argument many centuries later by Kant. Plato also believes (see the *Gorgias* and the *Republic*) that even in this life the unjust person becomes a slave to the passions, but that the just person has self-mastery and cannot be injured in the depths of the soul by external things. Justice results in well-being or happiness. We shall see something of the significance of these convictions in connection with the human search for well-being in the next chapter. Much later we shall see the fundamental change that occurs in moral philosophy or ethics in Kant who distinguishes morals from the search for happiness.

Another reason for belief in the immortality of the soul, and perhaps one more persuasive to Plato's contemporaries, relies on the Greek principle that like knows like. (The principle was of course disputed, but it did have wide currency and support.) Plato believed that since we know the Forms, we have an essential kinship with them, and thus share something of their permanent and unchanging nature. This is true, he believes, for that part of us that knows the Forms, for reason or mind (*nous*). But as we have seen, Plato is unsure whether the rest of our soul (our emotions and appetites or desires) also shares in this immortality.

Our ability to know ultimate reality and hence our kinship with it is a widely held assumption in Greek philosophy. That assumption may seem odd to us, but since the Enlightenment of the eighteenth century many people have assumed that we can know the nature of our universe by our sciences. The logical positivists in the twentieth century made this assumption explicit by insisting that there is nothing mysterious about reality. It can be understood by reason through and through. There is nothing in principle which cannot be understood by reason. So this Greek conviction is very much with us in a modern guise. It marks a decisive difference between Christianity and the dominant stream of Greek philosophy, particularly the Platonic tradition. In Plato, the handiwork of mind which we see displayed around us in the order of the visible universe is essentially like our own. Thus we have a capacity to know the visible universe (to the extent that matter can be rendered orderly by mind or by the craftsman), and the ultimate reality on which the visible universe is modeled. Plato hedges on our knowledge in this life of the Form of the Good which he seems less confident of in his later works, and our knowledge of the father and maker of all of the *Timaeus*. But however difficult it may be for us in this life to know the Forms and the Form of the Good which gives them their unity, there is nothing in principle to prevent it. Reason in us, reason evident in the visible universe, and reason as the ultimate basis of the visible universe are essentially alike, and so we have the capacity to know ultimate things.

But for Christian theology, God is above our intellect. Justin Martyr, one of the first trained philosophers whom we know of to convert to Christianity (about 130), clearly voiced the difference between the Platonists and the Christians on this matter. We can know that God exists by our reason, said Justin, but we cannot know the divine nature except by revelation. We can receive revelation only through the operation of divine grace and faith. Vision of ultimate reality, which is knowledge in the pure sense of knowledge for Platonists (*noesis*), is not achievable by use of the intellect alone, Justin insists. Over the centuries Christianity has developed many different conceptions of the difference between reason and revelation, but it has consistently agreed with Justin on this point.

3

The Platonic Tradition:
The Stoics, Plotinus, Pseudo-Dionysius

Socrates gave a decisive turn to philosophy. He turned philosophy from an investigation of the natural world to a concern for the well-being of our souls. Plato, his great disciple, discusses not only the nature of the soul (or human nature) but also its environment, for clearly our society and the natural world affect our well-being. Plato believes that all three—people, society, and nature—can be properly understood only by a recognition of the reality and primacy of an immaterial realm, the world of Forms. Human beings are members of both a material realm and an immaterial realm. Their well-being has to be considered in relation to both.

Plato often focuses his attention on our life in this world, describing the civic virtues of courage, temperance, wisdom, and justice in a well-ordered state. Such a life and society depend, however, on knowledge of the ordering principles of the cosmos, and those principles—the Forms—find their unity in the Form of the Good. A well-ordered society and life depend on knowledge of ultimate reality.

On the other hand, Plato could describe how we are to live in this world on the basis of life after we leave this world. We do not inhabit the ideal state on earth, and in many cases, not even a decent approximation of it. Nonetheless, a person is to pursue a knowledge of ultimate reality and to be just in this life. Such heroism is based on the belief that nothing external to us can injure that part of our person which is permanent or immortal. In Book 10 of the *Republic*

Plato argues that the soul can be injured only by a person's own acts of injustice. This is the only evil which can harm the soul. Clearly Plato is here thinking of the soul as a moral agent. We can be good or bad people morally only by our own actions, not by what people do to us. They can deprive us of the benefits of social life, and they can harm our bodies. But the only way we can be harmed morally is by our own action. Since the soul is immortal, moral injury is the most serious harm that can occur to us. We may suffer physically and socially because of others, but such injury is temporary. It ends with the separation of the soul and the body ("death"). In addition, the soul must face judgment after death, and we are rewarded or punished according to whether we have lived justly or not. One is here reminded of Jesus' remark, "And do not fear those who kill the body but cannot kill the soul" (Matt. 10:28a).

Plato's confidence that our well-being is in our own hands is based on the conviction that justice shall be done in the next life, even if it does not prevail in every case in this one. But for some people, this world is our home; there is no other realm. Plato's confidence in a world of Forms, an intelligible reality which is our true home and a knowledge of which gives us true and lasting happiness, was not shared by his greatest pupil, Aristotle. It was not too long before Plato's own Academy had lost an interest in this side of his teachings, so that from the time of his death in 348 B.C. until the great Platonist revival about 100 B.C., philosophy had no great representative who believed we have a home elsewhere. We could not look beyond this life for our happiness.

In addition, the *polis*—the rich life that could be found as a citizen in the city-state which Plato and others sought to revive after the ruinous Peloponnesian War (431–404 B.C.)—continued its generally downward slide. The fabric of city-state life was irrevocably damaged by the rise of the Macedonian Empire under Philip and Alexander the Great. From about 350 B.C. the moral and religious qualities to be found in intense loyalty to the traditions of one's city were becoming inadequate for many people. Where was a thoughtful person to look for a way of life that would ensure his or her well-being?

One answer was provided by the Cynics, whose founder, Diogenes of Sinope (d. 323 B.C.) was such a character that his name, like that of his hero Socrates, is still known to this day among people who have never studied any philosophy. He indeed did live at times in a vat, and at first sight his ideas seem to be an exaggerated version of Socrates' asceticism and a debased version of his irony. In actuality Diogenes had a rationale for his actions, one that enabled a tradition of Cynics to continue until the end of the Roman Empire.

The Cynic is the wise person in action. Philosophy is preeminently a way of life, indeed the life of a wise or sensible person. Its foundation is self-sufficiency *(autarky)* or independence. This is achieved by managing with the bare minimum, so that one is not dependent on anything or anyone. Diogenes once saw someone eating with his hands, so he threw away his only utensil with the word, "Slave!" Since the city-state was no longer able to provide security and a satisfying way of life within its customs and traditions, its demands on a citizen seemed alien to Diogenes. Its life, instead of being liberating, was a form of bondage to him and other Cynics. So the Cynics did not feel any loyalty to the city but wandered from place to place, spreading their teachings by actions and bold speech. They would perform bodily functions in public (shameless actions as they were called) on the grounds that animals did the same, and whatever animals did was natural. Thus they stressed life "according to nature" in contrast to the "conventions" of society, a theme played with many variations down through the ages. Their shameless acts earned them the name "Cynics" from the Greek word for dog, on the ground that they behaved like dogs. In speech they were fearless. Once Diogenes was visited by Alexander the Great who asked him what he could do for him. Diogenes replied, "Stand aside, you're blocking the sunlight." Their popularity was due largely to such fearless wit.

To live a simple life which gave one independence required training *(ascesis)*. So the Cynic had to toughen the body to be able to endure an outdoor life in all weather. By training the Cynic developed apathy *(apatheia)*, an indifference to cold, heat, and pain so as to be beyond the power of anything external. A life according to nature, then, gave one an imperturbable tranquility in the face of the changes and chances of fortune *(tyche)*. It was the surest course to happiness or well-being in an uncertain world. The early Church Fathers sometimes praised Cynicism as a way of life for its stress on simplicity as a positive virtue and because it enabled one to seek for genuine good instead of conventional worldly ones, and *ascesis* gave one endurance under all trials including persecution. Cynicism continued until the Roman world collapsed. There was little point in praising a barbaric life-style when the civilized world had become barbaric.

Stoicism was another response to the decline of the *polis*. It was much more significant than Cynicism, both because it appealed to more people than any other philosophy of antiquity and because of its influence on Christianity. A much glamorized Diogenes was held up by the Stoics as the ideal wise man, and his self-sufficiency, discipline, and apathy were part of their own outlook, but in their hands *tyche* or fortune became providence. For the Stoic there is only life in this world, but, following Plato's *Timaeus*, this world is glorious. It is good as a whole and in every detail of its operations. The universe is governed by a single principle which is rational and immanent. It is the vitalizing, directive force in all things. It is manifest as organism in plants, appetite in animals, and reason in people.

It is possible for us to have our well-being in our own hands. This orderly cosmos is our city or *poleteia*. Our life should be governed by its laws, and not by the petty laws of a particular city. Hence the Stoic is a citizen of the world, a cosmopolitan. This gives birth to that powerful idea in Western culture, "humanity." People by their nature as people have a natural bond which transcends their divisions along cultural and political lines because they are all under the laws of a single cosmos, ruled by a single immanent principle, which is also in each person. In the *Timaeus*, mind as the ruling principle of the physical cosmos supports justice as the governing principle of the ideal city and of the individual soul. But for the Stoic, reason as the principle of nature does not support the particular *poleteia* but the idea of an unwritten natural law which is the same for all people. Morals, human laws, customs, and traditions should conform to the unwritten laws of nature. Natural law transcends the confines of the particular city-state, or indeed of any political entity, and to go against it is to violate our very human nature. Thus in natural law there is an objective standard for both morals and law, which is based on reason and is to guide all wise or reasonable people.

The Stoic idea of natural law permeated the Roman world. It was taken up by Roman jurists and developed into a speculative body of moral ideas and principles to undergird Roman law (*ius civile*) and to rationalize the laws that governed the different people of their empire (*ius gentium*). This tradition was inherited by Christianity, related to God's eternal law, and greatly developed as a basis for ethics and politics during the Middle Ages, especially by Aquinas. It is much too complex to be treated here, but the long article on natural law in the *New Catholic Encyclopedia* gives an overview which is essential for any student of Christian ethics.

For the Stoic the notion of life according to reason or nature means the exercise of our own reason or nature. Colored objects are fitted to our vision and our vision to them just as a blade fits a scabbard and a scabbard a blade. Everything in nature has some use so each item helps make our universe a cosmos, a harmonious whole. Each creature fulfills its purpose by acting according to its nature. Human beings, because they have reason, have the task of discerning those purposes and rendering praise for the gloriously ordered whole.

The Stoics emphasize a point virtually ignored by Plato. All things do not go well for human beings in the operation of the cosmos. It is not only the actions of people but also nature's operations which can injure us. It is here that we find the distinctive note of Stoicism: providence. Greek Stoicism differs considerably from later Roman Stoicism, for which providence becomes fate and has overtones of dread. The most extensive source for early Greek Stoicism is Epictetus, who although he lived in Roman times (A.D. 50–138) was a Greek and was faithful to the original Greek Stoicism. So we shall rely on him for dealing with the Greek Stoic views on the untowardness of the cosmos to us as individuals.

Epictetus tells us that the goodness of the cosmos does not consist in everything going in accordance with our will, with all of our wishes and desires catered for. If we take a comprehensive view, we can see the marvelous fit of each item in the vastly interconnected whole. Many pleasant and unpleasant things happen to individuals because of these interconnections both in the physical universe and in the course of human affairs. But in every instance we can endure what happens to us. We have by nature been endowed with the faculties to bear whatever happens to us without being degraded or crushed. We can wipe our noses because we have hands; we can accept being lame as a small sacrifice toward the rest of the universe; we can even endure an unavoidable death with dignity.

All this can be achieved by recognizing necessity and by exercising the only real freedom we have. Our situation in the physical and social world is that of but one reality among many in a system of interconnected events, most of which are utterly beyond our control. What is beyond an individual's control can sometimes injure one's wealth, social position, body, and even bring utter destruction. In such circumstances an individual's only real freedom is the manner in which one responds to untoward events beyond one's control. One can complain about such misfortune; or bear whatever comes, without degradation by seeing its necessity and yielding to it courageously and magnanimously.

One thus makes *use* of whatever befalls one by using it to bring out these qualities of character. A person can thus be grateful to providence (reason or nature) whatever happens, for providing one with the capacity to recognize the universe as an ordered whole and for the capacity to yield to the adversity it brings—even death—with courage and dignity.

We thus see that to a Stoic, who does not believe there is another realm to go to after death as does Plato, *this* world is *home*. Not only is the cosmos orderly, but human nature and physical nature are related by a single principle which penetrates and gives them both their natures as part of one rationally ordered whole. With our reason, human beings can recognize its orderliness. Indeed, to recognize its orderliness is to live according to our nature, i.e., to make use of our reason. It is our home because of its goodness and because we are equipped to fit into it. Even when we encounter adversity, we have the capacity either to suffer as slaves or to endure adversity with the wisdom which recognizes the inevitable and yields to it calmly. We shall have to obey nature one way or the other, as slaves or as wise people. If we are wise, adversity need not penetrate the innermost fastness of our soul. Ready and joyful assent to the rule of reason by our reason is the whole human duty, the fulfillment of our nature.

The famous Stoic apathy or indifference which we think of as "grin and bear it" is considerably modified by Epictetus. Plato's tripartite soul allows for reason, the highest part of the soul, to govern the lower parts of the soul. Thus the emotions and desires are part of our being and are not to be eradicated but are to be controlled by reason. Greek Stoicism prior to Epictetus, by and large rejected the passions utterly. They were considered irrational, giving us wrong judgments as to what is good and what is bad for us. Freedom from all emotions and affections, or apathy, is the ideal. The Sage is utterly indifferent to all external things and without affections. But if the soul is tripartite, there is a place for our desires and emotions, as long as they are ruled or controlled by reason. It is still an austere ethic but not that of the utterly impassible Sage.

Among the Romans the modifications were carried even further. Drawing upon distinctions made by the founder of Greek Stoicism, Zeno of Citium (336–264 B.C.), the Roman Stoics said that not all external things have the same status. Virtue is not affected by external things, it is true, but some external things are to be "preferred," others to be "deprecated," and still others are "absolutely indifferent." Moreover some actions are "suitable" or "becoming" according to the station in life one occupies. Indeed one is to play the part upon the stage of life assigned to one by reason. Thus a Stoic could take part in public life even though he or she criticized all human institutions, laws, and customs on the basis of a belief in a natural or universal law. A Stoic need not withdraw from public life nor become a revolutionary reformer.

It is this much-toned-down version of Stoicism which Cicero endorsed and helped to popularize. Cicero (106–43 B.C.) was an active statesman who studied Greek philosophy as a refreshing avocation. His superb translations of many Greek philosophical works made him an important transmitter of Greek philosophy to the Latin West, both pagan and Christian, and especially to Augustine. Augustine tells us that his own pilgrimage began with a reading of Cicero's *Hortensius* at the age of eighteen. Reading it was for him a conversion (remember that Plato in the *Republic* describes the turn from this world to philosophy as a conversion). It gave Augustine a new purpose and a new concern: the pursuit of immortal wisdom. That quest, Augustine tells us, eventually led him to Christianity. In the *City of God* Augustine relies on Cicero for his definition of the pagan state, and for his view that it was the virtues of the early Romans which accounted for their success. Cicero was also important to the humanists of the Renaissance and Reformation era. We find that Calvin uses Cicero to support his conviction that "within the human mind, and indeed by natural instinct, there is an awareness of divinity" (*Institutes of the Christian Religion* 1, 3, 1). This is, of course, perverted and dimmed by sin, but still it accounts for the universality of religion in society and is used by Calvin to counter the charge made in his day that religion is an invention of the few to hold simple people in thrall. These are just a few samples of the remarkable influence Cicero had as a transmitter of the ideas of others.

The Stoic stress on providence, especially as viewed by Epictetus with his emphasis on everything having a function and thus contributing to a glorious cosmos, encouraged the development of this theme in Christianity. It is present in the Old Testament, but it is not the dominant way the Israelites think of God's providence. Providence in the Old Testament is seen primarily as God's provision of benefits for them over the course of time. God directs and leads the Israelites through various trials in history and intervenes on their behalf. Providence is thus viewed historically, in terms of what has happened or what is yet to be realized. The Stoics view providence as the unchanging goodness of the very order of nature, both physical and human, so that at all times we may praise "God" for its goodness and, by making good use of our capacities, realize our potential and endure all adversities. This idea was richly developed by Stoicism and popularized, so that it could even be used in catechetical instruction by Christian theologians such as Gregory of Nyssa. There is enough praise for the goodness of the cosmos in the Bible for Christianity to be able to absorb the Stoic view of providence into its own. Thus it is found in Christian worship. See for example the canticle *Benedicite, Omnia Opera Domini* in the Book of Common Prayer in which sun and moon, winds and fire, frosts and snow are said to praise and magnify God simply by acting in accordance with their nature. We who recognize God's providence in the very order of nature and give voice to it in song do as Epictetus and Gregory of Nyssa say we should do, for this is our function or the proper expression of our nature in the providential order. Thus Paul on Mars Hill can cite with approval a line from an old Stoic poem, "in him we live and move and have our being" (Acts 17:28). Stoicism was but one school among others which offered a rule of life, or a way to live rationally and well. We shall not deal with its great rival, Epicureanism because the Epicureans' influence on Christianity was negligible.

The Cynics, Stoics, and Epicureans were all "popularizers." Although Socrates, Plato, and Aristotle were deeply concerned with our well-being and believed that it was to be achieved by the rule of reason in us and a knowledge of the truth, the search for truth for them was a lifelong work. But the Cynics had no use for learning at all, and the Stoics and Epicureans studied only to find an unassailable tranquility. Thus their cosmologies were relatively slap-dash affairs compared to their great predecessors and not up to the standard of reasoning to be found among the academic philosophers of their day. The Stoics borrowed eclectically, and Epicurus, whose teachings were not modified by his followers, adopted the crude atomism of Democritus (a pre-Socratic we did not mention earlier). But it was to schools such as these, especially the Stoics, that educated people looked for guidance. Plato's Academy not too long after his death, turned away from his metaphysical and ethical concerns for several generations. Aristotle's successors became highly competent specialists. The academic type of philosopher was thus of no use to people who were looking for guidance on how to live, a situation rather like our own in twentieth century English-speaking philosophy. For most people today philosophy still bears the impress of Socrates; it is the search for a rational way of life. Academic philosophers then and now, however, take note of the popularizers and criticize their views with such devastating ingenuity as to lead their readers into radical scepticism concerning the possibility of knowledge. This was particularly true in ancient times. The Sceptics did, however, produce one of the most important sources we have for our knowledge of ancient philosophy. Sextus Empiricus (A.D. ca. 150–225), in order to show the contradictions between the various philosophies, had to say a great deal about them.

We also find something of their legacy in the mark they made on Augustine. He passed through a painful period in his early life when their Scepticism drove him to universal doubt. Augustine later very carefully and thoroughly refuted the sceptical position, searching for indubitable truth, which it is quite literally impossible to doubt. Unlike the Stoics and Epicureans, who are more concerned with a way of life that assures one of tranquility, Augustine is not satisfied until he can refute the Sceptics.

His reasoning is familiar to those of us who have heard of the type of argument used much later by Descartes: "I think, therefore I am." It is impossible to doubt that one exists because in order to doubt it, one must think, and to think one must exist. But unlike Descartes, Augustine only sought to refute the sceptical stance or position. He does not seek to build an indubitable philosophy on the foundation of the indubitable truths he uses to refute the sceptical position, for Augustine rejects the basic idea that only indubitable knowledge is admissible as knowledge.

From about 100 B.C. to about A.D. 200 there was a revival of Plato known as Middle Platonism, which reached its peak in the third century in the original work of Plotinus. It is genuinely Platonic but differs in many ways from Plato himself, developing matters he only touched on and showing the influence of Aristotle. Our only concern with this Platonic revival is as a background to the philosophy of Plotinus who deeply influenced Augustine and through Augustine subsequent theology.

The Middle Platonists viewed the human soul as belonging to another realm but as now fallen into the sense world. The object of life is to purify the soul by philosophy so we may return to a disembodied life in which we enjoy the vision of true reality. This is highly familiar to us from Plato himself. The departure from Plato that concerns us is some modifications of the *Timaeus*. Middle Platonism places a Supreme Mind as the supreme reality at the head of a hierarchy of beings. The manner of this transformation is easily seen if we recall that Plato in the *Timaeus* said that the "father and maker of all this universe is past finding out" (28c). So Plato told a story of a craftsman making the visible world by using the world of Forms as the pattern. Because according to the *Timaeus* the visible world is the handiwork of intelligence or mind, the Middle Platonists quite naturally describe the supreme principle as mind. In the *Republic* Plato had the Form of the Good as head of the hierarchy of Forms; Middle Platonists identify the Form of the Good with the Supreme Mind itself. Since the "father and maker of all" is remote, they fill the gap between him and the visible world with a hierarchy of beings. Plato gave them ample precedent, for whenever he had trouble connecting one thing with another, he would place something between the two (*metaxu*).

The identification of the Form of the Good with the Supreme Mind reinforces the remoteness of the Supreme Mind since, as Plato said in the *Republic*, knowledge of the Good is only possible for a few people after a lifetime of effort. For the Middle Platonists, knowledge of the Good is reserved for the next life, except for a few of them who thought that occasional flashes of vision of the Good are possible in this life. But the remoteness took on a decidedly different character under the influence of Aristotle's "unmoved mover." The Middle Platonists, as Plotinus after them, sought to reconcile Plato and Aristotle and took from Aristotle some of the features of his unmoved mover and applied them to their Supreme Mind. Aristotle's unmoved mover is mind but is so remote from this world (even though it is its top story) as to be utterly unaware of it. It is aware only of its own thought as it engages in perpetual contemplation. It affects what is outside itself only indirectly through intermediaries. The Middle Platonists adopted the view of the Supreme Mind as absolutely free of all external activities and exalted it to such a height that it has no direct contact with the material world. The Supreme Mind is still head of a hierarchy of beings, or the top story of the universe, unlike the Christian God, who as Creator transcends the universe. This is a point we shall stress later in connection with Plotinus.

One can easily see the possibility of an enormous increase or an inflation of intermediary powers between the Supreme Mind and the sensible world. The more one stresses remoteness of the Supreme Mind from the material world, the more ingenuity one can expend in populating the world with entities in decreasing gradations of ontological reality to connect the top to the bottom of the universe. Plato's charming "likely story" of a craftsman copying the world of Forms is turned into a realistic description.

Philo, an Alexandrian Jew who died about A.D. 50, was affected by Middle Platonism's stress on intermediaries between the Supreme Mind and the world. He was saturated in hellenistic philosophy and sought to reconcile the Jewish Scriptures with Plato. As a Jew, he believed God was active in creating and ruling the cosmos, but he also stressed God's transcendence and saw God as acting through various intermediary powers. Philo is vague about the relationship between these intermediaries and God, and he is not consistent in his description of them. Sometimes there are two, sometimes several, but often a single and great intermediary, the Logos.

Heraclitus first used the term *logos* in a philosophical sense. His *logos* is the principle or ratio or proportion that keeps a balance between the opposing pairs of things in the world process, and he described it as the principle of life and intelligence. The Stoics, in their eclectic physical theory of the cosmos, also spoke of a *logos* and used Heraclitus' image of fire for it. They believed that the formative principle of individual things in nature is part of a universal fiery principle. Individual things develop from "seeds" or *logoi*. For the Stoics, the seminal *logoi* are parts of the fire or *logos* (reason or nature) permeating all things, causing their growth, development, and action. The early Stoics believed in an endless cycle of worlds, somewhat as Heraclitus did, being generated by the divine fire of all things returning and disappearing in a great conflagration. After a pause the cosmos will arise once again. Combined with their view of necessity or fate, they held for a time to the theory that each world in the cycle was exactly like the previous one, so each individual appeared again and again in each successive world.

There are, of course, uses of the term "word" (*dâbar*) in the Old Testament. There are even poetical personifications of the Word of God in Psalms 33:4–7; 107:20; and 147:15. These are augmented in the Targums, the expanded traditions of the Old Testament. *Dâbar* is translated in the Septuagint as *logos*. So Philo had a term that was used in both of the traditions he was trying to bring together, Jewish and Platonic.

In Philo the Logos is not only an intermediary, or instrument by which God makes the world, but he frequently identifies the Logos with the Platonic world of Forms. We have just noted that Plato himself did not identify the world of Forms with the mind—either of the craftsman or the father of all things. The Middle Platonists did this. Philo follows them but in addition makes the important step of identifying the Logos with the Forms. Thus it is possible for the early Church Fathers to think of the three together: Divine Mind, Forms as the thoughts of the Divine Mind, and Logos as the Wisdom of God—the instrument of creation and the principle of its order. (See Proverbs 3:19–20; 8:22–31 where Wisdom is associated with creation.)

The identification of Jesus as the Logos in Revelation 19:13 (the Logos of God as eschatological victor and judge) owes nothing to Philo. The use of Logos for Christ in I John 1:1 and in John 1:1–18 has not been accounted for. But Philo clearly developed the meaning of Logos with an eye to Plato and the Platonists, whereas the Johannine material develops the theme by reference to Jesus. Still the term *logos* in both Heraclitus and the Stoics had cosmic import, and its tie to the Platonic world of Forms by Philo gave it even richer associations for theologians to explore. To connect Jesus with this philosophical material at all is to make Jesus not just Savior or Messiah in Jewish terms but to give him cosmic significance in hellenic terms. Clearly John 1:1–18 intends to elevate Jesus into a cosmic role, by relating him to the creation story of Genesis 1. It is by him and with him that the world was formed. This is the thrust of John, apart from any connection with the *specific* identification of the Supreme Mind and Plato's Forms, or the Logos, Supreme Mind, and the Forms. But Philo did make these specific connections, as did the Christian theologians who followed Philo's lead. As we said in chapter 1, we shall see the consequences of this specific identification in our discussion of the medieval and modern periods.

We come now to Plotinus himself (A.D. 205–270). He lived through one of the most politically unsettled periods of the Roman

Empire, but there is not the slightest trace of this in his writings. The political concerns of Plato are of no interest to him. The city-state of Plato's day is long since gone as the environment within which human beings are to realize their potential. Thus Plotinus draws mostly on those dialogues of Plato which stress that our proper life is to be found by a knowledge of another realm (the *Phaedo*, *Phaedrus*, and the *Symposium*) or on those parts of the *Timaeus* and the *Republic* which do the same. As for other Platonists, so for Plotinus the soul is divine and the object of life is to understand how we may restore the soul to its proper place. This can be done by a comprehensive knowledge of reality and our place in it. Unlike Christians, Plotinus shares the conviction of most Greek philosophers that human beings have the power to gain a satisfactory knowledge of all reality, including divine things because human beings are divine by nature and like can know like. Thus access to divine things is possible without a revelation. But unlike the Stoics and the other Middle Platonists, he is a philosopher of truly great ability. It is very difficult to understand his thought, but like all philosophy from Plato on, its double character is obvious. Philosophy is a complete account of reality that is at the same time a guide to life, and in Plotinus' case, to a life that is beyond the sensible world. To know that reality, for him as for Plato, requires purification or virtue, and not just mental ability.

What, according to Plotinus, is that reality which must be known if we are to live properly? We may approach this difficult question by recalling the problem of the One and the Many. The Ionian philosophers sought to discover the unifying principle behind the multiplicity of the visible world. Plotinus, in the Platonist tradition, seeks that unity in what is intelligible rather than in what is material. He inherited from the Middle Platonists the view that the supreme principle is Mind and the world of Forms is its thoughts. But Plotinus, who sought to reconcile Plato and Aristotle, draws upon a principle of Aristotle's theory of sense perception to get an even greater unity between Mind and its thoughts (the Forms). Aristotle distinguishes two major phases in all change; the movement from potentiality to actuality. He uses them in his account of sense perception. A sense organ, such as an eye, is not what it perceives. But a sense organ is *potentially* like its object of perception. It actually becomes like the object it perceives. It receives the *form* of the object, not the object itself. By receiving its form, the sense organ becomes like the object of perception. Plotinus uses this view in his account of the unity of the Supreme Mind and its objects, the Forms. Its awareness is like what it is aware of; in fact, it *is* what it is aware of since all it is aware of is its own thoughts which are the Forms.

The Supreme Mind and the world of Forms which are its contents are not the highest reality however. For Plotinus the unity between the Supreme Mind and the Forms is indeed immense, but it still involves the duality of subject and object. So we do not have an absolute and unqualified unity. So above Mind and the Forms there is the One. Following Plato, who in the *Republic* said that the Form of the Good is above the other Forms and is beyond being, Plotinus' One is beyond being and nothing can be said of it literally, not even that it is. But he also calls it Good, and claims that this is a name for the One and not an attribute or property of it. Plotinus is clearly influenced both by the unity given to the Forms by the Form of the Good in the *Republic* and also by Parmenides' notion of unity as absolute and unqualified oneness.

Multiplicity is the result of the overflow of the One "downward." This spatial term is not to be taken literally. It is an ontological term designating *degrees* of reality; the less unity, the less reality. So we move downward in that sense from the One. The One overflows by necessity, and this overflow descends level by level to the physical universe. Plotinus frequently uses the metaphor of emanation for this overflow, and uses the image of the sun radiating light. The One by its very nature radiates realities. It does not become less by this radiation, so this outpouring has no beginning or end. The total order and structure of the entire universe is unchanging or static, but it is not dead. It is full of life, and life at its highest is a life of intense, self-contained, contemplative activity, of which the life of movement, change, and production of things on the physical level are faint images. So although the total order and structure never change, there is a "flow" within it, which consists of a downward movement from the One and an upward movement back to the One.

How does this movement occur? For Plotinus there are three

main "hypostases" or individual divine substances which make up the intelligible universe: the One, Mind, and Soul. We have already distinguished the One from Mind by the fact that Mind in spite of its immense unity still contains the duality of subject and object. But we need to explain the mechanism which produces the flow or movement from the One to Mind. To start with, Mind emanates outward from the One automatically. Mind has the potential to know. By its activity of contemplation, the world of Forms arises. This happens because Mind seeks to be united with the One from which it has emanated or radiated, but it cannot remain itself as Mind and at the same time know the One. For then it is subject and the One is object, so the unity is not absolute. But what results from Mind's attempts to know the One is the world of Forms. The world of Forms is the way the One or Good is known by Mind. The absolute unity is known at the level of Mind as the multiplicity of the Forms. There is a high degree of unity at this level, for the Forms have a unity or order, and Mind in knowing its object becomes like it, so Mind is its own thoughts. But it is not the absolute unity of the highest level where oneness is unqualified.

The activity of contemplation (the Mind's attempt to know the One) is thus productive. Mind by its movement out from the One has the potential to know; by its movement of return, i.e., the actual attempt to know the One, it generates the Forms on its own level of reality. The Forms *represent* the One on the level of the contemplative mind. Mind or Nous timelessly emanates or radiates from the One as potency (ability to know) and timelessly Mind actually knows the One as the multiplicity of Forms. Mind cannot grasp the One in its own unity, on its own level, without losing itself. As long as it remains in its proper activity of contemplation, it can receive the One only in plurality.

The third great hypostasis is Soul. It also contemplates or thinks but it is distinguished from Mind because its thought is discursive, that is, its thoughts are successive. Mind's contemplation or thought is intuitive. For Plotinus, like Plato, the highest knowledge is intuitive. The Mind has a vision of the truth all at once, rather than having thought after thought. The level of Mind for Plotinus is thus *noesis*, or the realm of intuitive knowledge, in which the Forms are grasped all at once in a flash. Thus the unity is higher at the level of Mind than at the level of Soul, which is the realm of discursive thought (*dianoia*) in which the objects are known successively.

Soul is the most wide-ranging and various in its activities of the three hypostases. It is the cause of the sense world and represents the intelligible world to the sense world. Not only does it think discursively, but it also has the whole range of lower forms of sense consciousness. Although distinct from Mind, at the top of its range Soul reaches the realm of Mind, and with Mind it can rise in self-transcendence to union with the One. The mechanism for this will be explained later when we come to the human mind. But here let us only note that even though the three hypostases are distinct and hierarchically arranged, they are not utterly cut off from each other. The One and Mind are always present to Soul which is important for the return of human beings to the intelligible world.

The life of Mind is at rest. It is the life of thought in eternal, immediate, and simultaneous possession of all possible objects in knowing the Forms all at once. The Soul, like Mind, desires to be itself, i.e., to know. So Soul can be soul only by not having all things present to it simultaneously, but by having its objects one after the other. So there is succession to its awareness, a continuous series of thoughts. This is the same as time. Time is the life of the Soul, "moving from one way of living to another." Soul is thus the immediate source of the temporal physical universe, even though the radiation from One to Mind is the ultimate source. Soul plays the role of Plato's craftsman, operating directly on the physical universe with what it receives from Mind (the Forms). Plotinus describes the relation with the term *logos*. *Logos* often means in Greek philosophy the active, formative principle of something. Plotinus retains this but speaks of *logos* as an expression, image, or representation of a higher level of reality on a lower level. So Soul is the *logos* of Mind, and the active principles operating in the visible world through Soul are *logoi* of the Forms of Mind. Each level of reality for Plotinus is represented at a lower level, but each image of an image is a less powerful *logos* or formative principle. Reality is an unfolding from the top downward, so to speak, or from maximum unity to increasing multiplicity because the organizing principles (*logoi*) are less powerful at each level.

Soul governs the material world from the "inside." That is to say, Soul is not an external intelligence planning and arranging movement of mindless matter. The motions and order of the material world spring from the presence of Soul in its various *logoi* permeating the visible world and acting spontaneously without thought. So we have Forms springing forth as the spontaneous result of Mind contemplating the One, and Soul's spontaneous production of *logoi* of the Forms, which in turn move and order the physical universe. But Soul's own products are "dead," i.e., they are nonproductive. The *logoi* of the Forms in bodies are incapable of sufficient contemplation to produce images at a still lower level. So the downward process from the One comes to an end. Things are produced "horizontally," so to speak, in the physical world, but there is no production "downward" to a new level of being below the physical.

At the bottom of the descent from the One we reach utter negativity. The creative descent must bring everything into being which can have any kind of existence. The Good or One can only stop communicating itself when it reaches the level where there cannot be any image of goodness at all, or unity, or reality. This is to reach the quasi-existence of "matter," where the Forms (or their *logoi*) of bodies are like reflections in a formless mirror. The Forms do not unite with matter to make a single reality (as they do in Aristotle). Matter is a passive receptable in which the Forms are present but it remains totally unchanged and unaffected by the Forms. It can never be given any positive qualities or brought any nearer to reality or goodness. It remains always totally otherness, absolute privation, and negativity. Thus the "matter" of the sense world, below the sphere of the moon, is evil. The heavenly bodies are perfectly formed by their soul, and the light they give off is not a bodily thing but manifests their incorporeal activity.

We, who are souls, have knowledge of the *sensible* world but only because we can know the Forms of Mind. Our knowledge owes nothing to the body or the senses. It comes directly "from within" because of our contact and kinship with Mind which illumines us. The senses at best help us turn our attention inward and upward.

This higher knowledge of the Forms provides our discursive reason with the proper principles for making judgments about sense experience and guiding our life in the body. We also of course receive information, in contrast to knowledge, about the material world through our sense organs, but even sense perceptions, feelings, and desires are not purely corporeal. Sheer impressions on the body do not give them; only an ensouled body can have them.

But it is not knowledge of the material world which is significant for Plotinus. Humanity is *essentially* and *always* in the lowest of the three divine realms, that of the Soul. The One and the Mind are always present to Soul, and thus always present to our true selves. But Soul extends from the lower edge of the realm of Mind down through the sense world. Humanity is therefore double, with a higher soul close to and illumined by Mind and a lower soul. The lower soul is an expression or *logos* of our higher soul on the level of the physical world. We must discipline the lower soul as a prosaic but demanding duty. When we leave the sense world, if we are philosophical, our higher souls no longer have lower souls. Otherwise we are reincarnated with lower souls and perhaps with nonhuman bodies.

The procedure for getting rid of our lower souls is to gain knowledge. We presently are between our higher souls and our lower souls. That is, our intellects are stimulated by the action on us from above (whereby we attend to the Forms), and we also receive material from our senses. We can direct our attention upward or downward. That is, we can use the illumination of Mind which is always available to us, to expand to universality in the eternal world of truth and real being, or we can concentrate on the petty individual concerns of this world, of our bodies and earthly desires. (We can also fluctuate in our attention between the two.) Our entire way of living depends on the direction of our attention, and it is the function of philosophy to turn us and direct us upward.

Plotinus often describes "turning upward" as waking from our dreamlike obsession with the needs and desires of our lower selves in the world of sense. The way out of the dream is by vigorous moral and intellectual self-discipline. We move by degrees toward the realm of Mind as our discursive grasp of the world of Forms progresses from knowing *about* it to intuiting or contemplating the Forms themselves. The well-being of the true self, the higher soul, cannot be increased by an external good, nor can it be decreased by any external suffering or loss, however great. The body-soul complex can be distressed but the higher soul cannot be touched.

The philosopher can reach the goal of life, the vision and union with the Good (One) in this world and while he or she is still in the body. The philosopher who contemplates the Forms is filled with the object of his or her awareness and thus is like them. In that respect his or her soul is like Mind which has the same object for its attention and which is also like what it knows. Indeed, Mind *is* what it knows—or is united with it—and so too is the philosopher in attending to the Forms. Union with Mind is achieved by means of this common contemplation. Particular philosophical souls by being fully informed by the Forms are united with them and so united with each other.

It is at this point that Plotinus remarks that each soul is All. This sounds like the Hindu notion that release from multiplicity is to be found by recognition and realization that I am All. In Plotinus it seems to mean that each particular subject's union with all that it knows on the level of Mind—where the objects are the Forms, which are all the possible ways for things to be—is the same thing as to be identified with All. Plotinus can thus describe the object of life to be a realization of the soul and its proper relation to the All. To know thyself is to know thy place in the whole of reality.

From this level of union it is possible to reach the final vision and union with the One or the Good. For Plotinus this is a mystical experience and, as in the case of so many mystics, there are rival interpretations as to whether the mystical experience is one of absorption or of a union in which particularity remains. But if we insist on the ever-present distinction of Mind from the One, and note that Mind at the same time attains union with the One, we can perhaps get an idea of Plotinus' meaning.

For Plotinus we can be united with the Good because our intellect perfectly conforms to it and is thus made like it. This conformity can be achieved by love. Mind which emanates from the One by thinking, also seeks to know the One (to be united to it). Mind thus generates the Forms which are a representation of the One on the level of Mind. But besides knowing the One (Good) in this fashion, it also loves the One (Good). This love is the power which enables it to think and by thinking to produce the Forms as the content of its thoughts. But this love is itself a state distinct from the state of knowing. It is a state in which the contents of the Mind's own thought (the Forms) are not present to it. It is compared to a drunken state, in which one is outside oneself, in ecstasy. (Plato in the *Phaedrus* calls love a divine madness.) The Mind in love thus attains self-transcendence—as it is without the Forms as its content—and is united to the One by love. Mind is eternally and unchangeably in two states simultaneously, one "sober" and one "drunk," one knowing and one loving. It eternally pursues its proper activity of knowing while it eternally is raised above itself in the union of love with the One.

The philosopher who has attained the level of contemplation of the Forms by "looking upward" or "looking inward" (both are the same because they involve turning one's attention away from the world of sense as the object of interest and desires), and who is thus not just knowing *about* the Forms, can by love experience the ecstatic union with the One or Good, being joined to the eternal and unchanging love of Mind for the One. So the final goal can be reached while still in the body on earth. The higher soul can have the contents of Mind (the Forms) present to it, and by attending to the Forms, have Mind present to it or united to it. From this knowing union with the Mind, it can have the One, which is present to Mind be present to it as well by love. After death (the breakup of the soul-body complex) the higher soul is permanently in its proper place with no representation at a lower level. Embodiment (representation at a lower level) is a regrettable necessity of the full outpouring of the One or Good, but we are to seek to live even in embodiment as though we were out of the body, which is to live detached from material and earthly desires.

Plotinus himself had an intense and immediate sense of the splendor, strength, and solidity of spiritual reality. His writings, however opaque and difficult, had a powerful effect on those who studied them. Augustine pays tribute to their effect on him. They enabled him to realize that spiritual realities do exist and have priority over sensible ones. This was particularly important for Augustine, for it freed him from adherence to Manichaeism as the best explanation of the universe. Manichaeism was a popular religion, closely related to earlier Gnostic systems. It, like them, regarded Good and Evil as two independent forces engaged in ceaseless conflict. Both are material; one is material light and the other material darkness. God is a vast luminous body beyond the sky from whom proceeds an elaborate hierarchy of emanations. The material world is a kingdom of evil and darkness created by the Evil principle. Human beings are fragments of divine light imprisoned in bodies, from which they may be delivered after many incarnations by various ascetic practices and a purgatorial ascent through the upper regions of the universe. Thanks to Plotinus and also to the preaching of Ambrose which Augustine heard at the time he was becoming acquainted with Plotinus, Augustine was able to realize that God is not material.

Augustine (354–430) was one of the great Christian Platonists. Both he and Gregory of Nyssa (d. 394) as well as other theologians of the fourth and fifth centuries began to use the ideas of Plotinus about the three divine hypostases to gain a deeper understanding of God. The modifications they made to Plotinus are vital, and they arise because of Christian doctrine. The Christian doctrine of creation in particular made it impossible for them to think in terms of *degrees* of divinity. There is a sharp division between the Creator and all else in Christianity. One is either fully divine or not divine at all. (The Arians in the controversies over the relation of Jesus to God ran afoul of this principle when they tried to retain Jesus the Son as divine but to a lesser degree than God the Father.) So the hierarchy of degrees of divinity—the One, Mind, and Soul—is rejected, as well as Plotinus' view of the place of human beings on the lower end of the spectrum of divinity of Mind and at the top end of the spectrum of the divinity of Soul. Human beings are created in the divine image, but we are not divine, and we have so perverted our nature that we cannot be restored simply by knowledge, as in Plotinus, even if we include Plotinus' program of virtue and detachment from the sensible world in our understanding of knowledge, so that it includes all of our person. In other words, sin and the absolute necessity of God's grace mark an unbridgeable chasm between Christianity and Plotinus, and indeed all hellenic philosophies and religions which view human nature as essentially divine and merely caught or trapped somehow in the sensible world. Our problem in Christianity is not that we are divine and are in a nondivine place. That we have a destiny does not mean that the sensible world is not our proper or rightful place. For Christianity, unlike Platonism, the great division is between Creator and creature, not between the intelligible and the sensible worlds.

These are only a few of the differences between Christianity and Plotinus. Another which we need to explore more fully concerns Plotinus' claim that the One exceeds our thought and language. Christianity says this of God, and indeed Greek-speaking theologians and Augustine are influenced by Plotinus on this matter. So it is important to be clear about the way distinctive Christian convictions affect what is borrowed from Plotinus.

Plotinus seeks to account for the multiplicity around us. To account for it, he must posit a source for its unity. Then by further reasoning, he must determine how that source is to be characterized, if it is indeed to account for the multiple reality of which we are aware. He finds that the source of unity must itself have a unity that is absolute; for a principle that accounts for the unity in all the multiplicity of the universe cannot itself lack unity or be in need of further unification. It must be absolute unity. It cannot have the shadow of plurality. This is the element of Parmenides in Plotinus.

For Plotinus, to be is to be in some sense a unity. The degree of unification anything has determines its place in the scale of reality. At the top of the scale of reality there must be that which is the principle of unity, that which gives a degree of unity to each thing in order for it to be a single coherent whole-in-diversity, whether it be a blade of grass, a cow, a person. But the principle of unity at the top of the scale of reality must itself be absolutely one. Thus it cannot be Mind and Forms (a subject with the objects of its attention). This would introduce plurality, for although the unity between a Mind and its thoughts is very great, it still involves the duality of subject and object. All specifications as this or that are denied of the principle of unity for fear of compromising its unity, and so destroying its ability to give all else unity. The result is that we can describe the One only by negations. It is not Mind, it is not a Form, it is not any being, nor does it have the properties of any beings we have in either the intelligible or sensible universe. It is above all beings and above being itself.

This aspect of Plotinus is *not* acceptable to Christianity. It is not the reason Christian theologians say that God is beyond words and thoughts. They are influenced by the emphasis on unity because they too think that unity is necessary for anything to be something. A thing's properties and actions have to be held together in some fashion. God as Creator is the source of the existence of various kinds of things, so God is the source of the various kinds of unity we find in different created things. But they do not refuse all determinations to God for fear of compromising God's unity, as Plotinus does whenever he has the Parmenidean sense of unity in mind. Christian theologians believe that God's unity is not an absolute unity, which is the mere negation of plurality. God's unity is indeed beyond the kinds of unity created realities have. The unity of God is not that of a building, an organism, a genus or a species, or any other class or set. Thus it is beyond human thought. All we can say is that God is genuinely One and that divine unity is a rich one. But *how* God's power, wisdom, goodness, and other characteristics are united, we do not know. We thus do not fear attributing to God power, wisdom, goodness, love, and other attributes (such as being three persons, Father, Son, and Holy Spirit), as well as actions, (such as calling Israel to be a special people or becoming human in order to redeem us). The unity of God, divine oneness, does not prevent Christian theologians from affirming these specific determinations of God, however much they involve us in the mystery of being unable to grasp or specify the nature of the divine unity in them all.

This difference is largely due to the fact that Plotinus has the multiplicity of the things in the universe to account for, and to do so, he must find a principle of unity. That principle he feels cannot be compromised, for then he would fail in his project of accounting for the multiplicity around us. In this sense Plotinus' One is simply the top story of reality. It does not genuinely transcend it, however much he says it is beyond Mind, beyond the Forms, incapable of being given any determination, and the source of all else. A decisive reason to say that the One of Plotinus lacks genuine transcendence is that it radiates or emanates by *necessity*. It cannot exist *by itself*; there must be something in addition to it.

The Christian God is not initially affirmed to be because of some desire to account for the multiplicity around us. The people of Israel confess that they encountered God, who has called them to be God's people. God's actions in the course of their common life showed them that God is above all things and the soure of all. But God creates *freely*, not by any necessity. God can exist without any creatures. Yahweh can create freely and can exist without any creatures because the Godhead is complete in itself. The Christian conception of the completeness of God is described as consisting of life as Father, Son, and Holy Spirit. The trinitarian life is one of fullness and completeness, so there is no need to create or to communicate outside of it.

The completeness of God is the reason God is not the top story of a hierarchy of beings, profane or otherwise, which the mind discovers or postulates in its attempt to explain or understand the universe of multiplicity, or in its attempt to secure our well-being. God can exist fully without a universe at all and so is not its top story. It is in this sense that in Christianity God transcends all created realities. This sense contrasts with Plotinus' sense of "transcendence," which is largely that we cannot characterize the principle of unity or give it any determinations because it would then be destroyed as the principle that accounts for all the unity-in-multiplicity we find in all other things and the universe as a whole.

It is for this reason that Christian theologians of the fourth and fifth centuries who were influenced by Plotinus modified him. In brief what they did is to drop the notion of a divine hierarchy—descending from the One, to Mind, to Soul—and applied much of what Plotinus has to say about them to God as Trinity. The descriptions of the inner trinitarian life as one of coinherence or indwelling draw upon Plotinus' understanding of spiritual or intelligible realities. Material things cannot occupy the same place but exclude one another. Spiritual realities, not being spatial, do not exclude one another but may be fully present to one another. In their coinherence they are not a mixture, as are material things when unified. The circulation of reality in Plotinus' scheme of "movement"-"outward"-"return" is also exploited. Theologians make special use of what Plotinus has to say about Mind (his second hypostasis) by applying it to the second person of the Christian Trinity, the Son. The Son is the Divine Wisdom through whom all created beings are made and in whom the Forms—the exemplars of all created things—are present. All things thus exist only insofar as they are more or less representations or imperfect versions of God's perfections. It is only by so participating in God that they possess being.

The Bible says that the natural world's size and order reveal God's power and wisdom. But the identification by these theologians of the Forms with the Mind of God means that a far more specific knowledge of God can be given to us by the natural world than just impressions of God's power and wisdom. It is possible to move from the limited perfections of creatures to a knowledge of God's perfections, rather than to know God only from the act of calling Israel and from other saving acts in history. Nature and Scripture each yield the same truths about God's nature. Scripture gives us the names of God's attributes, which are the archetypes of all created realities and hence accessible to us from a knowledge of created realities.

The transcendence of God is expressible and was expressed by early Christian theologians by use of Plotinus' *second* way of speaking of the transcendence of the One. The One in Plotinus is also called Good. Plotinus was influenced here by Plato's remark in the *Republic* that the Forms have their unity from the Form of the Good. It stands above them at the pinnacle of the hierarchy of Forms, and Plato says that the Form of the Good is above being (*ousia*). Plotinus goes a step beyond Plato; the Good is not a Form at all, and so at times he speaks interchangeably of the One and the Good. The One-as-Good also cannot have (or does not have) any predicates or determinations. The One-as-Good is the source of all and is *more and better* than the reality it is the source of. Its excellence is beyond our language and thought, which are limited to the Forms, to their sensible images, and to Mind, Soul, and to lesser minds and souls. It surpasses the hierarchy of limited realities because it is infinitely perfect. This way of speaking of the One—the One-as-Good—by Plotinus comes closer to the Christian concept of God. Theologians also speak of God with negations when they say that God's goodness, power, and wisdom are not the goodness, power, and wisdom of created realities because they are perfect and without any limits. They cannot be grasped by the intellect because of their superabundance. But there is a difference. For Plotinus, the One-as-Good is beyond all thought because it is above the second hypostasis, the highest level of thought. But in Christianity, the second hypostasis—the Son, the Wisdom of the Father—is *fully* divine. To speak about the thoughts or mind of God is to be speaking of God, not something less than the ultimate reality. The reason created realities do not fully reveal God's nature to us is not because creatures reflect something that is less than the ultimate reality. It is rather because, in the first place, creatures are reflections, and reflections only, of ultimate reality. In the second place, it is because God does not have to create at all. God's fullness is such that God is complete without creatures. That fullness, as it is in itself, is unknowable to us. Such knowledge of the fullness of the divine nature as we have is given to us through God's revelation to us as Creator and Redeemer. God thus surpasses creatures, not only insofar as the goodness, power, wisdom, and other qualities they have are limited versions or reflections of the divine nature, but they are limited versions or reflections of that nature insofar as God has *chosen* to be related. It is not merely the fact that the human mind cannot characterize the unity and goodness of the Source of all that makes our characterizations of God limited. It is that the Source of all is more than the source of the unity and goodness of the created universe.

In spite of this important difference, Plotinus' notion of the second hypostasis as Mind and the Forms as its thoughts is used by theologians to give a basis for *some* knowledge of God through a knowledge of created beings. The natural world reflects the Mind of God *insofar as God is Creator*. God is all that they reflect and more, both because as their source God is more than their limited perfections, and because there is more to the divine nature than being the cause of the universe and the Redeemer of fallen human beings. A ladder of beings consisting of the creatures' degrees of perfection is established when the archetypes of creatures are identified with the Mind of God, and *some* knowledge of God in that relation is possible.

Plotinus also greatly influenced the description of the perfection of the soul and the spiritual life. Both Plotinus and Christian Platonists think of perfection or our final end in terms of our unity with the ultimate reality. For both unity is achieved by becoming like the highest. In Plotinus we become like Mind (before we move to the final union with the One) by a knowledge of the Forms (first discursively, then intuitively). But as higher souls, we are always close to and ever present to Mind. In other words, our *potential* to know the Forms is always present in us as part of our nature. Our proper place—on the level of Mind—is inherent in our nature and is not conferred on us. Nor can it be lost, even when we become embodied. Our restoration (or salvation) is thus simply a move from being *potentially* like Mind to becoming *actually* like Mind. That is, actually to know the Forms intuitively. Then with Mind we can move into union with the One.

In Christianity we do *not* have a likeness to God in the sense of being on the lower edge of the divine level of reality, even potentially. Although we are made in the image of God, we are creatures. Jesus, however, is divine and human. Thus he is the mediator between us and God. Our relation to God is established by faith and grace, for we are in a state of sin. We are thus raised by Christ to a participation in the divine life.

Because the Christian Platonists think of Christ as similar to Plotinus' second hypostasis (the divine Mind), they think of our ascent to union with God in a similar manner, namely as occurring by an increasing knowledge of God. Christ as the Wisdom of God enlightens our minds to give us knowledge of the principles of created nature, both physical and human, as well as God's actions in history. For us, to increase in knowledge of Christ, who is the Wisdom of God, is to grow more like what we know. To increase in our knowledge of the relations of the Father, Son, and Holy Spirit is to move more into their likeness. So however much faith and grace are involved in the revelation, wisdom is also involved in our spiritual ascent. The final goal is deification (*henosis*). We remain creatures, and so we do not become God; but we have such a *likeness to Christ as human* as to be united with the Trinity. That is to say, we share in the divine life, and this is the reason we were created.

The Platonist tradition, even when Christianized by faith and grace, has a tendency to overemphasize the part of an increasing knowledge of God in the soul's ascent. The knowledge is highly "spiritualized," that is, it encourages a steady movement away from the created universe in which we are to learn to live with one another as forgiven creatures. It tends to encourage a contemplative life as the Christian vocation *par excellence*.

Plotinus had one clearly unfortunate effect on Christian Platonists. We may illustrate this with Augustine. Plotinus thought of the soul as a substance, that is as able to exist on its own, unembodied. Augustine, as a Christian, knew that the whole person is not just a soul, but is soul and body (or spirit, soul, and body, if one follows some of Paul's remarks, but this does not change the point being made here). However, Augustine still regarded the soul as a separate, independent, and complete spiritual substance. We are rational souls which have a body we use.

We can see this view of the soul as complete in itself in operation in Augustine's theory of knowledge. In his refutation of the Sceptics, he relies on our knowledge of ourselves as thinking subjects. This knowledge is not gained through the senses. Indeed, following the Platonists, whenever we make a true judgment, it derives its necessity and universality from some illumination of our minds by the Forms in the mind of God. Thus it is from Christ alone, the divine Wisdom, that we gain truth, not only of spiritual matters but about this world. (Augustine never explains very precisely how our minds are illumined by the eternal truths, the Forms.)

This stress on soul as a spiritual substance with access to genuine knowledge, in contrast to the information provided by the senses, encouraged Augustine toward an "inwardness." Like Plotinus he tends to turn away from the external, material world (even though it is based on the archetypes of the divine mind) and to concentrate on God and the soul. This indeed tends to etherealize the Christian life. We shall see, however, from his great work *On the Trinity*, that

Augustine's Platonic inwardness can nonetheless bear positive results.

The Platonist revival which started about 100 B.C., did not end with Plotinus. It underwent a new phase which is often called late Neoplatonism to distinguish it from Middle Platonism. It greatly expanded the levels of intelligible realities and added complexities to the relatively simple hierarchies of Plotinus. Two aspects of the Platonism after Plotinus are of importance for us, and both stem from Proclus (410–85) who headed the Academy at Athens. First, Proclus rejects altogether the view that matter is evil and the principle of Evil which we found in Plotinus. For Proclus, matter is part of the universal order and therefore good. Evil is not matter but simply the absence or a deficiency of good. Evil does not have being, but it is always a defect or perversion in what is good. It is thus a parasite and is not a reality apart from good. This understanding of evil as privation is widespread in Christian theology.

The second point of interest to us is a series of works collectively known as the *Corpus Areopagiticum*. They were supposedly written by an Athenian convert of Paul, Dionysius the Areopagite. They enjoyed great esteem both in the Greek East and in the Latin West. Hugh of St. Victor (d. 1141) commented on the *Celestial Hierarchy*, and Thomas Aquinas wrote a commentary on the *Divine Names* in 1261. We actually do not know who the author of the *Corpus Areopagiticum* was, but they were clearly written long after Paul's time. Their author is often referred to as Pseudo-Dionysius. The outer limits of the time of their composition are after the Cappadocians (the fourth century) and before 528. Pseudo-Dionysius apparently drew upon Proclus, and if not, certainly upon fifth century Neoplatonists who had greatly elaborated the relatively simple hierarchy of Plotinus. Pseudo-Dionysius works out in great detail how we may know God from a knowledge of God's creatures, how that knowledge is limited, and how the soul may ascend to union with God. His influence on Byzantine Christianity was immense and considerable on the medieval Latin West.

Like Proclus, he describes two ways of approaching God, a positive way (cataphatic) and a negative way (apophatic). The positive way begins with those creatures which are most akin to God, or the best manifestations of God. It is truer to say that God is wisdom, life, and goodness than that God is air or stone. The names wisdom, life, and goodness refer to something which is actually in God but God is air or stone only in the sense that God is the cause of them. The negative way begins with the things which are least akin to God. We then deny that God is those things and mount upward to things that are more and more representative.

But in both cases—the positive or way of eminence, and the negative or way of remission—what we learn about God from creatures cannot be applied to God as God is in essence. We must deny all that we say of God. When we deny that God is, for example, wisdom, power, or goodness, it is not because God is *beneath* wisdom, power, or goodness but because God is *above* them. God is hyperwisdom, hyperpower, and hypergoodness. What these are in God and how they are united in divine reality we cannot know.

These two routes enable us, however, to move from the level of knowledge they provide to a realization that God in essence is unknowable. This is a positive state. Actually to reach the state of unknowing (*agnosis*) we move to union (*henosis*). The "divine darkness" of unknowing which we enter is not a failure of the intellect, but an extension of our minds so that we do not rely on their powers but by yielding them we encounter the One who comes to meet us.

The Greek Fathers and Augustine drew most extensively on the philosophy of Plato and the Platonists. But we have seen that other elements, such as Stoicism and Aristotle's psychology of perception and his notions of potency and act, played important roles in even the most Platonic of the Platonists, Plotinus himself. Nonetheless the Platonist revival so deeply shaped the outlook of many theologians that it is not always easy to make transfers from Greek Platonic categories of thought to Latin ones, especially after Aristotle is taken up in a big way by the Latin West in the Middle Ages. The stress on the One and its elevation above being itself in Platonism leads Etienne Gilson in his *History of Christian Philosophy in the Middle Ages* wryly to remark that "the subtle and somewhat laborious commentaries of Thomas Aquinas on *The Divine Names* ... make it abundantly clear that it is not easy to speak, at one and the same time, the language of the One and the language of Being" (p. 94).

4

Aristotle:
His Categories *and*
the Mystery of God

We shall divide our coverage of Aristotle into two parts. Here we shall cover Aristotle's *Categories* because it, along with another work in logic, *On Interpretation*, are his only works known from ancient times right through the Dark Ages (after the fall of Rome). It was not until the middle of the twelfth century that the rest of Aristotle's works started to become available in the Latin West. Before that the Greek Fathers had used him only sparingly within their Platonism; Basil of Caesarea (ca. 300–379) was an exception. We shall then consider a brief selection on the Trinity from the writings of one of the greatest interpreters and defenders of the Council of Nicaea (325). By putting this and the other philosophical material we have covered into action, so to speak, we shall illustrate its value for understanding theology.

Although Aristotle's *Categories* is far-reaching in its implications, its basic ideas can be stated rather simply. First, there are individuals, such as a particular person, a particular horse, a particular cabbage. We often refer to them by proper names, such as "Bill" or "Dobbin," or we point to them and say, "That cabbage!" Aristotle calls such individuals "primary substances."

Second, individuals such as people, horses, and cabbages have qualities, such as colors. Qualities are said to be "present in" primary substances, that is they cannot exist independently or apart from individuals. (For example, green cannot exist independently of individuals which are green.) To *predicate* a quality of an individual (to say, "That cabbage is green") requires words that are general. A word used exclusively to speak of one individual is not a predicate. It is a proper name, like "Bill" or "Dobbin." The word "green" is a predicate because it is used to speak of the color of anything which is green and not to speak of the color of a single object only. This is possible because colors such as the various shades of green are similar to one another. So we may use a word such as "green" to speak of all of them; and we may say, "That cabbage is green," predicating "greenness" of that cabbage because its color is similar to the color of other particular cabbages and indeed, to the color of other particular things. Thus we have a distinction between primary substances and accidents (substances, and qualities "present in" substances). It is also a distinction between subjects and predicates, things we say of subjects. Now we may make another important distinction. Individuals or particular substances not only have qualities but they can also be grouped into *kinds* of substances. Particular men are similar to each other and so, because they are alike, we can speak of all of them as "men." So too of horses and cabbages. We may say, "Bill is a man," "Dobbin is a horse," and "That is a cabbage." "Man," "horse," and "cabbage" can be predicated of individual substances then. They will tell us the *kind* of individual substance a particular substance is. We can consider the likeness between kinds of individuals—species—such as the likeness between men and horses, and so form the idea of the genus, "animal." These too may be predicated of individuals: "Bill is an animal," and "Dobbin is an animal." Or we may even make the combination, "Bill is a man, and man is an animal," "Dobbin is a horse, and a horse is an animal." Genera (the way species are alike) and species are called "secondary substances" in contrast to individual substances or primary substances. (Aristotle does not use the expressions "primary substance" and "secondary substance" in his other writings, but he retains the distinction. He speaks of substances and genera and species. But regardless of his terminology, the idea of *kinds* of substances is absolutely vital to his philosophy. It is worth remembering when thinking about "kinds" or "sorts" of individuals that "genus" comes from the Greek word *genesis* meaning "birth," so that the notion of secondary substance is closely related to *natural* kinds of things which are propagated by birth, in contrast to artificial things. But he applies the terms genus and species to both natural and artificial kinds of things.

The most important things we predicate of an individual (for philosophical purposes, as we shall see) are its genus and species. They give us its essence; they tell us *what* the individual is; they tell us the *kind* of being it is. (It is a man; it is a horse; it is a cabbage. The "it" in each instance refers to a primary substance; "man," "horse," "cabbage" refer to the kind of thing each "it" is.) The other things we predicate of a primary substance do *not* tell us the kind of thing it is. So there are two types of predicates: those which tell us the kind of thing each individual thing is and those which do not. Secondary substances tell us what a substance is *essentially*; the other predicates tell us what it is *accidentally*. (For example, Bill is five-feet tall and white. But a man may be six-feet tall and yellow. So in order to be a man Bill does not need to be as tall as he is or white.)

We may put the distinction in another way. We have a major division between substances and accidents (between individuals and what is present in them). We have a distinction between substances themselves: individual substances (primary substances) and *kinds* of substances (secondary substances). Genera and species, which group individual substances into various kinds of substance, and accidents are predicated of primary substances. But only genera and species give us what is essential to a primary substance, that is, tell us what a primary substance *must* have in order to be that particular kind of reality.

Altogether there are ten categories (the number varies in other works). Primary and secondary substances make up the first of the ten categories. Those attributes which are "present in" primary substances are grouped into nine categories, according to their similarities. The nine types of attributes present in substances are quantity, quality, relation, place, time, posture, having (for example, a coat on), action, and being acted on. These nine categories are the most general *kinds* of predicate terms (or classes of predicates). We may illustrate these nine categories by the following. "Bill is six-feet tall, white, across the market place, in Athens, in the morning, standing up, with a coat on, talking to someone, and feeling hot." None of these attributes is *essential* to "being a man" (species) or to "being an animal" (genus). They are ways a man, who is an animal, *may* be. But only the genus and species tell us what the individual Bill must be in order to be the kind of individual he is (a man, who is an animal). We do not, however, *define* an individual (Bill). We *identify* individuals, and define *species* (man). We define a species (man) by giving its genus and difference (animal, rational).

In the *Metaphysics* Aristotle says that the categories are the senses in which a thing may be said "to be." In one sense "being" (*ousia*) means an individual substance; in another sense, "being" means "what a thing is"; in still another sense it means "a thing is of such and such a quantity, quality, relation, etc." But to be an individual (primary) substance is the fundamental sense of being. There are kinds of substances only because there are individual substances; and "good" or "sitting" must be said of that which is good or sitting. Therefore, that which "is" *primarily and simply* (not "is something") is primary substance.

Now let us assume a person has this information about Aristotle's *Categories* and that he or she reads Gregory of Nyssa's Letter 38, written about 380, in which he seeks to inform his correspondents of the proper way to speak of the unity of the Trinity. It is my claim that he or she will be able to avoid an *incorrect* interpretation of Gregory and also be able to form a basically sound understanding of what Gregory is saying about the unity of God. We shall quote only the opening part of Gregory's letter, which was for many centuries incorrectly attributed to his older brother, Basil the Great. These two brothers, along with their friend Gregory of Nazianzus, referred to as the Cappadocian Fathers, are responsible for fixing the language and meaning of the Trinity as *mia ousia, treis hypostaseis*, the Greek equivalent of "one substance, three persons," which is a translation from Latin. Gregory writes:

1. Many persons, in their study of the sacred dogmas, failing to distinguish between what is common in the essence or substance, and the meaning of the hypostases, arrive at the same notions, and think that it makes no difference whether οὐσία or hypostasis be spoken of. The result is that some of those who accept statements on these subjects without any enquiry, are pleased to speak of "one hypostasis," just as they do of

one "essence" or "substance;" while on the other hand those who accept three hypostases are under the idea that they are bound in accordance with this confession, to assert also, by numerical analogy, three essences or substances. Under these circumstances, lest you fall into similar error, I have composed a short treatise for you by way of memorandum. The meaning of the words, to put it shortly, is as follows:

2. Of all nouns the sense of some, which are predicated of subjects plural and numerically various, is more general; as for instance *man*. When we so say, we employ the noun to indicate the common nature, and do not confine our meaning to any one man in particular who is known by that name. Peter, for instance is no more *man*, than Andrew, John, or James. The predicate therefore being common, and extending to all the individuals ranked under the same name, requires some note of distinction whereby we may understand not man in general, but Peter or John in particular.

Of some nouns on the other hand the denotation is more limited; and by the aid of the limitation we have before our minds not the common nature, but a limitation of anything, having, so far as the peculiarity extends, nothing in common with what is of the same kind; as for instance, Paul or Timothy. For, in a word, of this kind there is no extension to what is common in the nature; there is a separation of certain circumscribed conceptions from the general idea, and expression of them by means of their names. Suppose then that two or more are set together, as, for instance, Paul, Silvanus, and Timothy, and that an enquiry is made into the essence or substance of humanity; no one will give one definition of essence or substance in the case of Paul, a second in that of Silvanus, and a third in that of Timothy; but the same words which have been employed in setting forth the essence or substance of Paul will apply to the others also. Those who are described by the same definition of essence or substance are of the same essence or substance when the enquirer has learned what is common, and turns his attention to the differentiating properties whereby one is distinguished from another, the definition by which each is known will no longer tally in all particulars with the definition of another, even though in some points it be found to agree.

3. My statement, then, is this. That which is spoken of in a special and peculiar manner is indicated by the name of the hypostasis. Suppose we say "a man." The indefinite meaning of the word strikes a certain vague sense upon the ears. The nature is indicated, but what subsists and is specially and peculiarly indicated by the name is not made plain. Suppose we say "Paul." We set forth, by what is indicated by the name, the nature subsisting.

This then is the hypostasis, or "*understanding;*" not the indefinite conception of the essence or substance, which, because what is signified is general, finds no "*standing*," but the conception which by means of the expressed peculiarities gives *standing* and circumscription to the general and uncircumscribed.*

Gregory writes this letter, he tells us to keep people from using *ousia* and *hypostasis* interchangeably. If one fails to distinguish the two terms, the Father, Son, and Holy Spirit, who are one *ousia* are also one *hypostasis*. As one hypostasis, they would be one individual, and this would fail to acknowledge that Father, Son, and Holy Spirit are irreducibly distinct. On the other hand, one who accepts three *hypostaseis* (that Father, Son, and Holy Spirit are distinct and irreducible to one another) would think that they are three *ousioi*, and thus destroy the unity of God. Gregory draws a distinction between *hypostasis* and *ousia*, between individuals and their common nature, so that *hypostasis* and *ousia* are not to be used interchangeably.

Some nouns, he writes, are predicated of more than one subject, such as the noun "man." The noun refers to a common nature (humanity), and it is not confined to any one man in particular. Peter is no more man than is Andrew. Gregory refers to the common nature as "essence or substance" (as this translation renders *ousia*). "Man" corresponds to Aristotle's secondary substance (*deutra ousia*); "man" for Aristotle refers to a species.

Other nouns which are names, Gregory continues, denote individuals, such as Peter, Andrew, Paul. Gregory refers to an individual as *hypostasis*. His use parallels Aristotle's primary substance (*protê ousia*) or individual beings. Should anyone ask for the essence or substance of "humanity," Gregory points out, he or she will not be given one definition for Paul, a second for Sylvanus, and a third for Timothy. The same definition will be used to give the essence or substance of all men. They are of the same essence or substance (*homoousioi*). So Gregory claims that *ousia* and *hypostasis* are not to be used interchangeably: *ousia* refers to essence or substance; *hypostasis* refers to individuals, who may have a common *ousia* or a common nature.

---

* From *Nicene and Post-Nicene Fathers*, 2d ser., ed. Philip Schaff and Henry Wace, trans. Blomfield Jackson (Grand Rapids, Mich.: Wm. B. Eerdmans Publishing Company, 1955), 8:137–38. Volume contains the works of Basil.

This much of Gregory we can follow easily because it runs parallel to Aristotle's distinction between primary substance and secondary substance. But Gregory does not apply the words *ousia* and *hypostasis* to God in precisely the same way as he does to individuals such as Peter, Andrew, Paul, Silvanus, and Timothy. Father, Son, and Holy Spirit are distinct and yet united. This is similar to but not identical with saying that Peter, Andrew, and Paul are individuals yet they are united because they have a common nature. Gregory makes the distinction between individuals and the nature they share in the case of people and ordinary things to keep us from using *hypostasis* and *ousia* interchangeably in speaking of God. But when it comes to speaking of the *unity* of Father, Son, and Holy Spirit, *ousia* does not mean the same as it does when it refers to the common nature of Peter, Andrew, and Paul. Peter, Andrew, and Paul share a common nature as men—they are of the same *ousia*—but they are not so united that they are *one man*. They are *three men*. Father, Son, and Holy Spirit have a common nature as God—the same *ousia*—but they are not *three Gods*. They are *one God*. So the *ousia* of the Father, Son, and Holy Spirit is not a secondary substance, that is, a genus or species.

We thus see that Gregory transcends Aristotle's *Categories*. It is a mistake to think that he believes God's unity is identical with the unity between individuals (e.g., men) who have the same *ousia*. But it is only by a knowledge of Aristotle's *Categories* that we can understand the charge commonly made that Gregory tries to account for the Trinity along Aristotelian lines (and thus so emphasize the distinctiveness of individuals as to fail adequately to preserve the unity of God). Gregory knows that the unity of individuals sharing a common nature is at best only analogous to the distinctiveness and unity of Father, Son, and Holy Spirit. Even if one interprets him with a Platonic understanding of common natures in which particulars participate in a single Form (so that the unity between individuals is greater than that to be found in Aristotle), Gregory clearly believes that the unity of individuals is only a reflection of the unity of Father, Son, and Holy Spirit. He writes,

> Yet receive what I say as at best a token and reflection of the truth; not as the actual truth itself. For it is not possible that there should be

complete correspondence between what is seen in the tokens and the objects in reference to which the use of tokens is adopted.*

His stress on the distinction between *hypostasis* and *ousia* when we are dealing with people is intended to keep us from using the terms interchangeably; for if the terms are used interchangeably, we are either led to deny the distinctions between Father, Son, and Holy Spirit or led to affirm three gods. On the other hand, the way we use *hypostasis* and *ousia* for people is only an analogy for their proper use for the Father, Son, and Holy Spirit. The *ousia* of Father, Son, and Holy Spirit is not a secondary substance; for Father, Son, and Holy Spirit do not *have* the same *ousia*, they *are* the same *ousia*. They are one *ousia* because they are one God. Neither of the two kinds of unity—that of an individual (a *hypostasis*) and that of a common nature (having the same *ousia*)—is the unity God has. There is only a similarity between the unity of several individuals that have a common nature and the unity of the Father, Son, and Holy Spirit.

We shall not seek here to give an extended account of Gregory of Nyssa's views on the unity of the Father, Son, and Holy Spirit, for our purpose is merely to give an example of how the philosophical material in this book can enable us better to understand a major doctrine and a major theologian. The text we selected is particularly suited for our purpose and such a rich return cannot be expected with every doctrine and theologian that one examines. On the other hand, the text we have examined is a famous one by a theologian whose work on a central doctrine of Christianity was critical in establishing its meaning.

An understanding of Aristotle's *Categories* also makes the questions raised about the Council of Nicaea more intelligible. Did the Council understand the oneness in substance (*ousia*) to mean a generic unity, so that it is the *likeness* or *coequality* of substance (*homoiousia*) that is affirmed? Or was oneness in substance intended to mean a *unity* of substance (*homoousia*)? These issues are also raised about Athanasius' understanding of the nature of the unity of the Father, Son, and Holy Spirit, as well as about the understanding of all three of the Cappadocian Fathers.

---

* Ibid., p. 139.

There is one other very important point which the brief text from Gregory of Nyssa enables us to make about the nature of theology. The hiddenness of God, or the mystery of the divine being, which must permeate all theological reflection, is not to be called on *arbitrarily*. It is rather at specific junctures when we recognize that we have reached a point where the truth is beyond our capacity to comprehend that we may ascribe our ignorance to mystery. One of these junctures is well illustrated by Gregory's reflections on the unity of the Father, Son, and Holy Spirit. Their unity is beyond the concepts we use to characterize the unity of people and things. Our understanding of God arises from our reflections on God's operations or actions (*energeia*) by which God relates to us.* Some conception of the divine nature is available to us from divine operations, and God's works are believed to be faithful to God's essence. But our conceptions do not exhaust God's being nor enable us fully to comprehend it. From our apprehension of the divine operations—and not from some philosophical notions or some mystical ideas about the absolute transcendence of God—we recognize that God is Creator and Redeemer. We can understand that our redemption is achieved by God's incarnation. We also understand from an examination of revelation that the Creator and Redeemer (God the Father and Jesus Christ) are not reducible to each other. It is also clear in the Bible that God is One. It is the *way* these things are connected that is beyond our comprehension. Mystery arises then, not because we cannot understand various things about God's nature, such as that God is Creator and Redeemer, but that God is One in all the diversity of divine actions. It is rather that we have no concepts or models which enable us to understand the *way* God is united in all the diversity of divine actions, or the way God is One. So it is by means of God's operations which reveal God's nature to us as Creator and Redeemer that we also know that God's being is a mystery to us.

---

* Christian theologians changed the terminology that Plotinus used. He has the pattern of One (*mone*)—emanation (prodos)—return (*epistrophe*). In its place they put Being (*ousia*)—power (*dunamis*)—act (*energeia*). Since God's thoughts are never frustrated but achieve actualization, power or the capacity to act and its achievement or act are frequently coalesced and referred to together as *energeia*. We are thus left with *ousia*, the divine essence or nature, and the divine *energeia*, divine operation or act.

Even though the divine unity is unique and cannot be reduced either to the relations between various creatures (like a genus that unites various individuals) or to the type of unity exhibited by an individual (so that the diversity of God's operations as Father, Son, and Holy Spirit is collapsed into one individual), some understanding of that unity is possible by means of analogies. That God has acted and that some of the relations between those actions have been revealed are not at issue in such reflection. So its tentative and even speculative nature casts no doubt upon the truth of what has been revealed. Although it is speculative, it is sometimes religiously rewarding. Since God is the object of our thought, the better God is apprehended, the greater is our joy.

This kind of theological inquiry will be illustrated by a brief examination of Augustine's reflections on the unity of the divine Trinity. It is indeed "faith seeking understanding." Engaging in this kind of reflection on the mystery of God does not in itself commit a person to the Platonist's tendency to associate an increase in knowledge with an advance in spiritual condition. Nor does it commit us to the Platonist's goal of passing beyond conceptual knowledge to a vision of the Good, as in Plato, or to union with the One, as in Plotinus. It is rather that we can get some knowledge—conceptual knowledge—of God by reflecting on the revelation of God by means of some analogies. And we can also come to see that God is beyond such analogies, and so recognize that God transcends our conceptual knowledge and the creatures which we use in our analogies in order to gain some understanding.

In the selection we examined, Gregory of Nyssa started with three individuals and worked from diversity toward unity; we shall see that Augustine begins his reflection with the consciousness of a single mind and works toward diversity. These starting points are said to be quite typical of the Greek Fathers and of the Latin Church which follows Augustine, the greatest western theologian of ancient times.

Augustine, no more than Gregory of Nyssa, thought that God, Jesus, and the Holy Spirit are One because they are primary substance (an individual as you and I are individuals) or a secondary substance (united by sharing a genus or species). Gregory looked to secondary substances—to the way things share a common nature—to find an analogy for the unity of God. Augustine, however, looked to primary substance, in particular to the mind of human beings, for an analogy for the diversity and unity of God. Augustine used the human mind as his analogue because human beings are created in God's image. Physical nature reflects the greatness and goodness of God, but only human beings are said to be made in God's *image*. So a human being is the best creature to examine in our thoughts on the Trinity; we should be able to find in ourselves "trinities" which are images of the Trinity.

Augustine distinguishes three things: (1) the human mind, (2) its power to know and love, and (3) ourselves as the object of our knowledge and love. Each of these is distinct and irreducible to the others. There must be a subject to exhibit its powers of knowing and loving; there must be an object to know and love. When we know and love ourselves, we are both the subject of knowing and loving and the object of knowing and loving, and it is our knowledge and love by which we are related to ourselves as subject and object. All three—(1) knower and lover, (2) object of knowledge and love, and (3) knowing and loving—are *relations*. That is they do not exist without each other. If there is a knower and lover, there is knowing and loving, and there is also an object known and loved.

The three are substantive and not properties of a subject, as are color and shape. Color and shape are in a body; they cannot be transferred and belong to another body. But the mind can know and love not only itself but also objects outside itself. So knowledge and love do not belong to the mind like a property does to a body. Knowing and loving are as substantive as the mind itself.

Although distinct, the relations of subject, object, and knowing and loving are inseparable and wholly involved in each other. They are thus a substance. Its oneness is not the *subject* to the exclusion of being the object or to the exclusion of being its powers; nor is the oneness the object to the exclusion of being the subject and powers; nor powers to the exclusion of being subject and object. What is the substance? It is subject, object, and powers.

This forms an analogy for the unity of the Father, Son, and Holy Spirit. It is not that one is subject, another object, and the third powers which relate subject to object. Each is a power (acts); each is an object (of the other's acts); each is a subject (with the others as objects of its acts). They are thus one *God*, who is Father, Son, and Holy Spirit.

Our material on the Platonic tradition enables us to realize how seriously the notion of an *image* is taken by Augustine as a way to increase our knowledge. Analogies are not mere chance similarities. Since every creature is a limited version of a greater perfection, similarities are guides to genuine knowledge or realities beyond the material world. In Christianity human beings alone bear God's image; all other creatures are only reflections of the divine. Thus for Augustine as a Christian Platonist, limited human trinities yield genuine knowledge of the divine Trinity. The Platonic tradition reinforces the conviction that our knowledge is always limited since any representation is always less than its exemplar. In Augustine in particular, the "trinities" to be found in us, who alone are made in the divine image, are not enough like God's Trinity to enable us to comprehend the unity and diversity of God. The agents we are give us some idea of the unity to be found in God, who is Father, Son, and Holy Spirit, but the agents we are do not enable us to comprehend a unity that can include such an act as the incarnation. Or put in another way, God's unity in diversity so exceeds ours that we do not even have an image of the most important feature of that unity, namely the unity which includes the capacity to become incarnate.

Augustine's predilection for looking to the inner relations of the mind as the main guide for understanding is natural for one influenced by Platonism. For although nature is the handiwork of mind, and so reflects the divine mind, human beings because they have minds are more like it than its other handiworks are. So the unity and diversity of the human mind is a better guide than the unity and diversity of ordered objects in the world. Such a stress on the *individual mind* (or rational soul) in isolation from others neglects the way Genesis describes the image of God. The text reads, "So God created man in his own image, in the image of God he created him; male and female he created them" (Gen. 1:27). This suggests that a better image for the Trinity may be that of the relationship *between* man and woman, rather than the diversity and unity to be found *within* the individual soul. It may well be that the doctrine of the Trinity, though expressed accurately enough in terms of the Platonic tradition, ought also to be expressed in other ways as a corrective. People in a different historical era, facing different issues, may find theological illumination from different analogies. Our search for community today may receive guidance concerning what true community is, and what prevents it and what enhances it, from an examination of the relations between man and woman as the divine image, rather than from the isolated individual.

Another place where the mystery of God is encountered is the unity of the divine and human natures in the person of Christ. It is maintained that Jesus is the mediator between God and humankind. We cannot reach God, so God must come to us if we are to be redeemed and to share in the divine life. But we do not know how divine and human natures can be united in one person. We can become a different *kind of person*, but we cannot become a different *kind of being*. We cannot become a tiger—not just have a tiger's body, but become one—and still retain our own identity. But the second person of the Trinity can become another kind of being, a human being, and yet retain identity as God. How the Word of God remains unchanged in the union of the divine and human natures was one of the issues in the Christological controversies in the early centuries of the Christian era.

One tendency was to speak of the Word of God as though human nature were external, as though God were making *use* of a body. But this was immediately challenged by many theologians as utterly inadequate because God can raise us to the level of the divine (be a mediator) only by genuinely becoming what we are, human beings. So it is stressed in the final formulation of the Council of Chalcedon (451) that the Word of God is fully united to human nature. Jesus is still the same Word through which and with which God created the heavens and the earth. The Word retains the same personal identity in the change. But the Word now has besides a divine nature, a human one. Our existence as creatures is derived, terminable, and must be sustained; the existence of the Word of God is not derived from, nor terminable by, nor in need of sustenance from any creature. Both remain true when the Word of God becomes human. The existence of the union itself requires Mary's cooperation; and the union of God and humankind can be terminated by the actions of creatures (Jesus can be killed); and it must be sustained by creatures (air, food, and drink). Thus, human nature is not changed by the divine nature. The Word of God is "impassible," but the *union* of the Word of God with human nature is subject to passions (can be affected, or be passive), threatened with termination, and in need of sustenance, just as we are. How we are to conceive of these two natures both fully present in a union is not known. We do not know the divine nature or the being who can so act as to unite divine nature with human nature.

Theological reflection on the ways God has related to us thus encounters matters which are beyond the intellect. The notion of mystery is not invoked haphazardly. It is rather the being of God, full and complete in itself, which leads us to invoke mystery at specific junctures in our reflections. It is by means of the intellect that we understand where it is impossible for us fully to understand. Such mystery does not lead to unbelief or agnosticism. As Gregory of Nyssa said, it leads to awe and silence in the presence of the divine *ousia*.

5
Aristotle and the Creation of Scholastic Theology

We do well to recall that our intention is to present only the philosophy one needs to understand theology, for the medieval period abounds in great thinkers and it would be impossible to cover them all in such a short book. Aristotle was the dominant new philosophical force of the period. The Platonic tradition continued with some very important representatives, such as Bonaventure, and elements of Platonism were usually present in the Aristotelians. Still, it is the impact of Aristotle which dominates the era.

Another significant shift was that learning was no longer confined to the monasteries. A new type of teacher arose. Like people of trade, carpenters, and masons, who organized themselves into guilds, the new master of learning had the consciousness of belonging to a profession. His trade was learning and teaching in the classroom. He was a Schoolman, a "Scholastic." It was this type of master of learning who turned avidly to Aristotle. The *Categories* and *On Interpretation,* which had been known for centuries, were now called the "Old Logic" in contrast to the rest of Aristotle's writings, which became available during the second half of the twelfth century. They became known as the *Novum Organum* or new instrument or tool for knowledge. As they absorbed these new texts, the Scholastics became aware that there were other works known to them by their names only. This led to a search for the hitherto unknown Aristotelian works as well as for other writings of antiquity. We cannot here trace the effects of the successive acquisition of texts, commentaries and steadily improved translations. We shall instead merely present those ideas of Aristotle which will enable a person to better understand the issues with which theologians wrestled and the philosophical terminology they used. For the most part we shall ignore the modifications made to Aristotle's philosophy by theologians and their different interpretations of him since a knowledge of Aristotle himself gives one a benchmark whereby to recognize these modifications and interpretations in one's study of theology.

We must, however, touch on the attitude of the Schoolmen, in particular those of the faculty of arts at the University of Paris. They were not content simply to transmit the traditional wisdom, as had been the case in the West—with a few notable exceptions—since the fall of Rome. They wanted to learn and master the knowledge of antiquity and to rub together Scripture and the Church Fathers with the ancient pagans, especially in the natural sciences of medicine, astronomy, metaphysics, and physics. Aristotle's spirit of curiosity and criticism of others' views matched their own growing confidence.

When in 1255 the faculty of arts of the University of Paris adopted a new syllabus that imposed the study of all the known works of Aristotle on its students, Aristotle occupied a position which no other philosopher had ever achieved in Christian circles. With Aristotle's corpus as the basis of instruction in the arts faculty, sharp distinctions between philosophy and theology, faith and reason, nature and supernature, which had not hitherto existed in Christianity, soon developed. These have significantly marked Western theology, both Protestant and Catholic, from that time until the present. We find it said very early on in the Middle Ages, for example, that the resurrection of the body is a miracle and, since it is beyond nature's laws, it does not belong to the subject matter of philosophy. Likewise whether we are the cause of our good and bad actions was answered both philosophically and theologically; *philosophically* speaking (and it was still a manner of speaking since they knew that the truth lay with theology), we are the entire cause of both our good and bad actions; *theologically* speaking, we are not capable of good actions but must receive grace. The Schoolmen in the faculty of arts thus introduced a new approach, and the potential for controversy was not long in being realized. The early Church Fathers who used Greek philosophy to better understand the Christian revelation did not draw such sharp distinctions because for them their *reason* thoroughly depended on divine faith and grace. There was no such autonomous discipline as philosophy for a Christian mind.

The reason for the change was the distinctive focus of Aristotle. Plato and the Platonists had not emphasized a study of the sensible world. Aristotle, the son of a physician, and one of the greatest biologists of all time, had a *cosmos*-centered philosophy. His achievements were so great (and achieved without divine revelation or grace) that a place had to be made for *human* knowledge, and then of course one had to consider the implications of that knowledge for theology. Thus the attempt to relate human knowledge to the Christian revelation took on a different character when it was Aristotle and not Plato who was the prime representative of human capacity and achievement. So the boundaries between nature and grace, faith and reason, philosophy and theology were drawn and redrawn again and again. The Protestant Reformation was a determined but only partially successful attempt to escape from the framework of discussion created by the Schoolmen.

We shall briefly illustrate the new forces at work by reference to Thomas Aquinas (1224–74). Theologians had traditionally sought to unveil the truth revealed by God in Scripture with the help of councils and the Church Fathers. The function of teaching belonged to the church acting through the clergy rather than to the individual. So a corporate transmission of the traditional wisdom was the ideal. It presumed a concordance of the fundamental authorities. Any discrepancy among the authorities was a stimulus to the theologian to make greater efforts to find a harmony. This contrasted with the attitude of the arts master studying Aristotle who was not dealing with an infallible guide and so could recognize deficiencies and irreconcilable conflicts in his teachings, and even hope to go beyond him to discover new truths. Thomas Aquinas attempted to establish a new harmony. He included not only Christianity and Aristotle in his scope but also Islam and Judaism which had come to the theologians' attention as the transmitters of so much of antiquity.

Thomas met the challenge by making room for philosophy *within* the subject matter of theology itself. God revealed not only strictly supernatural truths but some truths which are philosophically demonstrable, such as God's existence. Such rationally demonstrable truths are natural theology. A concord between philosophy and theology is partly achieved by the creation of *natural theology* as a domain within theology, and the claim that some revealed truths are accessible to reason or philosophy. Harmony between philosophy and theology is further enhanced by the discovery of natural analogies for supernatural truths which transcend the intellect, philosophy thus aiding our understanding of theology. Finally, philosophy is used to order both natural and supernatural truths into a deductive system in an Aristotelian manner with knowledge of the natural world and Christianity intertwined. Philosophy thus becomes the handmaiden of theology.

The task of harmonization was made especially difficult for Thomas because the Muslims who were the transmitters of Aristotle to the Latin West had also interpreted his work. Sometimes their interpretations were incompatible with Christianity. Averroës (1126–98), known as "the Commentator," was especially troublesome because he held a special status among some philosophers at the university of Paris as explicating genuine Aristotelianism, even though some of his interpretations were at variance with Christian faith. Thomas, who took Aristotle as the true philosophy, thus had to show that Aristotelianism did not necessarily involve the interpretations given to it by Averroës. With these intimations of the complexity of the medieval theological scene, we shall now turn to an exposition of the philosophy which was most responsible for directing it into new paths.

We shall begin with a few remarks about Aristotle's logic because it supplies some of the terminology of the period and because it is the source of the problem concerning the ontological status of universals. We have already examined Aristotle's *Categories*, but we now need to see it in relation to his *Topics*, especially as interpreted by Porphyry (A.D. 232–304), a disciple of Plotinus. Porphyry wrote

an introduction (*Isagoge*) to Aristotle's *Categories* which was pre-
served in a commentary by Boethius (480–524) and known in the
Latin West before the recovery of Aristotle's works in the middle of
the twelfth century.

In the *Topics* there is an account of five things which may be
predicated or said: definition, property, genus, differentia, and accident. A definition signifies a thing's essence, and consists of the
genus in combination with differentia. (When we add to the genus
"animal" the differentia "rational," we have the definition of person.
In Porphyry, "definition" is replaced in the list of predicables by
"species.") A property was explained as that which belongs to a
thing *exclusively* (for example, capacity to read belongs exclusively
to humankind), but it does not define it or give its essence. (In "a
person can read and whatever can read is a person," the terms are
convertible, but no definition of person is given.) That leaves us with
accident. It is said to be "none of the others," and it is what may or
may not belong to a given individual (such as being seated).

Boethius believed that there was a need to harmonize the *Topics*
(the "predicables," as they are called) with the *Categories* (the
"predicaments"). (Actually the predicaments of the *Categories* are a
list of the types of answers that can be given to the question, "What
is it?" when asked of an individual substance. The *Topics* is concerned with how a predicate is related to a subject in a sentence. The
Topics is thus part of Aristotle's logic in *our* sense of logic, namely,
how we associate terms in expressions.) Nonetheless, Boethius says
that according to the *Topics* the term "rational" is classified as a
differentia, and hence is not an accident. But it is a quality. According to the *Categories*, whatever is not a primary or secondary substance (including the category of quality) is classified as an accident.
Boethius tried to resolve this apparent difficulty by separating qualities into two types: those qualities that are differentia of substances
and those that are not, calling only the latter accidents.

Boethius uses the distinction between *being predicated of* a subject and *being in* a subject, which is found in the *Categories*. The
main division in the *Categories* is between substances and accidents,
and Boethius aligns differentiae with substances by saying that they
are predicated *de subjecto* (of the subject) and so contribute to a

knowledge of the subject (contribute to a "theory" of the subject). *In subjecto* predicates (in the subject) do not belong to a theory of the subject. This distinguishes qualities that are differentiae from qualities that are accidents.

Finally, Boethius distinguishes predicates that are in *eo quod quid* (in respect of whatness). They answer the question "What is it?" These are genus, species, and differentia, and are called "quidditative." Other predicates are qualifying predicates (*eo quod quale*) and are accidents. That is, they come and go without the subject perishing. One should also note that the five predicables—species, property, genus, differentia, and accident—*can be predicated of many things*. They thus fit Aristotle's definition of a universal. So the five predicables are frequently known as "the five (types of) universals."

Porphyry raised the problem of universals in the *Isagoge* with his remarks concerning the referent for genera and species. That is, what does a genus such as "animal" and a species such as "horse" refer to? He himself declined to say (1) whether they are realities in themselves or simple conceptions of the mind; (2) if they are realities, whether incorporeal or corporeal; and (3) if they are incorporeal, whether they exist apart from sensible things or only as united in them.

A proper understanding of the Platonic and Aristotelian views of universals was not possible until the middle of the twelfth century because some of their important works were not available. Boethius added to the problem by apparently harmonizing the two. In his commentary on Porphyry, he says that Plato believes that genera and species and other universals are known separately from bodies and also that they exist outside bodies and extramentally. The ontological reality they correspond to is Forms. Sensations are known only because the intellect (the soul) is aware of the impressions on the body, and the sensations only cause us to turn to the Forms. Aristotle, Boethius claims, thinks that universals are objects of knowledge but exist only in sensible things. It is because the intellect abstracts from sensible things that it can *think* a universal apart from sensible things, even though universals do not *exist* separately from sensible things. Boethius says that he "supports" Aristotle because he is commenting on Porphyry's Introduction to Aristotle's *Catego-*

ries! But then in his *Consolation of Philosophy*, Book 5, Boethius supports a Platonic view. His readers for a long time interpreted him as trying to harmonize Plato and Aristotle. With their limited knowledge of Plato and especially of Aristotle, some early medieval theologians took it that to believe in the reality of universals was to hold that universals are realities both *in themselves* and *in sensible things*. Not to hold this, they believed, was to reject their reality.

It is impossible to present the long course of the various controversies over universals in the Middle Ages. But to guide one who studies medieval theologians, I shall outline the major philosophical positions on universals. Let us begin by noting what is at stake.

If we begin with individuals—such as particular persons—and with particular qualities—such as the particular color of someone's hair—we could not keep track of all the particulars there are. So we group particulars and form the idea of species, such as the species of person. But there are too many species to keep track of unless we group them into genera (such as the species person, horse, and dog into the genus of animal). We do the same thing for qualities, as we saw with Aristotle's nine categories of accidents. These "general words," or universals as they are called, enable us to talk about many particulars or individual substances and qualities, which otherwise we would be unable to do. We would simply be flooded with particulars, able to point but not able to predicate or to say anything about the particular. We are also able to reason about many particulars and to come to conclusions about them in this way.

The question then arises concerning the ontological status of these general words, especially genera and species. What is their status in reality, and how do they relate to the concrete particulars we experience? Our various answers have very different epistemological consequences. For example, Plato thought that universals or general words refer to Forms. These Forms exist apart from sensible particulars, and we have knowledge of sensible particulars only because sensibles are "copies" (*Timaeus*) of the Forms. But as copies, sensible particulars do not represent the Forms very well. They are comparable to *reflections* of objects seen on the surface of water, with the distortions and limitations of reflections. Sensible particulars are just enough like the Forms to enable us to recall them from latency in our memory but we do not receive the Forms from sense experience.

The first solution to the problem of universals by some of the early medieval thinkers is known as extreme realism or ultrarealism. It is not actually Plato's position even though people often refer to extreme realism as Platonic and many medieval thinkers who held the position thought they had Plato's support. In extreme realism the universal (genus or species) is a *thing* which exists extramentally and prior to sense objects. When present in sense objects it exists in the sense object *in the same way* as it is thought in the mind. For Plato, as we just saw, the Form of person does not exist *in* persons; persons are but copies of the ideal, and as copies they only approximate it. Extreme realists thought that the concepts in our minds must exist in objects in exactly the same way; otherwise the concepts are purely subjective. This is the only way in which we can have knowledge of objects. There has to be an exact correspondence between objects and our thoughts of objects. In addition, because Porphyry had asserted that an individual is a unique collection of attributes, the difference between two human beings consists in the fact that Socrates (for example) is constituted by a collection of attributes which is different in at least one member from the collection of attributes which characterize any other human being. On this view, the individual is literally derived from the species; the universal nature (person) becomes an individual person (Socrates) simply by adding accidental characteristics to it.

Plato himself raised a crucial objection to the view that universals are things in his dialogue *Parmenides*. We use the same general name (person) to apply to a number of particular things (persons) because the particulars resemble each other. This practice is explained on the basis that the general name applies to each particular as well as to the resemblance of the particulars because there is a single Form in which the particulars participate. If this is taken to mean that one and the same Form is *in* particulars (persons), we have a dilemma. How can the Form be single and undivided and still be *in* the several distinct individuals? Either the Form will be divided and multiplied as many times as there are individuals, or the individuals will not be distinct. The former alternative destroys the Form;

the latter, the plurality of individuals. (See Julius R. Weinberg, *A Short History of Medieval Philosophy*, Princeton, N.J.: Princeton University Press, 1964.)

Abélard (1079–1142) made good use of Plato's own criticism of Forms as things, and went on to affirm that universals are significant words or concepts only. He forced William of Champeaux (1070–1121) of the Cathedral School of Paris to abandon the view that individuals differ from one another by a diversity of accidents. He went on to show that since all attempts to predicate things of things fails, universality is to be ascribed only to significant words. One significant word can be predicated of many things because of their common likeness. Individuals are distinct from one another both in their individual essences and in the diversity of their accidental differences. The justification for predicating the same universal term (person) for several individuals is that the individuals themselves are like each other, and this resemblance does not involve anything—such as a common nature—distinct from the individuals in virtue of which they resemble one another.

The second view is known as moderate realism (quite often it is referred to simply as realism). As more of Aristotle's works became available, it became the dominant position, and it was not seriously challenged until the rise of nominalism in the fourteenth century (which we shall look at in Chapter Seven). In moderate realism, genera and species very definitely have a foundation in extramental reality. Things are like one another, having the same essential nature. The intellect is able to *abstract* from sensible particulars their common natures. It is not the "image," the passive result of the impression of sense objects on the mind, but a concept formed by the intellect itself, using the data supplied by images. The concept is a concept of the common nature present in many individuals. Genera and species *as thoughts or as concepts* are universals (that is, they apply to many individuals). Through concepts we conceive what is in particular objects apart from their matter. But they have no independent existence as do Plato's Forms. Universals, as concepts, exist in our minds; they are not subjective because their foundation is the common natures in extramental reality.

This last point—common natures in extramental reality—distinguishes moderate realism from Abélard and the third position, conceptualism. In conceptualism universals (in the sense of general words) do exist, but they are mere concepts. There is a gap between our thoughts and objects. Our knowledge is thus of doubtful validity when it goes beyond the particulars which we have experienced and studied. There are many different kinds of conceptualism, depending on how the relations between thought and reality are conceived. Conceptualism and moderate realism are the two main rivals in modern philosophy. We shall give a fuller characterization of them in Chapter Seven where we describe the rise of nominalism and its challenge to the great philosophical-theological synthesis of Aristotle and Christian doctrine.

The fourth view is nominalism. Universals are said to stand for names (*nomina* in Latin). This is to say in effect that universals have no reality at all; their reality is simply the sound of the voice. This kind of nominalisn is not really defensible, but it existed both early and late in medieval thought (Roscelin ca. 1050–1120, for example, was reported to have held this view). It was not the main challenge to the synthesis of Aristotle and Christianity. In the fourteenth century that challenge was really conceptualism even though it is usually referred to as "nominalism." "Terminists" is really a more accurate name for these conceptualists since their work treated universals as terms in logic and language.

The moderate realism of Thomas Aquinas is still prominent among Roman Catholics. It is not exactly the same as Aristotle's position and includes Plato in a modified form. The notion that the Forms are divine ideas or thoughts, passed on to the medieval thinkers by Augustine, is continued in Thomas' moderate realism. They are said by Thomas to be exemplars used by God to create the world. That is, God, knowing divine essence, knows it as *imitable* by a plurality of creatures (*Summa Theologica* 1.15,1,ad1). We have no direct knowledge of the divine thoughts or exemplars. Our only knowledge is of the *expressed* universal, and this expressed universal exists *externally* only in particulars and in our minds as abstract. This position thus affirms the *universale ante rem* (the universal exists *before* there is a thing). But it does not exist independently, as in Plato, but as an exemplar in God. The *universale in re* is the concrete individual essence alike in the members of a species. The abstract universal concept is referred to as the *universale post rem*. Although various forms of moderate realism predominated in the thirteenth century, the earlier rejection of extreme realism made the principle that only individual substances exist as subsistent (independent) realities a firmly held tenet, and so set a direction which led away from realism.

As more of Aristotle's works became available the role of logic in his philosophy became more clear. Logic for Aristotle was not a "science" or body of knowledge. He divides the sciences into the theoretical (whose purpose is the knowledge of truth), the practical (which concern the conduct of the good life and the ultimate end of every human being), and the productive (whose purpose is to make useful and beautiful things). Logic is a *preparation* for the study of these sciences. Logic teaches us to reason rightly so as to gain knowledge. It is thus not concerned merely to construct internally valid patterns of thought with no reference to anything outside, as it is today.

Sentences or propositions have to have *formal* concepts, those outside all the categories such as is, is not, all, no, some, and, if-then, or, hence, and number words. The medieval logicians called them "transcendental terms," not objects, but the terms which make other terms join into a sentence or proposition which can be true or false. They were also called "syncategorical." They go with categorical terms but they are of another type. For example, what makes *Soc-* a syllable in the word *Socrates* is not the other letters but the arrangement or form; so too we join subject and predicate to make a sentence or proposition, and the joint can be "is" or "is not."

Aristotle, as we have seen, begins with terms (the categories into which terms fall), then analyzes the meaning of propositions, which involves a study of formal terms, and lastly he analyzes the syllogism, which is an arrangement of several propositions. The syllogism is the form of rational arguments. Given premises, it can be shown that a further proposition follows *necessarily* from them as conclusion. Such an argument, when valid—that is, when the conclusion really does follow by necessity from the premises—does not of itself prove anything. The premises must be true in order for the conclusion to be not only valid but also true. Then the conclusion has been demonstrated. To be a *scientific* demonstration, however, the major premise must be a principle of the particular field of inquiry. Such a principle is itself not demonstrable (not itself the conclusion of a syllogism). It is rather immediately certain or self-evident. So Aristotle's ideal is that of a *deductive* science, where we go from the general to the particular, showing that the particular follows from the general by necessity.

Aristotle recognizes that even though premises are *logically* prior to conclusions, the order in which we come to know things (their epistemological order) is not the same as their logical order or their "order in being." Objects which are sensible are the first to be known by us. Our knowledge starts from sense experience, this is, with the particular, and finds there the general (by means of a knowledge of essences). We reason inductively. This is the crucial point in all of Aristotle's philosophy. He believes that the general or universal can be apprehended in the clearly known sense particular. This is because of his understanding of "form," which we shall examine in a moment. But for now let us note that the ideal is a deductive system of knowledge in which the particular is demonstrated to follow by necessity from the general. This is the "order of being," the way things are causally related, and is distinct from the order in which we first come to know things. The order of being is truly *scientific* knowledge. But the way we come to know something (know it incompletely) is by grasping in the sense perception of particulars the form or essence or universal, which holds for many particulars. It is only then that we use that knowledge to work toward the ideal of a demonstrative science. Whatever Aristotle's actual practice may be, and it does not usually fit this ideal, a deductive science is his goal.

Perhaps the easiest way to get to the heart of Aristotle's philosophy is to explain one of his remarks about the soul. The care of the soul was the fundamental concern of Socrates, Plato, and Plotinus; they all believed the soul is immortal and is capable of existing without a body. Aristotle, however, said that the soul is the *form* of the body. This does not mean "shape" as we may be tempted to think. It is to be understood in terms of the most far-reaching and fundamental distinctions in Aristotle's philosophy, that of matter and form, potency and act.

Parmenides argued that change was impossible. On the one hand, being cannot come out of nonbeing (out of nothing comes nothing). On the other hand, being cannot come from being since being would already be. Thus fire could not come out of air since air is air and not fire. Aristotle's reply was to make a distinction between potency and act. Fire does not come out of air, but out of air *which can be fire* and is *not yet fire*. Fire does not come from nothing nor from air as such, but from what has a *potentiality* to become fire. That potency exists, not as fire but as air with the potency to become fire. So it does not come into being from *nonbeing*, nor does it come into being from being. It comes from a being which is not the thing which it *comes* to be. A being lacks what it is to become. Aristotle calls this privation. But it has the potential (capacity or power) to become what it lacks. Change is the movement from potency to act, from potency to the realization of the potential. This is Aristotle's answer to the difficulty Parmenides raised about change, namely that it is impossible.

The other side of the difficulty with change is that something must remain the same through change and give order and stability ("being") to sensible change. Otherwise we have flux (a stream of sensibles). Aristotle dealt with it by using the same set of concepts. Unlike Plato who was driven away from the sensible world to the world of Forms, Aristotle found the permanent and the sources of order *within* the cosmos. As a person who studied plants and animals in great detail and number, Aristotle took with profound seriousness the obvious fact that plants and animals change in an orderly and patterned way from seed to mature plant, from embryo to mature animal. The reason for this orderly and patterned change is not that things are copies of Forms but that there are *active principles* present *in* things. Orderly and patterned change occurs because each thing has a form; that is, *what* a thing is to be is present at first potentially and gradually realizes itself as the form comes to full actuality.

In addition it is obvious that plants and animals regularly produce successors that are like themselves. What a plant or animal is to become is present in it right at the start, and when it is fully actualized in the mature plant or animal, it is passed on to a new generation and in time the older generation passes away.

What makes sensible individuals what they are is not that they are copies of what is truly real—Plato's transcendent Forms—but active principles in them. These too are called forms, but these forms are not remote, requiring a turning away from sense particulars, so as to recall forgotten knowledge from a previous existence. They are right before us in the various genera and species of sensible plants and animals which come to be, mature, and die, and are followed by the same kinds of individuals as themselves. Forms are indeed real, but they are present *in* things.

We come to know them by a process of abstraction (as we pointed out in talking about universals). The mind is able to receive the form present in a particular object, that is, it can grasp or understand *what* the thing is, leaving out of consideration its matter. So the form is present in the understanding in an *abstract* way, that is, apart from the matter. But the form actually exists inseparably from matter, making matter *what* it is, a particular kind of reality.

For Aristotle the actual particular, the concrete individual being, is a substance. It is the prime reality or being on which all else depends in order to be (as we saw in the *Categories*). But *knowledge* is general. It is about the *kinds* of individual beings there are and the relations between them. To gain knowledge one is not interested in the skeleton of this horse but in the skeletons of *horses*, in what is true of the *kind* of being a horse is. The starting point of science is thus accurate *definitions* which give us the *essence* a group of particulars has in common. So we have the interesting situation in which particulars are substances—that which is—but knowledge is about *kinds* of substances. We *sense* individuals (*this* horse) or particular items (*that* yellow patch); to *know (episteme)* is to connect general terms. (Medicine or carpentry are arts, not knowledge. They apply to and make judgments about *this* patient or *this* chair.) Knowledge, however, is not remote from sensibles because the forms we know do not exist apart, as do Plato's Forms. Aristotle's forms exist as the active principles of sensible particulars, enabling them to move from potency to act, enabling them to become and be the kinds of things that they are.

To say that the soul is the *form* of body thus means that the soul is the active principle which enables some matter (the kind of matter which has the potential for being a living being) to actualize or realize that potential. The souls of plants, animals, and persons (with an exception to be noted later) exist only as the form of matter, making it the kind of individual substance it is. (As it is put by medieval theologians, all creatures are composed of matter and form. This is called the doctrine of hylomorphism.) The human soul is thus not on a journey, seeking release from the body in order to return to its place of origin, for the soul by itself is not a substance. Soul—including the human soul—is the actualization of matter which is able to become a living substance.

Let us now examine systematically the crucial terminology of matter, form, potency, and act. Every individual is a member of a class, or is a kind of substance. It is hylomorphic, that is, composed of form and matter. Its form makes it what it is and enables us to know what it is; the fact that it is a particular body that is informed makes an individual distinct from all other individuals of the same kind. Unlike Plato's Forms, Aristotle's forms have a built-in *telos* or end. Aristotle detects or specifies a form by means of ends or goals achieved. Take a pen. If we ask what it is, we may reply that it is something designed to be used for writing. That function, use, purpose, or end tells us *what* it is. Thus purpose or end tells what a thing's form is. Natural things move to realize their form or end unconsciously unless they are rational beings, but an end is present in them *potentially*, and it enables them to move in an orderly and patterned way to a *realization* of their form or end.

Matter too is a complex notion in Aristotle. If we mentally abstract from matter all forms, including the forms that make it one kind of matter rather than another (take from our body not only its soul, but even the forms that enable it to be a corpse, so that it becomes decomposed into various elements, such as iron or calcium, and then remove the forms of iron and calcium) we would be left with something that cannot be characterized at all (this was later called "prime matter"). There is no such thing in nature as matter utterly uncharacterized. The lowest we may go in the sublunar sphere according to Aristotle, is to four principal elements: earth, air, fire, and water. These four elements are of course informed; that is, they are what they are because of their forms. They possess the potential to be transformed into each other, and from such compounds to be informed still further and gain the potential to become the matter for still other things.

Matter then is viewed as what can receive forms. That is, it is potentially one or more things. No matter exists that is utterly uninformed. What forms it may receive, that is what it is potentially and so is able to become, depends on what it *now* is (what forms it now has actualized). Matter and form are thus able to be viewed as potentiality and actuality: matter as potency, form as the realization or actualization of potency. But matter as potency is always matter as actualized, that is, as informed. It is always something. Because it is a particular kind of thing, it has the potential for receiving certain other forms and becoming something else.

Matter and form when viewed in terms of potency and act are applied to a particular being in terms of whether we are looking upward or downward in the scale of being. A brick, for example, is both a form and matter. It is a brick because the form of brick has been introduced into clay, so that a brick is actualized. The clay had the potential to become a brick. From the point of view of a brick (looking downward) clay is matter; from the point of view of clay (looking upward) a brick is an end or a realized form. A brick is a realization of one of the potentials of clay. A brick, however, can be used to build a wall. It has that potential. From the point of view of a wall (looking downward) a brick is matter. Thus a brick can be regarded both as an end (a form) and as a means (matter). Every individual thing thus has two aspects, it is both a means and an end. It is both matter and form. Matter is the term used to refer to *whatever* is a means to an end and form is used for whatever is an end.

This example deals with artificial things, not natural kinds, and the terms—form, matter, potency, act—are used by analogy as principles of natural beings. Let us see how matter and form are related to potency and act with natural beings. Natural beings develop in time toward the actualization of their potential. At any time during a process a thing is formally what it shares with other beings. So its form may be an acorn. But in another sense, its form is an oak tree.

This gives us its direction of development, its natural goal. The form is its inner drive to direct its development and organization of the matter it takes in (air, water, and other nutrients) toward a certain end. Aristotle calls forms in natural things *entelechies*. They are the inner drives and directions in things which enable things to actualize their forms which are present in them potentially, or that enable them to actualize their potential.

In the *Categories* Aristotle pointed out that the most characteristic thing about substances is that they are capable of admitting contrary qualifications (4a, 10–12). That is, a particular man, for example, can change without ceasing to be a man; whereas "white" and "round" cannot change without ceasing to be what they are. A substance that was cold can now be hot; one that was here can now be there; one that was small can now be large. The substance is still the same *kind* of thing (a person, a horse, a dog) so its essence is the same. Its changes are all accidents (quality, place, quantity). Aristotle calls this sort of change "alteration."

Some change is "substantial." Let me first illustrate this with an artificial object. Wood can be made into a chair, that is, an artifact. The change is a change in the *kind* of thing we have. One substantial form has replaced another; the form of chair has replaced the form of wood. The only thing which remains the same is the material. We have the same wood before it was made into a chair and after it was made into a chair. So the *substratum*, as Aristotle calls it, which allows us to have change by giving us continuity through change, in this case is the sameness of the material.

Substantial change with natural things is similar, but it requires us to call upon "prime matter" to provide the substratum. When a horse eats grass, the grass is digested and takes on a new substantial form. It becomes part of the horse. The destruction of the grass is not complete, however. Prime matter, which does not exist precisely as prime matter but is always in conjunction with form, is nonetheless a real element in every material object, including the grass the horse ate. That element remains even when grass loses its form and becomes an element of the matter of the horse's body.

This leads us to the generation of new individuals. In generation, the matter of sperm and the matter of ovum of two mice, for example, are combined to become the matter or the potential for a new individual. That matter when realized will be a mature mouse. We have a new substance, that is a new individual distinct from its parents but the same in kind; it has the same nature as its parents. There is continuity because the matter of the parents (the ovum and sperm) and the offspring (the ovum and sperm combined) each contain the same prime matter as an element even though the forms of sperm and ovum, and sperm and ovum combined are different.

We have now covered every type of change in Aristotle but that of locomotion or change of place. Before we look at this and its far-reaching implications, we need to complete our account of the concepts of matter and form, and the closely related concepts of potency and act. Aristotle tells us that the highest knowledge is that knowledge which is sought for its own sake and not because it may be used as a means to produce something else. It is higher because it is desirable for its own sake. The science which is desirable for its own sake is the science of first principles or causes. This science first arose because people wanted to know the explanation or the cause of the things they saw. "First Philosophy" or metaphysics (as we call it because his book on First Philosophy was placed after—*meta* in Greek—*Physics* in Aristotle's edited corpus) arises then from wonder or the desire for understanding, a desire natural to human beings. This natural desire to know has enormous implications for Aristotle's view of the proper realization of our nature, or more specifically for ethics, as we shall see. But for the present we want to see its connection with his concepts of matter and form, potency and act.

Aristotle tells us in the *Physics* and *Metaphysics* that the explanations or causes of things are four in number: their matter, cause of motion, essence or form, and end. Aristotle seems to have a craftsman in mind. For a craftsman to make something, he needs something out of which to make it; he must supply the power to make it (it must be made *by* something); he must make it *into* something; and he must make it for some purpose or use. These are Aristotle's famous four causes. They are called material, efficient, formal, and final causes, respectively. For natural things, in contrast to artificial things made by a craftsman, the four causes reduce to two. There is no need for an external agent, such as a craftsman. A natural thing's own form or entelechy is the efficient cause. The end or purpose or final cause of a natural thing is not conscious except for rational beings. It is simply to move from potency to act. Thus we are left with form and matter in the explanation of natural things because the form—what a thing is—is the efficient cause, and it is distinct from the final cause only in that when the form has completed its realization, moved from potency to act, it has achieved its end. Aristotle uses the terminology of matter and form, potency and act in every subject of inquiry, making suitable adjustments for the particular subject matter. Let me illustrate this briefly from the *Physics* because this will enable us to treat local motion, which we have not yet covered.

The subject of physics (which simply means "nature" in Greek) is that which is sensible and changing in ways besides pure locomotion. This means the substances we perceive, excluding the heavens (since for Aristotle the stars' and planets' only change is place) and also excluding artifacts. Natural things—stones, plants, and animals—are natural objects because the impulse to change is within themselves. (Stones fall naturally—by their nature—as they move to their natural place.) Artifacts need an external mover. (A table falls not insofar as it is a table, but insofar as it is wood.) Physics then is concerned with three kinds of change: (1) qualitative change (a substance that is cold becomes hot), (2) quantitative change (an increase or decrease in amount), and (3) locomotion (change of place). Coming-into-being and passing-away (generation and corruption) are treated in biology (the study of living things), a subdivision of physics. We have already treated qualitative and quantitative change (alteration), so we may now turn to local motion.

Local motion is motion in our present-day sense of the word. It presupposes place and time. There must be "places" so that what is in a place can be displaced by something else. Because the four elements—earth, air, fire, and water—have their natural place, they must be kept from it by force of violent motion. But remove the obstructions (pull the plug), and they will move to their natural places (the water will drain out). So place is not something relative to us. For Aristotle "up" is the place to which fire moves and "down" is the place to which water moves. Aristotle defines place as the limit within which a body is, a limit understood as immobile. Everything in the physical universe is thus in a place. Local motion occurs through a change of place. The universe itself is not in a place, so it does not move forward or backward. It simple turns.

A body can be moved only by a *present* mover in contact with it. The problem of projectiles—cases of motion in which there is no present mover in contact with what has been thrown or shot—was never solved satisfactorily in Aristotelian terms. (It became the starting point for Galileo, and his work became a major factor in discrediting Aristotle in the seventeenth century.) Aristotle took it that natural motion accelerates (as is evident from falling bodies) but that unnatural motion or compulsory motion tends to decelerate.

Plotinus thinks of time primarily as a mental phenomenon, but for Aristotle time is very closely associated with local motion or change of place. Only things which are in movement or capable of movement are in time. What is immobile and everlasting is not in time. What is everlasting but in motion is in time. Aristotle does not simply identify time with the movement of bodies because he believes that we can recognize a lapse of time with a change in our state of mind. Time, however, is an aspect of the element of change, and it is a measure of *uniform* motion. The natural movement of earthly bodies accelerates, but the natural movement of the heavenly spheres is circular and uniform. So we measure time by their motion. Were there no minds to measure motion or to be aware of time, there would be no time strictly speaking, but there would be the substratum of time.

According to Aristotle, the universe consists of two distinct and very different parts: the sublunary and the superlunary. The earth is spherical in shape and at rest at the center of the universe. Around it is a series of invisible spheres—one inside the other—on which are placed the various heavenly bodies. The moon is the nearest sphere to earth. The moon, the other heavenly bodies, and their spheres are not composed of the four earthly elements—earth, air, fire, and water—but of a fifth and vastly superior element, ether. It is incapable of any change but change of place in circular motion. That is its natural motion, as the natural motion of earthly elements is in a straight line. (One of the most devastating criticisms of the Aristotelian cosmology and astronomy was Galileo's stress on the fact that changes besides that of place did occur in the heavens so that the universe does *not* consist of two distinct parts, one with generation and decay, the other imperishable.)

Aristotle postulated a total of fifty-five concentric spheres (elsewhere thirty-nine) in order to account for the observed motions of the planets, as they were at that time believed to be, and in addition an outermost sphere for the stars; and beyond that dwelt the First Unmoved Mover.

Aristotle's cosmos is thus one in which there is a gradation or a scale of being (and value). As the scale is ascended, form is ever more predominant (one is reminded of Plotinus, in which the scale is determined by degrees of unity). In the *Physics* and *Metaphysics*, Aristotle argues that there must be at least one being which is pure act–that is fully realized form and hence without any matter–to account for movement. As pure act, it would itself not move since movement is a change from potency to act. This means it would not be acted on by anything since it would have no unrealized potency (one sort of potency is the ability to be acted on by something else). It would be an unmoved mover. Let us see first why Aristotle thought there must be at least one unmoved mover and then how it would cause the motion of the universe as its final cause.

Now for motion to occur there must be a mover. The mover must either be the object itself or some other object. If some other object, then it too must be either its own mover or be moved by some other object. Eventually we must conclude that there is a first mover who is unmoved, or a cause of change which itself does not change from being unmoving to moving (it is without any potency). This is perhaps more apparent when we ask how the first cause causes motion. In Aristotle, all qualitative and quantitative motion needs locomotion. So the unmoved mover must be related somehow to locomotion. But as pure act, it cannot shove or push things, for it would then itself be changed and thus not be pure act. The locomotion to be everlasting must be circular, for motion back and forth is composite motion, and so must have a reason for a change from one direction to the other. On earth we do not have everlasting circular motion; the natural motion of earthly matter is up and down and from side to side. But we can see circular motion in the heavens. Heavenly matter must be different from our own. Aristotle calls it "ether." The eternal motion in circular form by heavenly bodies is the result of their being attached to moving spheres which are solid but invisible. Generation on earth is caused most immediately by the heat of the sun. The material vehicle of this action is called *pneuma* ("breath" or "spirit" in Greek). It is not heated air, but it is life-giving and permits the soul to act on the body. *Pneuma* is present in seeds and is the active principle in generation (the passive principle being moisture). This odd intermediary had a long career and is what is referred to in physiology as "animal spirits" well into the seventeenth century.

We still have not connected the unmoved mover to the spheres and hence indirectly through the sun to the motions on earth. Aristotle is difficult to interpret because he does not seem to be firm about whether there is only one unmoved mover or several. He sometimes has only one, but in very late writings he has several—one for each sphere—as well as one in the outermost sphere (that of the stars) and also the First Unmoved Mover beyond the outermost sphere.

The principle, however, is clear. There is motion because every good thing is desired insofar as it is known. The First Unmoved Mover is a perfect and eternal being, and so is particularly an object of desire. The first sphere of fixed stars, which seems to be alive and intelligent, desires the perfection of the First Unmoved Mover. It imitates that perfection as best it can by moving with the most perfect of all motions, in a circle. So the First Unmoved Mover acts as a cause by being the *final* cause of motion.

But it is unclear how the motion of the outermost sphere is transmitted to the other spheres. It would be possible by some form of local motion caused perhaps by *pneuma*. But the location of the heavens cannot be caused by the rotation of the sphere of the fixed stars because the spheres rotate in different directions. Thus Aristotle speaks of several unmoved movers, one for each sphere, with each sphere's circular motion caused by imitation of its own unmoved mover's actuality.

The First Unmoved Mover's activity is thought, but not discursive thought since that involves a move from not knowing to knowing and so a motion from potentiality to act. Its thought, then, is intuitive or perfect and its object can only be itself. It is this unmoved mover which the Middle Platonists and Plotinus adopted as the hypostasis Mind. It is also the being which medieval theologians who sought to relate Aristotle to Christianity sought to adapt and relate to the God revealed in Scripture. The First Mover in Aristotle, however, is not an object of worship. It does not know anything outside itself, and it is not a creator. It is posited simply as a necessary consequence of an analysis of motion as a change from potency to act, and a study of earthly and heavenly motions.

Aristotle's treatise *On the Heavens* in which he presented his theory of the heavens as consisting of concentric spheres nesting in one another with the earth at the center, utilized the most up-to-date astronomical observations available. In the High Middle Ages Ptolemy's *Almagest* (late second century A.D.) with better observations became available again. Its theory of eccentrics and epicycles was incompatible with Aristotle's theory of concentric spheres. Medieval theologians were troubled by this contradiction between Ptolemy's mathematical astronomy, which best accounted for the observed phenomena in the sky, and Aristotle's physical theory, which they assumed was deduced from first principles.

Thomas Aquinas supported Aristotle. Aquinas granted that Ptolemy's hypotheses were supported by experience but experience does not and cannot demonstrate a hypothesis. Ptolemy's account, though it is harmonious with the appearances, is not the only possible astronomical theory. Phenomena may perhaps be accounted for in another way yet to be discovered and which, unlike Ptolemy, would be harmonious with Aristotle's theory of the heavens. Thomas' defense of Aristotle suggested that the harmony between philosophy (Aristotle) and revelation need not be disturbed by contrary data from experience. When the sixteenth and seventeenth century revolution in science destroyed Aristotelian physics, it implied for many the falsification of Thomas' approach to revelation and philosophy.

We have pointed out that Aristotle's cosmos was a hierarchical one, with an ascending scale of being in which form is ever more predominant. That is, the potential in matter is more and more realized or actualized, so that at the very top there is pure act, or perfect being. This scale of being is evident in his biology and ethics, and both are integrated with his physics and metaphysics.

As we have mentioned, Aristotle was a great biologist. He left us detailed information on some five hundred living beings. He seems to have studied physics as the material factor, and soul as the formal factor, of living objects. Thus arose the phrase we mentioned earlier, the soul is the form of body. In keeping with the general principle of hierarchy as ascending according to the greater realization of the potential of matter, living bodies are also arranged hierarchically. Since this has implications for his ethics, we need to look at it briefly.

A natural body which is potentially a living body must be organic, that is, have the necessary instrumental parts for the performance of life functions. The lowest type of body is that of plants. This level of life is able to take in nourishment and thus to increase or decrease in size. The next level of life is that of animals, which not only have the power of nutrition, but also of sensation and local motion. Thus they have desires and the ability to move in order to gratify desires. The next level is that of living beings which possess the powers of both plants and animals and also reason. Each type of living being at a higher level possesses the powers of what is below its level. The living body is a unity, not a soul and a body. Matter and form are aspects of one thing, and are separable only in thought. So life for the soul after a living being dies makes no sense since the soul is the form of the body.

This picture is greatly complicated, however, by Aristotle's view of reason. There are several aspects of it which we have already touched on. We mentioned that Plotinus utilizes Aristotle's view of perception and knowledge. The eye or ear is unlike its object, but it is potentially like it, and actually becomes like it by receiving the form of the perceived object. But there is a step in this which we have not treated before. The five senses receive some sensations which belong to them exclusively. It is by "common sense" that we associate the specialized sensations of different organs with the same object. Some perceptions, such as size, shape, duration, rest, and motion, are not perceived by any of the special senses. These are also perceptions of common sense. Abstraction, which is so important to Aristotle, involves the production of images by a faculty of the mind. Sensations are received and formed into images (*phantasmata*). These differ from sensations in that they can last after the object causing them is no longer present. Images are the raw data from which concepts are formed. This is the highest activity of the rational soul. It is the reception of the intelligible form just as sensation is the reception of the sensible form. It is here that the mind becomes what it thinks; that is, the form is entirely abstracted from the matter of sensible things and it actualizes the mind's potential for thinking it. The form is then actually present in our minds and exists in our minds.

The mind is not wholly a passive potency waiting to be actualized by forms in sensible objects however. It is the passive intellect which becomes what it knows. Act always precedes potency, so actually existing and active power are required to illumine the mind and actualize the forms which exist in the mind potentially. Sensible objects are not sufficient causes because they do not actually yield intelligible forms (concepts) but only the raw material of sensations, which produces images, a raw material again which an active agent must use to produce concepts.

Aristotle calls the active intellect *nous*. He says little about it. It is always in act, without potency, and so it is unchanging, everlasting, and is able to exist apart from the body. So it is not the realization of the body. It enters from without. It clearly gives us a kinship with the First Unmoved Mover and the other intelligences, but Aristotle never explores this. We do not know whether there is one active intellect common to all human beings, or whether there is an active intellect for each individual. But the survival of our death by the active intellect in us does not mean that we survive. Memory is a necessary condition for personal identity, or for the continuity of personality. Memory is a function of the soul/body unity, and memory cannot survive its demise.

This, of course, caused considerable difficulty for Christian Aristotelians since Christianity affirms personal life after death. According to Aristotle what individuates each substance so that it is different from the other individuals of its kind is its matter. *What* an individual is, its essence, is common to all members of its species (more precisely its *infimae species*, the lowest division into kinds of individuals). Individuals do not differ from each other because of their specific form since it is the same. A person is "this" person rather than "that" person because the matter of each person is different. They differ from each other only because of their accidental qualities. Once an individual person is no longer embodied, that is, the living body dies, all that is left is *nous*. Without any matter, there is no way to distinguish the *nous* that was active in a particular departed individual. Aristotle is not clear about its status. As I have said, it may be that each individual in active thought is simply part of the action of a single Agent Intellect (as the active intellect or *nous* is called) that resides above the earthly sphere.

This is indeed the interpretation Averroës gave to Aristotle. Our active intellect is not an essential part of us. Our rational activity is the result of *an* Agent Intellect, which is a separate and unitary intelligence in the lunar sphere. The passive intellect of each individual person is acted on by the Agent Intellect, so that we may form concepts and engage in intellectual activity. With the death of a particular human being, the Agent Intellect simply does not have that individual to illumine any more. So the belief that we survive death cannot be based on the incorruptibility of our rational activity, and on the ground that it is active and thus distinct from the soul which is the form of the body.

Aquinas argued that a *consistent* Aristotelianism must regard the intellect of each individual as itself a distinct intellect. Otherwise all individuals would have the same intellect, yet people think and reason differently. In addition, our *nous* survives bodily death by *its own nature* (so we have a basis of immortality by nature), and the body will be resurrected. This way each individual *nous* can be distinguished from the others. That our rational principle by its nature survives bodily death can be demonstrated; that our body will be resurrected is revealed and is supported by probable arguments.

Some theologians disputed Aquinas' claim that our *nous* survives by its very nature, or that this can be demonstrated. But what Aquinas and other Christian Aristotelians had to fear was Averroës' interpretation of Aristotle according to which our rationality is not part of our specific form. Hence, on the basis of philosophy, the possibility of immortality could be denied.

Quite apart from the issue of personal survival, reason plays an important role in Aristotle's ethics. Ethics for Aristotle is not a theoretical discipline but one concerned with practice, the conduct of the good human life. It is based on our nature. Given what we are, some practices are good for us; that is they enable us to fulfill our nature. Right is defined in terms of those actions which are conducive to good ends. Thus right is defined as a *means* to good ends. There are many things which are good for human beings, and so part of the task of ethics is to order them in terms of their being conducive to the chief or highest good for us.

Aristotle claims that everyone agrees that the chief good for us is happiness, and he proceeds to argue that happiness for human beings is to be found by doing what is peculiar to human beings. This cannot be growth, reproduction, or having sensations since these are all activities we share with plants and animals. It is rather in the practice of a life *in accord with reason* since reason is distinctive to our nature. Moral virtue itself is not the end of life, for it can go with misery. So Aristotle distinguishes moral virtues (such as courage, temperance, and justice) from intellectual virtues (such as prudence) since reason must be used to live a life in accord with reason. Thus the use of reason in seeking a life which fulfills our nature requires good judgment in practical matters (*phronesis*). Virtue for Aristotle means "excellence" (*arete*), as we saw earlier in discussing Plato. It is to engage in those practices that result in an *excellent* or virtuous human being and are the activities of an excellent human being. The form of humanity, so to speak, becomes realized in a virtuous person so that we have an excellent specimen, just as we have an excellent tree or cabbage.

Moral virtue involves the formation of character; that is, a person develops or has a virtue (an excellence) by forming a habit of acting in a particular way when it is appropriate. We form these habits by practicing good actions just as a person learns a craft by practice. Thus moral virtues are defined in terms of the habit or disposition to choose the mean response in action and/or feeling which avoids the extremes of either too much or too little. It is a disposition to choose a rule which a truly virtuous person, possessed of practical wisdom, would choose. For example, a person should have self-respect and should not go to the *excess* of vanity nor to the *defect* of humility. Not all virtues have two extremes. Nor should it be thought that virtues are a precise midpoint between extremes, nor that the proper mean is the same for every person. A person who is a manual worker needs more food than an office worker, so if an office worker ate the same amount of food as a manual worker, he or she would be a glutton. A person who is truly virtuous, possessed of practical wisdom, is the one who can determine the proper response in a given circumstance.

Intellectual virtues are divided into two kinds, according to two intellectual operations. One is the intellectual operation which relates to moral and political activity. As we mentioned, the use of reason in seeking a life which fulfills our nature requires good judgment in practical matters (*phronesis*). Practical wisdom is concerned with determining the means to ends. No virtue can exist without the virtue of prudence (right and reasonable choice). The other intellectual virtue is the pursuit of theoretical knowledge. It concerns only those objects which are necessary. The virtues are those habits or dispositions by which we can demonstrate or prove, and also the developed capacity to grasp a universal truth after experience of several particular instances. Together these give *sophia* (theoretical wisdom). It is here that human beings find the highest part of their nature fulfilled. For our *nous* finds its fulfillment in theoretical knowledge. We have here an affinity to the pure intelligences of the spheres and to the First Unmoved Mover whose activity consists in thinking. Our highest activity and hence happiness is to be found in the pursuit of scientific knowledge—the knowledge of the cause of things—or in short, a knowledge of ultimate reality. The whole of moral life is supposed to be ordered to this end. Moral virtues are good in themselves and also are a necessary condition for intellectual investigation and contemplation of theoretical knowledge, for a person must be free of the disturbing vices of our lower nature in order to engage in such activity. Likewise a person lives in society and must develop the intellectual virtue of "good sense" (*phronesis*) to live well with people and also to have sufficient goods to live without want and to be hospitable. These are all indispensable conditions for happiness, even if they are not part of happiness itself.

For Aristotle happiness does not consist of pleasure. But pleasure is necessarily involved because it accompanies any well done, free activity. The practice of virtues thus is pleasurable. But both Aristotle and Plato before him feared the easy pleasures of the body. These pleasures do not require repeated activity or the formation of character before they can be enjoyed. Virtues, however, and the pleasure which accompanies their exercise require the development of character *before* they become pleasurable to practice. People are thus immediately attracted to the pleasure of bodily gratification and, unless they are restrained, they will not develop the virtues and thereby be able to recognize from personal experience that the practice of virtue is to be preferred to undisciplined bodily gratification.

Aristotle's ethics contain so much good sense that they have been adapted and incorporated into Christian ethical theory, especially by Roman Catholic theologians. The notion of the development of "habits" has played a large role in the conception of spiritual formation with a stress on repetition and denial of appetites. Aristotle's ethics, of course, must be modified to be acceptable. For example, besides moral and intellectual virtues, which are *natural*, one must add the theological virtues—faith, hope, and love—which are infused by grace. There is the problem of original sin and its relation to the natural virtues. Also the stress on happiness (*eudaemonia*) or well-being as the goal of life and the basis of ethics is a source of theological controversy. Our desire for happiness is considered by some to be at bottom a selfish concern. Even if our goal is God, the knowledge of whom gives us happiness, the motive is questionable unless it can be distinguished from the desire for personal well-being as the determining aim. This is often discussed in the contrast between *eros* (the selfish desire for well-being) and *agape* (the spontaneous and unselfish love that comes from God's grace). It is part of the longstanding difficulty in Western Christianity of specifying the respective domains of nature and grace.

Aristotle claims that politics is the chief of the practical sciences since it is concerned with human beings living together. Ethics deals with individual character and behavior and is therefore subordinate to it. He thinks that the good life for the individual can be achieved only in and through the community. So he has a positive view of the state and is one of the continuing influences on that type of political theory, in contrast to laissez-faire theorists who tend to regard government in a negative way. Aristotle says that the state seeks to serve the supreme good of human beings, unlike the family and clan which come into existence to serve the bare ends of life. The state is a *natural* society because it serves our nature, and it is prior (in the sense of taking precedence by nature) to the individual, family, and clan.

Aristotle's positive conception of the state and the way his philosophy generally supports the integrity of natural things were major forces in the development of natural law in the Middle Ages. They also created much of the basis for the controversies over jurisdiction between church and state. The Christian belongs to another community that is higher than the state, namely the society of the church. The end of the church is higher than that of the state, and so the state is rightly subordinate to the spiritual end of human beings and so too to the church. Still natural law and the natural character of the state give the state its own integrity. Its place and role needs to be defined relative to the eternal law of God (which, because God is the Creator, underlies natural law) and to the church. These matters had been raised earlier, of course, but with the rediscovery of Aristotle, they were discussed in terms of philosophic conceptions drawn from him.

6

Aquinas' Program and Two Critics:
Karl Barth and Process Theology

We shall now illustrate how Aristotle's philosophy gave theology a new direction by a brief look at Thomas Aquinas and thus show once again the value of philosophy for understanding theology. We can get a sound idea of the immensity of Aquinas' achievement by an examination of his program in natural theology. It will enable us to understand on the one hand, the objections to natural theology by the greatest Protestant theologian of this century, Karl Barth, and on the other hand, the proposal of process theology, a contemporary movement, to replace this natural theology with a version of its own.

In the *Summa Theologica* (la, 2.3) Aquinas gives five proofs of the existence of God, or "five ways" as he calls them. A proof is needed because it is not immediately self-evident to us that God exists. A self-evident proposition is a proposition in which the predicate forms part of what is meant by the subject. "God exists" is a proposition in which the predicate ("exists") is part of what the subject means. It is this fact which Anselm tried to make use of in his famous ontological argument (which we shall look at in connection with his modern critics). Anselm tried to show that God's nature is such that from the essence of God (from *what* God is) we may conclude *that* God exists. But, Aquinas says, the proposition "God exists" is not self-evident *to us* because we cannot grasp the divine essence. So the route of an ontological argument, an argument from the being or essence of God to the existence of God, is impossible.

We can see this more clearly if we note that in Aristotle a demonstration involves the use of a syllogism. Subject and predicate are shown to be connected by use of a middle term. (An example of a middle term in a syllogism would be: "All *x*'s are *y*'s. *P* is an *x*. Therefore, *p* is a *y*." The middle term is *x*.) If we knew what causes existence (the predicate) to belong to God (the subject), we would have the proper middle term. But God's essence is unknowable to us, so the middle term which connects the predicate to the subject is unavailable to us.

But God as Creator has *effects*. We can demonstrate the existence of God by showing that there are effects of which God is the *cause*. So, unlike Anselm who connects the predicate (exists) to the subject (God) by means of the cause of their connection (God's essence), Aquinas connects them by proceeding from an *effect* (the creation) back to its cause (God). When we reason from effect back to cause we do not reach God's essence. That is, God is far greater than the world God produces, and so from God's effects we cannot comprehend God's nature or essence. But we can establish *that* God exists and characterize God accurately.

In early Christian doctrine, God is referred to as ungenerated (*agenetos*) and incorruptible. God and only God is "unborn" (*agenetos*) and undying. Everything else depends on God for its existence; God depends on nothing in order to exist. Not only is God the Creator, but God creates freely since God is complete and full in the divine life. We cannot comprehend this life, for that would be to comprehend God's essence. We described this conception of God as Creator as the ontological foundation of theology. We can understand Aquinas' program by relating it to this doctrine.

Aquinas insists that the Christian doctrine of creation, which asserts a beginning for the world, is not demonstrable. Philosophy can show that all things depend on a God who exists and that we know *something* about divine nature. We cannot fully grasp or comprehend the divine essence or nature, but we may know that some things are true of God's essence by use of Aristotle's philosophy, which for Aquinas was the same thing as to say by the use of philosophy or reason.

Thomas' five ways or the traditional proofs of God's existence (as they are often spoken of today in the philosophy of religion) rely above all on Aristotle's conception of motion as the actualizing of potency. We shall not go into them rigorously because an examination of them is not necessary for understanding this part of Aquinas' theological program. The conclusion of the first way gives us the existence of a being who is pure act (in whom there is no potential). This is similar to Aristotle's First Unmoved Mover, and indeed Aquinas adapted Aristotle's argument for the existence of at least one being who is pure act. But the second way goes further than Aristotle. Using Aristotle's concepts, Aquinas shows that God is also the first *efficient* cause, so that all efficient causes within the world are dependent on God's efficient causality all the time in order to be causes. They are thus called "secondary causes." Likewise, Aquinas proceeds to characterize God as necessary being in the third way. Aristotle distinguishes between beings which come to be and pass away and those which are everlasting. For Aristotle the heavenly bodies and the First Unmoved Mover are everlasting. In that sense he considers them to be necessary beings and calls them gods (as the Greeks did with whatever was not mortal). Aquinas goes far beyond Aristotle here. Granted that there are everlasting beings, they nonetheless are *contingent* or dependent beings because in them essence (what they are) and existence (that they are) can be distinguished. Even if they exist always, it is *possible* that they might not be since what they are (their essence) does not enable them to exist of themselves. There must be a being in whom essence and existence are the same in order to explain or account for beings in which essence and existence are distinct. This being is God who is distinguished from all other beings as a necessary being because God is not only everlasting, but God's perpetual existence grounds itself in the divine essence, being identical with the divine act of existing.

Aquinas does not assume that we have a knowledge of God's essence so that we may, from that knowledge, show that God exists. This would be the ontological argument. Instead, he shows that the existence of contingent beings and everlasting beings entails the existence of a necessary being in whom essence and existence are the same. God's existence is not treated as an attribute of divine essence. God does not exist from divine essence. God's essence *is* a pure, subsistent act of existence. God is sheer existence, the only being who can be said to be existence. God is being in God's self (*esse per se*).

Until Aquinas, Christianity had conceived of God's difference from all other beings and the world as a whole as consisting in God's being ungenerated and incorruptible, so that a temporal dimension was involved in distinguishing God from creatures. God does not begin or end, as they and the entire cosmos do. But, as we mentioned, Aquinas does not believe we can demonstrate by reason (philosophically) the revealed truth that the world began. But in the third way God is shown philosophically to be *esse per se*, the one who is of oneself. This achieves what the characterization "Creator" achieves; it marks God off from the whole world as self-sufficient. This remarkable achievement was broached by Anselm, who also thought of God as self-existent. But Aquinas argues the point in a different way, and in addition he makes it clear that existence is not an *attribute*, but that God's being is an *act* of existence.

The fourth way, taken in conjunction with the third, enables us to characterize God as the source of the limited perfections (such as good and truth) which we have in the world. In the Platonic tradition, the Forms, put into the mind of God, are God's perfections. They act as the exemplars of created things. God, in knowing the divine essence, knows that essence to be imitable by creatures. God's perfections exist in creatures as limited perfections and imperfectly reflect the divine being. And finally, God is known as the final cause or the continuing source of the orderly motion of all things from potency to act. The regularity of their motion requires intelligence, and since many things which so move do not have intelligence, God guides them.

In his five ways Aquinas has characterized God in ways that go far beyond Aristotle's First Unmoved Mover. God is not only the first cause of motion as pure act (the first way) and the final cause of all things (the fifth way), but God is also the first efficient cause (the second way) and the exemplar or formal cause of all perfections (the fourth way). Furthermore, for Aquinas God is radically different from Aristotle's First Unmoved Mover in his third way. God is sheer existence; God is being in God's self (*esse per se*). God is thus not one term in a contrast to other beings which are the other term, as is

Aristotle's First Unmoved Mover, who even as pure thinking and highest being nonetheless is part of the world. God as being in God's self (*esse per se*) is marked off from the whole world as self-sufficient. God is able to be without a world at all.

The doctrine of creation in the Bible describes a God who creates freely. God can do so because divine life is full and complete in itself. Aquinas claims we may also reach this understanding of God through the five ways which give us God as one who is being of oneself and utterly complete. The One who is pure act, for example, is not composed of potency/act, does not depend on anything in any way. There is no composition of essence and existence, so again God does not need anything in order to be. (This independence of God is what is meant by God's *aseity*). So the view of God as one who is absolutely independent and self-sufficient, whose life is full and complete in itself, which is the result of revelation, can also be reached by philosophy. Aquinas never wearies of pointing out that God, who is *esse per se* according to philosophical reasoning, is self-revealed as "He who Is" (cf., Exod. 3:13–14). Even though it is now acknowledged that Aquinas' interpretation of these verses is somewhat far-fetched, the exposition of his program which we have given makes it clear that it does not stand or fall on a piece of biblical interpretation.

Aquinas proceeds from demonstrating God's existence by reason to demonstrating many of the divine attributes by reason. From God as being itself, that is from God's aseity, all other perfections can be deduced, such as unicity, truth, infinity, immensity, ubiquity, and eternity. A distinction is drawn between these attributes as *entitative* (since they do not involve any relation to contingent beings; they tell us how God is in essence), and those that are *operative*, which concern God's nature as related to others. They too are demonstrated by natural reason. They concern God's intellect and will, and thus enable us to conceive of God as a personal being. Aquinas' program in natural theology then is one in which we may gain a limited but genuine knowledge of God as God is in essence and as God is related to us, without revelation. This knowledge is gained by demonstration, and so natural theology is a science.

This program was inspired by Aristotle's *Metaphysics*. Aristotle there says (among a large miscellany of things, for the *Metaphysics* is not actually a single treatise) that First Philosophy is a study of being *qua* being. For Aristotle the primary kind of reality is substance. But besides the individual substances which are subject to change, there are substances which are free of change or which are pure actualities. These are the most completely real things that there are. So First Philosophy concentrates on the study of being in its most perfect form. It has its culmination in a knowledge of the attributes of the First Unmoved Mover, or theology, as Aristotle calls it. But, as we have seen, Aquinas' ingenuity is such that he can by his five ways arrive at a characterization of the primary being that is far more than the First Unmoved Mover and above all not a being among beings. In Aquinas our knowledge of God is nonetheless limited. God is far more than we can grasp because God cannot be *defined*. Created beings have a genus and species (they are *kinds* of beings). But God, as being itself, in order to be defined would have to be placed under the genus of being. Being, however, is not a genus. A genus is *determined*, or made specific by those differentiae which are not contained within it. Nothing, however, can be added to being since outside being there is nothing. Or, put in another way, God is not *a* being but being itself. The divine essence is not that God is this or that sort of being, but God is an act of independent existence. So we have no categories by which to define God.*

Even though we cannot define God, we may have *some* knowledge of God. But our characterizations do not apply *univocally*. That is they do not mean the same thing when applied to God and to creatures. We must *negate* any characterization we give God in order to emphasize that these characterizations are not what the divine

---

* This point is so fundamental that we need to go into technicalities for a moment. "It was Aristotle who first demonstrated that Being is not a genus at all, and so, *a fortiori*, not the *summum genus*. All the differentiae of any genus must have being. But, Aristotle held, it is impossible for a genus, taken apart from its species, [for example, *animal* apart from *human*, *cow*, and the like] to be predicated of its own differentiae [to say, for example, that *rationality* is an *animal*]. If the differentiae *rational* and *brute* divide the genus *animal* [that is, every *animal* is either *brute* or *rational*], then it is impossible that *animal*, when taken apart from the species *rational animal* or *brute animal*, should be predicated either of *rational* or of *brute* [that is, to say that *bruteness* is an *animal*, or that *rationality* is an *animal*]. If being is a genus, Aristotle therefore argued, it follows both that its differentiae must have being, and that being must not be predicated of them. Now since that is self-contradictory, the hypothesis that being is a genus must be false (*Metaphysics* B, 998b, 21–27)." (Alan Donagan, *The Later Philosophy of R. G. Collingwood*, Oxford: Oxford University Press, 1962, p. 281). It is perhaps Hegel's failure to honor this which allowed him to talk about *Being* in contrast to *Nonbeing*, sublated into *Becoming*.

nature or essence is. (The way of negation is familiar to us from Christian Platonism.) On the other hand, some characterizations fit God better than others. Positive attributes of creatures such as goodness and intelligence are attributed to God. They exist in creatures in a limited way, but in God, their source, they exist eminently. Since God's essence or being is unknown to us, we cannot know how they exist in God, but we can assert them properly of God.

Since God and creatures differ so drastically in being, the perfections of creatures are applied to God by analogy in a *particular* sense of analogy. It is called the analogy of proportion. The likeness between God and creatures is based on their proportionate participation in the reality signified by the concept. They participate in the perfection according to the nature of their being. To say God is intelligent, therefore, is to say that there is something that bears the same kind of relationship to the divine nature as intelligence does to human nature. The analogy is the expression of a *parallel* in the relationship between the divine intelligence and the divine nature on the one hand, and between human intelligence and human nature on the other. The perfection attributed to God and creature is really present in both, but not in the same way. God has it eminently; in the creature it is present in a limited way. (Recall Aquinas' fourth way in which the divine perfections are exemplars imitated by creatures.)

Another kind of analogy is that of proportionality. For example, we see by our eyes, not by our minds. But there is a similarity between the way the eye is related to vision and the way the mind is related to apprehension. Because the two *relations* are similar we may rightly speak of the mind's apprehension as a kind of vision. Aquinas favors the analogy of proportion over proportionality. (It can become very confusing because today the analogy of proportion is called the analogy of attribution, and the analogy of proportionality is called the analogy of proportion.)

Thus for Aquinas our knowledge is very limited indeed, for we do not know the divine nature. We only know that certain perfections are applicable to it and that the nature of their reality in God is not known to us. We cannot form a concept of pure being (existence) as such; we always know being *as this or as that being* (genus and species). The analogy of being is not a way of discovering the nature of the divine being by moving from creaturely perfections to divine ones, but of knowing that certain perfections are to be attributed to God.

Aquinas and other theologians emphasize that the divine attributes are one, not multiple. For they designate one entity or reality which we understand under multiple or diverse aspects. We may confirm that they are united by showing that the divine attributes may be derived from one or another of the perfections. Commonly the other perfections are derived from aseity; that is, one shows how they are implied by it. (Scotus shows their unity by deriving them from infinity.) But this does not mean that one perfection is more fundamental than the others in God. It is only that such a perfection appears to be prior to any other attribute *to us*. Thus when it is said that the ontological foundation of theology is creation, this does not mean that power and goodness are more constitutive of God's nature than other perfections.

Aquinas' project of natural theology, which is intended to give us knowledge of God by philosophic means, thus recognizes impenetrable mystery. We can by philosophy (reason) know that God exists, that God is one, good, perfect, intelligent, and the like, but what these are in the divine essence is not knowable either by philosophy or by revelation. Nonetheless, Aquinas has gone much further than the Fathers of the ancient church, both East and West. He has not only admitted philosophy within theology (as natural theology) but, by his identification of God's essence as God's act of existence, he has been able to attribute a great deal to God, to specify the meaning of those attributes analogically, and to relate them to one another in a demonstrable science.

This is just an indication of part of Aquinas' theological program. The achievement of it is marvelously impressive regardless of one's final philosophical or theological estimate of its adequacy. There have been no shortage of critics both in the Middle Ages and today. I want to look at two contemporary ones briefly and then, in the next chapter, at the fourteenth century criticisms of the attempt to wed Christianity and Aristotle.

We begin with Karl Barth. He rejects natural theology as such because it is a *philosophical* construction. The deity in it is not the God of Abraham, Isaac, and Jacob. The God who is self-revealed can be known *only* by revelation and not apart from it. Aquinas' God, in spite of many differences, is no more God than is Aristotle's First Unmoved Mover. That god is the creation of human reason, and so is an idol. There is no way to reach God from human reasoning; God must come to us.

This criticism may be significantly mitigated if one interprets Aquinas' theology as an attempt to *think* God, rather than to reach God, that is to say, to understand his project as a *rational* theology which seeks to understand *what* it means to say that God is complete and full in essence. The mind which seeks to determine what we may know of God need not be an unbelieving mind. One need not interpret Aquinas' five ways as demonstrations leading us to faith but as the ways a believing mind achieves a rational apprehension of God. What is apprehended by the believing mind in the natural world's existence and operations is no less there, and no less apprehended if it is not apprehended nor acknowledged to be there by nonbelievers.

A far more telling matter is the interpretation of the Christian God in Aristotelian terms or concepts, expressly as pure act and as the one whose essence is the act of being. The issue may be put this way. One of the tasks of theology is to relate the metaphysical and moral attributes of God, that is, to relate what God is in essence and what God is self-revealed to be in relation to us. Aquinas has demonstrated by reason (philosophy) that God has certain attributes, both entitative and operative. The question is whether these demonstrated attributes are to take precedence over biblical descriptions so that the biblical descriptions would be treated as accommodations to popular understanding when there is any tension between the two. That the attributes are demonstrated is not decisive since we do not know precisely what the characterizations *mean* in their application to God. If in our interpretation of the attributes we take Aristotelian philosophical terminology as our guide, we seem to give to unaided reason the power to interpret the Bible. It seems to subordinate revelation to reason.

Barth, in his *Church Dogmatics,* speaks of God's being (essence) as God's acts and also of God's acts as God's being. But in volume

2/1 where he treats the relationship between the metaphysical and moral attributes, he insists on interpreting all the attributes in terms of God as *trinity* (which is, of course, God as self-revealed). This means to interpret all the attributes in terms of the Bible. To speak of God's intelligence and power, for example, one does not rely on the way intelligence and power are found in limited perfection in creatures. Rather one relies on the way God is revealed in Scripture. What God is found to be in revelation is used to inform us of the proper sense in which to understand divine intelligence and power. There is no claim to know what God is in essence. We know God only as God is self-disclosed to us. We believe by faith that God is in essence not less than God is self-revealed to be, or that God would in any way contradict what God is self-revealed to be. (Yet sufficient linkage between the language of Scripture and the rest of our discourse must be presumed.)

Another objection to the Thomist enterprise has been launched in recent years by process theology. It too frequently objects that the God of "classical theism" (the name given to the Scholastic deity by process thinkers) is not the God of the Bible. For the deity of classical theism is unaffected by anything outside. As complete and self-sufficient, that God is an absolute. (This would also reject the Christian doctrine of creation, as we shall see, but let us continue with its criticism of classical theism.) Following Aristotle's *Categories*, what we predicate of a substance is either the kind of being it is or the way it *may* be. The way a substance may be is not essential to its nature, and so is an accident. In classical theism God's relations to anything outside are not essential to God's being and so are accidents.

More damaging is the claim that the God of classical theism has no *real* relations with anything. A substance may, for example, be unchanged in itself, and something else move closer to it. Their relation is now one of nearness. Only one of the substances has changed. The relation of closeness is purely external and not real as far as the substance which is unchanged is concerned. Because God is unchangeable, the God of classical theism is not really related to the universe or its members. God could at best be like Aristotle's First Unmoved Mover, which is unaffected by anything outside itself. Other beings are moved by it only because they imitate its perfection. It is only an external final cause, and the relation to it is purely external and not real, for it remains utterly unaffected by the relation. The biblical God is active and has real relations. Besides, the view of God as unchangeable, which means God is nontemporal, is incoherent, according to process theologians.

Those who follow Alfred North Whitehead (1861–1947) and in particular Charles Hartshorne (1897–) who gives a theological interpretation to Whitehead's few remarks about God, have their own natural theology or philosophy. Although they claim that it does much more justice to the Bible than does classical theism, the biblical view of God is not the decisive factor in process thought. This can be briefly indicated by reference to the doctrine of creation as the foundation of Christian theology. Whitehead does not even consider the ontological status of the universe as posing a question. He takes the existence of the universe as given, indeed as everlasting. (In this he is very Greek.) His concern is to explain its workings. To do this he postulates only what must be postulated in order to account for its workings. His categorical scheme, as he calls it, demands a "principle of limitation." This is because there is an infinite number of possibilities which might be realized, and not all of them are in fact realized. So something must act to limit possibilities. (This is a version of the argument that there must be a designer for the order of the cosmos because the beings we have are not in themselves sufficient to account for its order.)

My main point concerns method. Whitehead posits only what he must posit to account for the world's order, just as Plato does in the *Timaeus* (which in fact is one of Whitehead's main sources of inspiration). Thus, Whitehead's "God" is postulated as a principle of limitation. But Whitehead says in a famous remark, that we are not to pay God any "metaphysical compliments." That is, we are not to attribute various perfections to God and certainly not to an infinite degree. God is not the Creator of the universe; God is not unlimited in power, knowledge, and goodness. To say these things of God would be compliments because they are utterly gratuitous. There is no basis whatsoever for asserting them since they are not required in an explanation of the working of the world (in particular physical nature). This procedure is perfectly in order for a philosopher and in the construction of a philosophy. But Christianity is not *bound* by this methodological requirement.

As we pointed out in the Introduction, the Bible is not engaged in philosophical speculation concerning what we need in order to account for the world's workings or even for its existence. It is a witness to God's action in the redemption of a people from Egypt, the establishment of a covenant, and their witness to God as Maker of heaven and earth. The Bible does not consider the attribution of the power to create and indeed to create freely "a metaphysical compliment." It is the way God has shown God to be to the Israelites. God creates freely because God alone is complete and full and has no need of anything else. God is indeed related to the universe, for God is its Creator and Sustainer, but the relation *between* God and the world is less basic than one of the *terms* of the relation, namely God, who is more fundamental than the *relation* between God and the world. It is precisely from the reality of that relation to the world as Creator that the *primacy* of God's independence and completeness is affirmed. The biblical and Christian belief in God as complete in essence and not in need of a universe is not the result of Greek philosophy. However much Greek philosophy has been employed by Christian theologians, it is the biblical view of God as Creator which is the basis of the conviction that God is complete and full in essence and in no need of being related to anything outside.

It may be that neither a Christian theology guided by ancient Greek philosophy nor process theology (which is itself a variant form of the themes of Plato's *Timaeus*) will do. For clearly Christianity views God as active in creation and redemption, and indeed as Father, Son, and Holy Spirit in communion with us. On the other hand, only because God is complete in essence is God's love in creation and redemption utterly gracious. My own guess is that we need to recognize that God, who is full and complete, has the power to become *less* in at least some respects; that is, God has the capacity to condescend to the position of being like a creature, acted upon and in need. This is certainly what the incarnation suggests. However that may be, both Barth and process theology have at the very least encouraged a fresh consideration of the nature of God. Their attacks have stimulated conversations between Catholic theologians and others, with the consequence that both philosophers and Protestant theologians have come to recognize the fruitfulness of engaging themselves with Scholastic theology.

7

The Beginnings of
the Modern World:
Nominalism, Humanism,
the Scientific Revolution

To treat the nominalism of the fourteenth century in a chapter called "The Beginnings of the Modern World" may seem strange. It is part of the world of the Middle Ages and not part of the Renaissance or the Reformation, which are usually regarded as the beginning of the transition from the medieval to the modern world. But I take it that the scientific revolution of the late sixteenth and the seventeenth centuries is the most significant point of division between the medieval and the modern mentalities. The eminent historian, Herbert Butterfield, gives this assessment of the scientific revolution:

> It outshines everything since the rise of Christianity and reduces the Renaissance and Reformation to the rank of mere episodes, mere internal displacements, within the system of medieval Christendom. Since it changed the character of men's habitual operations even in the conduct of the non-material sciences, while transforming the whole diagram of the physical universe and the very texture of human life itself, it looms so large as the real origin both of the modern world and of the modern mentality that our customary periodisation of European history has become an anachronism and an encumbrance. (*The Origins of Modern Science: 1300–1800*, revised ed., New York: Free Press, 1957, pp.7–8).

The rise of modern science is of particular significance for us because modern science repudiated the concepts of potency/act, matter and form—or Aristotle's view of change—on which his view of physics was based. It was with Aristotle's concepts that the Scholastic synthesis of natural theology (philosophy or reason) and theology was achieved.

It is because of its repudiation of Aristotelian categories or concepts that I regard nominalism as part of the beginning of the modern world, even though it is very much a medieval Scholastic phenomenon and did not of itself have the power to bring about the reorientation we call the modern world. We shall also restrict our treatment of the humanism of the Renaissance. We shall consider only its contribution to the rise of modern science.

Let us look first at nominalism. The foundation of the thirteenth century syntheses of philosophy and theology, of reason and faith, of nature and grace, was attacked by the movement known as the *via moderna* (the modern way). Its greatest representative was William of Ockham (ca. 1285–1347). The great rival schools of Thomas Aquinas and John Duns Scotus (ca. 1266–1308, who revised in a more Aristotelian direction the outlook of Bonaventure, the great contemporary rival of Aquinas), as well as the school of Giles of Rome, were all referred to as the *via antiqua* (the old way). As we have seen, the introduction of the philosophy of Aristotle to the Latin West formed the main challenge to the leading theologians of the day. They sought to harmonize Aristotle with Christian doctrine. There were several resulting syntheses (the *via antiqua*). They all accepted Christian doctrine as normative and considered philosophy to be autonomous in its own sphere. Philosophy did not receive its principles from theology. When Aristotle was at variance with Christian doctrine, there were two possibilities. One was to eliminate the contradictions by a reinterpretation of Aristotle, but a reinterpretation which left the Aristotelian system intact. This was the route taken by Aquinas. The Franciscan theologians considered this inadequate. Indeed, Bonaventure, whose inspiration was fundamentally Platonic, never thought of reason as utterly unaided in its operations (in the tradition of Augustine). Scotus, whose work superseded his great Franciscan predecessor, exploited the more Platonic elements within Aristotle along the lines of the Middle and Neoplatonists of the ancient period, to develop his own theological synthesis. Aristotle was thus much more seriously revised and not left as an intact philosophical system. This then was the other route. So there were deep and significant differences in the philosophical-theological syntheses of the *via antiqua* of the thirteenth century, but they all depended on some version of moderate realism.

Moderate realism is the philosophical position which holds that we are able to abstract from sensible particulars their essences. These essences, or specific forms, are ontologically present in sensibles and when they are abstracted we can demonstrate necessary truths concerning sensible beings and their relations to each other, and so achieve demonstrable knowledge of the causes of particular beings. In addition we can gain demonstrable knowledge of God's existence and attributes as we just saw with Thomas Aquinas.

William of Ockham rejected realism, the fundamental epistemological and ontological basis of the great thirteenth century syntheses. Thus he, and others who rejected realism, were followers of a "new way." The philosophical issue here is so important for theology that we need to look once again at the problem of universals.

One way to approach the problem is to think of the three divisions of Aristotle's *Categories*. Primary substance and secondary substance involve a distinction between individual substances and genera and species. Genera and species specify the *kinds* of individual beings there are and so are *general*. (They apply to more than one individual.) A quality such as the particular white of a person's hair is also an individual, even though it is not a substance. But "white," which is predicated of many individuals, is as general as a genus or a species. It can be predicated of more than one individual instance of white. In Aristotle, knowledge as we have seen, is general. It is primarily a knowledge of genera and species, that is a knowledge of essence, which is a nature common to several individual beings. The problem of universals is how the objects of thought are universal (apply to more than one individual) and yet everything that exists is a particular or an individual.

Moderate realism was the answer given by most theologians once the main part of Aristotle's corpus became available in the Latin West. We abstract by our intellect from our sense experience of individuals their common nature. The common nature of several individuals is distinct from what individuates them as different individuals. Moderate realist theories can be divided into three types, depending on how they regard the *distinction* between the common natures (the specific forms which make each individual the *kind* of individual that it is) and what makes each individual an *individual*, different from others of its kind.

One type of moderate realism holds that there is a *real* distinction between the common natures and what individuates. The common nature is one thing, present in many individuals, and so it does not distinguish one individual from another of the same kind. Ockham argues that if the human nature of Socrates (the specific form, which is the common nature present in him) is *really* distinct from him, then it is not Socrates' nature or essence. For a thing cannot be said to be *essentially* something it really is not. On the other hand, if the common nature (specific form) is not *one* but many (so that it does individuate Socrates and is not really distinct from what individuates him) then the *commonness* of the common nature is lost. Unacceptable consequences thus arise whether one makes the specific form really distinct or really not distinct from what individuates.

Duns Scotus created the second type of moderate realism. The *haecceitas* (or individuating differentiae) "contracts" the common nature to singularity. So the common nature is really identical with what individuates, but it is "formally" distinct, as genera and species are distinct from differentiae which "contract" them. Against this position, Ockham argues that even a formal difference is either a real difference or a real identity. There is no intermediate ground. So we are back where we were with the first type of moderate realism.

The third moderate realist position, articulated by Aquinas, is that the same thing is singular and universal, according to the way it is considered. We gave this position earlier, without mentioning this feature, when we said that it is the *concept* formed by considering the likeness of individuals that is universal. Its basis in reality is the common nature *in* sensible things, which is distinct in various individuals. The universal (the concept) exists only as an abstraction; for though the common nature can be abstracted from matter in thought, it does not exist apart from matter in reality. So what is referred to by universals and common natures is neither individual nor singular in itself but is made singular by being received in individuating matter and is made universal by being received into the mind. Ockham scornfully replies that anything is a singular thing because of itself, not because something (individuating matter) is added to it.

Ockham's rejection of the reality of common natures or specific forms present in things is thus an attack on the foundation of all of the thirteenth century theological syntheses which rely on Aristotelian terminology. The main causal principle of Aristotle's philosophy is destroyed, for matter and form, related as potency and act, are Aristotle's linchpin.

With the rejection of forms, matter for Ockham is not a potentiality, but it is actual in its own right. Form for Ockham is no more than the shape or structure of material parts. Final causes whereby nature is said to be teleological through and through (the purposive movement of each thing from potency to act) is regarded by Ockham as metaphorical. Causality becomes efficient causality and is knowable by repeated experience of a regular sequence. That is, one thing is the cause of another if, when it is present, the effect follows, and when it is not present, the effect does not occur. Such a causal relation can be known only by experience. There is no possibility of inferring from a knowledge of one thing that something else must result from it, as is the case with essences, which once abstracted permit one to go beyond the particulars that have been experienced. Ockham's view of causality thus makes demonstration impossible, for our knowledge can extend no further than our experience. Beyond our experience there is only probability. Deductive ontological constructions that begin with experience but can be carried beyond present experience because of essential attributes of various beings are impossible. Aquinas' project of a natural theology as the crown of all natural knowledge becomes impossible. This consequence indeed follows when the reality of substantial forms is denied. Without Aristotelian conceptualty, the proofs of God's existence and a demonstration of divine attributes as a preamble to faith is utterly undermined. Aquinas had believed that a natural theology is *presupposed* by revelation. But now Ockham relegates the existence of God, along with everything else in theology, to the sphere of faith.

It also means that natural law as a basis for morals and politics is seriously weakened. The moral order established by God can be known only by revelation. It may be approximated through natural reason only by reflection on the needs of individuals and society. It is thus possible that at any time the reasoning of Christian people on morals and politics and the teachings of revelation might diverge so that the harmony of faith and reason, philosophy and theology, nature and grace are no longer guaranteed. Although Ockham rejected moderate realism, he was not a nominalist. That is, he did not, any more than did many others of "the modern way" hold that things called by the same name have only the name in common since there is no extramental basis for calling a number of things by the same general term. He rejects common natures but the universal concept is appropriately applied to each of a set of individuals if they resemble one another and if the concept resembles each individual. Ockham was what we now call a conceptualist. His work on how general terms are used in propositions is philosophically of a very high quality. He turned the problem of universals from the ontological problem of common natures present in various individuals to a question of language and logic. He deals with the terms of propositions and how they signify.

Ockham was not sceptical about our knowledge of the natural world. He believed that things operate in an orderly way because of God's will, and we can therefore rely on probable reasoning. He also believed that we have *direct* knowledge of particular beings and their qualities in perception. This view of perception (a direct intuition of sensible beings' existence and properties) is called "realism" in modern philosophy. It should not be confused with the realism that concerns the ontological reality of common natures in things. It is conceptualism, which denies the reality of common natures in things and which is a rival view of ontological realism.

Ockham's own theological views are also positive. They are based on revelation and faith, rather than philosophical demonstrations, so there is no room for a natural theology. Nor is theology a science. On the other hand, theology can no more be refuted by philosophy than it can be demonstrated by it. God is omnipotent and free because there are no "essences," and God's nature does not

include exemplars of them. Thus the order and structure of beings—
the natural world—has no necessity in itself. The created world is
sheer fact, utterly contingent on God's will with no metaphysical
ground of necessity on which to construct a demonstrative philosophy with which theology must cohere. This stress on the sheer
creative novelty of God's actions is the last shadow of Plato's Forms
as ontologically independent realities whose independence had
already been modified by making them the thoughts of God and so
part of divine nature.

Although himself a Scholastic, Ockham represented a powerful
attack on Aristotle. It was no longer possible to think of Aristotle as
"the Philosopher," as Aquinas and others spoke of him. The philosophical situation was rendered more fluid by the *via moderna*, so
that different ways to explain nature's order and movement had a
better chance of receiving a hearing. Thus Ockham contributed to
this extent at the very least to the scientific revolution which is above
all responsible for a new division in human history.

Before we turn to the scientific revolution, we need to consider
the humanist movement from the standpoint of its contribution to
that revolution. Humanism is primarily a literary and philosophical
movement which began in the latter half of the fourteenth century
and spread throughout much of Europe. Its very name "humanism"
suggests the value it placed on humanity. This meant in part the
recovery of human beings as *natural* beings. Humanists sought to
reintegrate us into the world of nature and history as the proper
realm for the realization of our capacities.

This is not in itself contrary to Christian Aristotelianism. It too
recognized the integrity of human beings as natural beings with natural ends to be realized. But Renaissance humanists, who by and
large continued to believe in the supremacy of the supernatural end
of human beings over the natural end, nonetheless felt that aspects
of our natural realization had been neglected by Scholasticism. Their
ideal was the Roman *humanitas* (rooted in the Greek *paideia*) which
means the "education" of a person into true human excellence (virtue or *arete*). The instrument to educate human beings as human
beings was not the "sterile" logic and dialectics of the Scholastics
nor Aristotle's physics and metaphysics. The instrument of educa-

tion was the literary arts of classical antiquity: poetry, rhetoric, history, ethics, and politics. These would free a person to take part in human affairs as a genuine human being.

The importance of human personality as original and as an autonomous center of achievement, and confidence in human initiative are essential features of humanism. Earthly happiness is a genuine goal, and this formed a powerful motive in the scientific revolution or search for useful knowledge (as Bacon put it) that would give us power to bend nature to our purposes. This attitude contrasts with Aristotle's *theoria*, which is to be contemplated as an end in itself.

The passion for classical antiquity in the early fifteenth century led to a greater recovery of Latin manuscripts than had ever been realized before. This was taking place even before the fall of Constantinople in 1453 which led to an influx of Greek manuscripts. For all humanism's enthusiasm for the harmony between Plato and Christianity, it did not create any philosophical ideas which we have not already treated and which are needed to understand theology. Its influence on the scientific revolution was in some of the texts it uncovered. It provided, for example, a much more complete knowledge of Archimedes (ca. 287–212 B.C.), whose work in statics became widely available in scientific centers, especially after its translation into Latin in 1543. His work showed how nature could be studied mathematically (or more precisely geometrically) and showed the value of such an approach. It had a direct influence on Galileo (1564–1642), whose work on projectiles and falling bodies created an entirely new approach to the problems of motion that Aristotle's methods had never been able to handle properly. In addition, new texts made people aware of the heliocentric doctrine of Pythagoras—that the earth went around the sun. The Platonic-Pythagorean view that nature is written in mathematics was an inspiration to Copernicus and especially to Kepler (1571–1630) whose work became an indispensable pillar of the Newtonian synthesis. In medicine the work of Hippocrates (ca. 460–377 B.C.) and other ancient physicians became available for the first time and bore fruit in the faculties of medicine in the Italian universities.

Many features of Renaissance humanism helped create our modern world. But it is the two which we have emphasized which were relevant to the rise of modern science and that is the reason we have restricted ourselves to these two aspects. Since the term "humanism" is used today by some Protestants as a term of reproach, a few more remarks are in order.

The term "humanism" has a number of different meanings. Originally it referred to the literary movement of the Renaissance, with its devotion to Greek and Latin classics. It has been extended to refer to the movement in the twelfth century when there was also a recovery of texts from antiquity. People speak of the humanism of the High Middle Ages. In the twentieth century it has been used by William James and John Dewey, two of America's leading philosophers, to refer to their ideal of joining scientific concerns with the nobler elements of human life. Others have used it in our own century as an antidote to vocational specialization and a narrow view of science in education. But perhaps what some Protestants object to is the kind of humanism which puts itself forward deliberately as an alternative way of life to a Christian or to any other religious one, explicitly excluding a belief in the existence of God and at times criticizing Christianity for the irrationality of its beliefs and its crippling of human development.

One should remember, however, that there is such a thing as *Christian* humanism, so that the term "humanism" should not always be considered a rival to Christianity. Christian humanism is the view that human culture is valuable to the Christian life, and although it is subordinate to Christian teaching, nonetheless it can enhance our Christian life. It avoids both philistinism—the vulgar denigration of genuine human achievements—and also the pride of attaching more importance to human culture than is compatible with a creaturely existence. The theological foundation of Christian humanism is that human beings are made in the image of God. As *creatures* we have natural goals which are valuable, and which can only be properly achieved within a culture which recognizes, even if only implicitly, the sovereignty and graciousness of God.

In spite of the *via moderna*'s opposition to the Christian-Aristotelian theological syntheses, and the Renaissance humanists' rejection of much of Aristotle as inimical to the proper development of a human life, a basically Aristotelian conception of nature continued to dominate people's thinking. The cosmos was still viewed by theologians, scientists, and humanists as hierarchical. The earth, at the center of the universe, is the only place in which things are born, mature, decay, and disintegrate. The matter of the heavenly spheres is imperishable. The only motion beyond the moon is uniform circular local motion. Ptolemy's understanding of the motions of the heavenly bodies was rendered "compatible" with Aristotle's. There had been so many epicycles and other adjustments made to Ptolemy's system in order to fit the apparent motions of the heavenly bodies that it could not be taken seriously as an actual physical description of the heavens. It was used simply as a means of calculating the positions of the stars. Aristotle's physics was taken to be the actual physical description of nature. Its picture of a scale of being, extending from plants, animals, and human beings on earth, up through the various spheres and their intelligences, to God beyond the outermost sphere, was widely held. Aristotle's categories or concepts of matter and form, potency and act, still dominated the universities.

What is of particular importance for us is the union of science (or "natural philosophy" as it was called well into the eighteenth century) with human values. The hierarchical structure of nature was regarded as society and morals writ large. Everything in nature had its proper place, so that the universe was orderly and harmonious. This provided the ancient Greeks a confirmation of their belief in a properly ordered human life. For things to go against their nature was harmful and disruptive. This had been absorbed into Christianity. It is consonant with Genesis 1–3, in which the world is created and ordered by God's Word, and human disobedience introduces disorder, decay, and death.

It is not only physical nature, then, but all human relations which have a natural and proper order. To violate this leads to social disruption and harmful consequences. This underlies some of Shakespeare's plays. The basis for the action of *The Taming of the Shrew* is the conviction that woman's role is to be subordinate to her husband since this is the only way either of them can be happy. Their relation is a microcosm of society and of the physical universe which also have natural orders. People supported the legitimate sovereign, not primarily out of sentiment, but on a rational basis, for some are born to rule. To go against nature, as does Macbeth in his ambition to rule, leads to civil disorder and personal tragedy.

The idea of a hierarchical order both in the heavens and on earth, in nature and in social relations and politics, was taken for granted well into the sixteenth century. Human beings were the meeting place of all that is above as well as below; we are microcosms of the entire universe. We are thus mortal and earthly, but we are made in the divine image, and so by God's grace we can overcome the effects of the Fall and rise to an imperishable realm. Thus Copernicus' theory that the sun, not the earth, is at the center of the universe, is not a mere scientific hypothesis. It is socially revolutionary and threatens the entire Aristotelian rationale for the social and moral order. Not a mere physical theory but an entire civilization is at stake.

Copernicus himself was not a revolutionary. He wanted instead to improve on Ptolemy, to make the old better. Ptolemy was able to maintain the fundamental assumption of Aristotle's astronomical theory—that perfect motion is circular and uniform—only by a bit of cheating, for the observed motions of the heavenly bodies were not perfectly circular. Ptolemy's addition of epicycles to get them plotted in circles was acceptable to Copernicus. But even with epicycles, to get *uniform* motion Ptolemy had to invent a point called the *punctum equans*. It was simply a point in empty space around which a planet supposedly moved. Copernicus wanted motion in *circles with uniform* velocity, without any such hanky-panky. To get it, he put the sun, not the earth, at the center of the planetary orbits.

This did not cause any particular stir because of a disclaimer in the preface (added by Osiander) to Copernicus' book *On the Revolutions of the Celestial Spheres* (1543). It suggested that he had placed the sun at the center of the universe only for the ease of making mathematical calculations. It was not a claim about the actual position of the sun in relation to the planets. This was no different from the use made of Ptolemy's astronomy itself. It too was said to be used for purposes of calculation. So because of the preface, Copernicus did not pose a serious threat, even though he personally believed that the sun was at the center of the universe. (He also was aware that the system he devised was not mathematically accurate, even with the retention of epicycles.)

Kepler, a much greater astronomer, was far more radical. He was inspired by the Platonic-Pythagorean belief in mathematics as the means to understand nature. It led him not only to view the sun as the actual center of the universe (*Mysterium Cosmographicum*, 1596), but also to abandon uniform circular motion for the planets. This was truly daring, for it meant that the heavens did not move because of their natural circular motion (in imitation of an unmoved mover). They moved in elliptical orbits, and accelerated and decelerated along the path. This implied that some *physical* explanation had to be found for their motion: a physical explanation outside of those possible in Aristotelian physics.

Kepler was led to his view of the planetary orbits by the most meticulous concern for mathematical accuracy. For some years he had tried to work out the orbit of Mars, the most difficult of the planets. He had at his disposal the best observational data of the time (the work of Tycho Brahe, 1546–1601). After years of work he plotted a circular orbit for Mars. It differed from the observed data by only eight minutes (there are 360 degrees to a circle and 60 minutes to a degree). This was so small a discrepancy that it could easily have been dismissed as owing to the limitations in accuracy of observation. But Kepler chose to sacrifice six years of work and start all over, looking now for an elliptical orbit which would fit the observed data better. It was not until Newton's *Principia Mathematica* (1687) which relied so heavily on Kepler's work, that the fruitfulness of such mathematical accuracy was thoroughly vindicated. At the time, Kepler's work, and in particular his three laws which included elliptical orbits, did not break the hold of the Aristotelian hierarchical world view.

Aristotle received his fatal wounds primarily from Galileo's work on falling bodies and projectiles and from Descartes' philosophical analysis of the essential properties of bodies. Galileo and Descartes, for different reasons, considered only the *mathematical* properties of bodies as essential and objectively present in bodies. All other properties of bodies *as they appear to our senses*, such as color, texture, smell, taste, are the result of the size, shape, and motion of matter on our sense organs. These subjective appearances are called secondary qualities—secondary powers which bodies have to produce in us these secondary appearances. But matter objectively consists of nothing but extension, figure (shape), and capability of motion or rest. These are called primary qualities.

Thus change for Galileo and Descartes is local motion only, not a motion from potency to act as a specific form moves to realize itself. Descartes referred to specific forms as "occult" (or magical) explanations. There are neither formal nor final causes in matter (or nature). All qualitative changes (such as color, sound, texture) are caused by *impact* in local motion of matter, whose essence is extension. He devised a view of the entire cosmos as a vast machine, with mechanical causality (impact) as the sole cause of all change. Nature as a vast clockwork mechanism became the dominant image of the universe and replaced the friendly hierarchy of Aristotle. It was utterly impersonal, unlike Aristotle's world which was interpreted as operating the way our minds work, with purposes, and with the sensible appearances of things as objective and part of the nature of bodies. Individual substances or beings are no longer the prime reality. Nature consists of nothing but matter which is utterly uniform in its essence.

Galileo broke with the Aristotelian conception of motion (as a change from potency to act) by addressing himself to the motion of projectiles and falling bodies. There was nothing new in his choice of this point of entry. This was the weak link in Aristotle's theory of motion and in the fourteenth century a rival explanation—the theory of impetus—had been fashioned. For Aristotle a moving thing has to have a mover acting on it *while* it is moving. Motion requires the *continuous* action of a mover. But an arrow continues to move for some time after it is no longer in contact with a bowstring, and falling bodies, although seeking their natural place (the center of the earth), *accelerate* instead of moving uniformly. Aristotle and those who followed him had tried various expedients to account for these anomalies, but none was satisfactory. According to the theory of impetus—which broke with Aristotle's principle—a projectile continues to move even though it is no longer in contact with its original mover because it acquires an impetus. An impetus is supposed to be something inside the projectile itself. Just as a poker absorbs heat from a fire and thus keeps heat for a while after it is withdrawn from the fire, a projectile acquires an impetus of motion from its contact with a mover. A falling body, in moving to its natural place, gains from its very motion an acquired impetus, which it *adds* to its natural motion, and this continues to build up, so that a falling body accelerates.

What makes Galileo original is not beginning at Aristotle's weakest point but his development of a radically new conception of motion. Archimedes had studied centers of gravity and the lever and had treated them mathematically. The study of Archimedes encouraged Galileo to treat quantitative relations as more important than qualitative ones. (The latter had primacy in Aristotle.) Galileo gave a mathematical relation for bodies in motion. The crucial revolutionary element was to treat time as an abstract parameter of motion. That is, time is freed of all associations with the mind and all associations with growth (a passage from potency to act). Time is treated simply in relation to velocity and distance. It is simply a mathematical term in relation to velocity and distance. Thus Galileo could express in a general way the relation of velocity to the distance a body falls in terms of time. He found a ratio so that the three are convertible. With this shift Galileo could give a precise and general mathematical statement of a law applicable to all falling bodies.

Descartes' conceptual analyses (in contrast to experiments) of matter and motion led him to the concept of inertia. (Galileo himself never quite reached it in his work.) It utterly subverts Aristotle's principle that whatever moves has a mover continuous with the motion (or has something always in the state of act). For the principle of inertia (which became Newton's first law of motion) is that a body at rest or in motion (in a vacuum) continues to be at rest or to move uniformly in a straight line *indefinitely*. To continue moving uniformly in a straight line does not require a mover continuously acting any more than to be at rest requires something to keep a body at rest. What needs to be explained are departures from rest and from such motion. Thus there is no need for an external mover (something always in the state of act, and ultimately something always in a state of pure act) in order to explain the motion of bodies. Nor is there any need of an internal source of motion, a form, causing bodies to go from potency to act. The motion of bodies can be accounted for by their impact on each other and the principle of inertia.

The mechanical philosophy in which all nature is to be explained in terms of extension, figure, and motion, was felt by many people, and not just Aristotelians, to be a threat to our conception of human beings and to Christianity. It suggested that nature operates blindly by mechanical action, and that nature's motions are self-sustaining. Nature, as a great self-sustaining machine, is not related to God in its operations; this appears to support atheism. Human beings are an anomaly. We act to achieve goals or ends but the world we act in supposedly operates mechanically. Instead of our being in a cosmos like that of Plato, Aristotle, the Stoics, or Plotinus in which things are mindlike in their operations, reflecting an ultimate reality that has affinities with our own minds, nature is utterly alien to us. It simply is extension in motion. In the seventeenth century the expression "brute matter" attained widespread currency, for matter is absolutely devoid of any mindlike qualities. Here I wish to inject a comment made to me by my teacher Jesse De Boer:

> As for the breakdown of Aristotle and Stoic natural law ... this I've learned not to feel sorry for. I think that Augustine—apart from his constant leaning on the Platonists—was the discoverer of personality and he also saw that a person as an agent in history *makes* himself and affects other folk and so helps create a culture. Forget about nature's apparent hierarchy. We must *choose* what to do, remember where we are, look ahead, and choose our aim, and act *now*! This is human historical existence. We can remember all the way back to Adam—repent of our sins back to Adam—and anticipate the Kingdom. This outlook—and it *is* being worked out by the rejection of Aristotle—is closer to biblical thinking than the Scholastic scheme.

The severity of the new mechanical picture of nature was diluted and made acceptable by several factors. To begin with, the success of the new scientific explanations was itself immensely appealing to many people. The Aristotelianism of the universities was frequently obscurantist and generally on the defensive. Francis Bacon's *Novum Organum* (1620) was very successful in making a contrast between the uselessness of Aristotle's understanding of nature, which did not enable one to change anything, and the value of the study of nature free of his concepts. The new science could uncover *useful* knowledge, that is, it gave us the "springs of nature" so that we could control nature and make it serve human purposes. The title *Novum Organum* was deliberately chosen to suggest a new instrument for the investigation of nature in contrast to Aristotle's logic. Bacon's own methods for the study of nature proved to be of little use, but he was successful in promoting the value of the new science of nature and in portraying Aristotelian concepts as an impediment to scientific progress. The promise of knowledge which would be used to improve human life on earth became a widespread and powerful motive in science.

The scientific revolution also opened the way for new intellectual investigations into the foundations of morals, society, law, and politics. Christian Aristotelianism had respected the integrity of nature and had developed foundations in nature for morals, society, law, and politics, and then related them all to our supernatural end. But with a new conception of nature, these human activities had to be rethought from the ground up. The seventeenth century is thus a great era for political theory, as witnessed by the development of the social contract theory of the state by Thomas Hobbes (*The Leviathan*, 1651); John Locke's treatises on government; and the great work on international law by Hugo Grotius (1583–1645). As nature was considerably more independent (a pure act always present to keep it running was no longer needed) the foundations of human activities were less closely related to God than in Christian Aristotelianism.

Deity was not wholly excluded by the new mechanistic science. God's continuous presence was not needed, but nonetheless a deity was required. Although nature was able to keep moving once set in motion, it had to get its *first* push from somewhere, and indeed its very existence. So God was thought to be its Creator, and to give it the first push, and then to leave it to run on its own. The workaday God was superseded by the God of the sabbath, as the historian of science, Alexandre Koyré put it so graphically. The work of creation done, God now rests, leaving nature to itself.

This conception was achieved after considerable opposition. Indeed, Isaac Newton (1642–1727) himself did not subscribe to the self-sufficiency of nature's operation. Many gaps remained in the scientific accounts of its operation. So Newton, as others, with the best of intentions, inserted God into those places where our science had no explanations to offer. In doing this, he ran together natural and supernatural explanations, or put into the same framework quite disparate explanations. This violates the transcendence of God, who is not a being among beings. Natural causes are to be given for natural processes. That completely natural accounts of natural processes are to be sought and given does not imply that there is no God. They are compatible either with a belief in a transcendent God or a belief that nature is self-sufficient. The difference between a believer and a nonbeliever is that the nonbeliever thinks that natural processes are "just the way things are," whereas a believer claims they are the way they are because of God's wisdom and benevolence.

But Newton and others sometimes used God when they could not find a natural cause for some natural phenomenon. Leibniz (1646–1716) was quick to point this out to Newton. (The letters have been published as the *Leibniz-Clarke Correspondence*.) But Leibniz was misunderstood by Newton and others, for the distinction I have just given was an insight that had not been achieved by many of Leibniz's contemporaries, and indeed one which some religious and nonreligious people today still have not achieved (as can be seen in the recent treatment of the Genesis creation stories and the theory of evolution as if they are *rival* accounts of the origins of life). So Leibniz was widely misunderstood. He was thought to make the world completely self-explanatory in terms of natural causes. Newton and others who think of explanations of natural processes which refer to God and those which refer to natural causes as being on the same plane and interchangeable actually cause needless conflicts between science and religion, for it means that God and some natural causes are rivals for the same place in an account of a natural process. As science progresses and finds a natural account where before it had none, God, who had been used to fill the gap, is pushed out. It now looks as if science has discredited belief in God, as if belief in deity is a belief which developed in more primitive times, but as our knowledge grew, we saw our mistake and corrected it by giving up belief in God. Newton thus did a great disservice when he put God into his accounts wherever there was a gap in the science of the day. As science progressed, God was pushed out of place after place into which Newton and others had put him. When Napoleon asked Pierre Laplace (1749–1827), who had presented him with his work on celestial mechanics, why there was no reference to God, Laplace could respond, "Sire, I have no need of that hypothesis."

In spite of God's insecure position as God of the gaps, God retained a secure place as Creator and source of the world's order in the new mechanistic science. New forms of the cosmological and teleological arguments were devised in the seventeenth and early eighteenth centuries. A cosmological argument is one in which God's existence is inferred from the existence of the world. A teleological argument argues from the order of the world to an intelligent designer of the order. Neither of these arguments mixes together natural and supernatural explanations. They were widely accepted by intellectuals as sound arguments until near the end of the eighteenth century. In fact, during the scientific revolution, they were the backbone of Deism or natural religion, a newly created rival to Christianity. It claimed to be a rational religion, without superstition and mystery. Many of the exponents of the new mechanistic science of the seventeenth and early eighteenth centuries were not atheists. In fact, never in the history of Western culture did the teleological argument enjoy such widespread popularity, for it seemed utterly improbable that "brute matter," moving by collision, could arrange itself into such intricate order. Some great mind must have designed it. It was either that or chance. But this is also why the problem of evil attracted so much attention and led to so many theodicies (attempts to explain how evil is compatible with a benevolent designer). If belief in God is based *solely* on the order of the world, then any "disorder" (pain, suffering, unhappiness) counts against the wisdom and goodness of the designer. If they cannot be satisfactorily accounted for, then the hypothesis of intelligent, benevolent design may have to be withdrawn. The explanation, moreover, has to be achieved in terms of the necessity of evil *for the world order itself.*

This very much limits the scope of a theodicy. Alexander Pope's remark in his poem, "Essay on Man" well summarizes the principle which a theodicy in natural religion has to sustain: "Whatever is, is right."

As long as the order being unveiled by the new mechanistic science was novel and fresh to people, "design" seemed the only possible explanation. Belief in the "rightness" of the natural order was secure, but as the novelty wore off and nature seemed "natural" to many intellectuals, the teleological argument became less compelling, and eventually was seriously discredited by David Hume's *Dialogues Concerning Natural Religion* (1778). Immanuel Kant's *Critique of Pure Reason* (1781) did the same to the cosmological argument. But this is to go beyond the beginnings of the modern mentality.

The new mechanistic science, then, led to a radically new conception of nature. It very nearly gave nature a self-sufficiency, so that it became a quasi-deity in its own right, and God was pictured more and more as the God of the sabbath rest. New categories began to replace the older Aristotelian ones in people's thinking, and the search for new foundations for all human activities was launched. God's existence could still be affirmed with confidence because it was solidly based on the existence and order of nature.

8

Early Modern Philosophy:
Rationalism, Empiricism, the Enlightenment

Modern philosophy, which is said to start with René Descartes (1596–1650), is primarily concerned with epistemology. The search for certainty and the grounds for certainty are its driving force. Theory of knowledge and ontology always interact with each other, to which the philosophical material we have covered bears witness. There is serious and significant concern with the grounds and nature of knowledge in the ancient and medieval periods. Plato's criticism of sense experience and his stress on the powers of the intellect to know the Forms, and Aristotle's doctrine of abstraction are both clearly in the domain of epistemology. Nonetheless, the emphasis on the nature of being, the elaboration of a scale of being, and the study of the properties of being are preeminent in premodern philosophy. It is simply a matter of emphasis. In the modern period the emphasis is on epistemology.

This can be shown by a look at Descartes' search for certainty. Both the continuity and novelty of modern philosophy are evident in Descartes. We have seen that Aristotle's concept of scientific knowledge is that of a demonstrative syllogism, based on first principles, the truth of which is self-evident. To deduce the particular from the general means that we know that the particular cannot be other than it is. This gives us certainty. Descartes repudiates the syllogism as a method for gaining knowledge. Nonetheless, he accepts the ideal of certainty, that is the demonstration that something is so and cannot be otherwise. He is also like Aristotle in saying that we must have self-evident principles and in believing that substance is the prime metaphysical notion.

Descartes differs from Aristotle in that for Decartes, and indeed for all the rationalists of the seventeenth century, *mathematics* is the ideal of all knowledge. He was deeply impressed with the clarity and certainty which are achieved in mathematics, especially in geometry. Its precise definition of terms, self-evident axioms, and clearly formulated demonstrations were unmatched in any other subject. He sought to achieve the clarity and certainty of mathematics in other subjects. His program was to adapt the procedures of mathematics into a method suitable for the search for first principles (metaphysics) and then, on the basis of first principles, to study nature.

How to make the transfer from mathematics to philosophy was not obvious. Descartes did not adopt the form of geometric demonstrations as did Spinoza (1632–77), who set out his greatest work, *Ethics*, literally in the form of geometry, with definitions, axioms, demonstrated theorems, and corollaries. It was rather the *certainty* obtained in mathematics which gave Descartes the standard to be achieved (indeed even to be surpassed) in metaphysics. Much of the history of modern philosophy concerns the attempts to attain truth which is *necessary* and hence certain, and the various adjustments that are made when such knowledge is thought to be impossible. As we go along, we shall see the implications that these various theories of knowledge have for theology.

Let us begin with an examination of Descartes' procedure. In 1641 Descartes published his masterpiece, *Meditations on First Philosophy*. Most of it is written in the first person, in an easily accessible style, inviting the reader to retrace the steps which led the author to arrive at indubitable first principles: the existence of God, mind and body as distinct substances, and the essence of matter as extension. His method of arriving at certainty is to begin by doubting everything which can be doubted until he finds that which cannot be doubted even by making the most farfetched and improbable assumptions.

His purpose in doubting all that can be doubted is to free us from our dependence of sense perception and other prejudices so that the mind can operate unimpeded. By its own powers—by its "natural light"—we can discover truths which are absolutely certain and which form the foundations for all other fields of inquiry. These truths are not derived from sense experience but are innate to reason itself. Hence the label "rationalist," that is, one who believes that our reason has access to general principles which neither have their origin in nor can be established by sense experience.

Descartes seeks to convince people that this is true by having them go through the reflections he describes in his *Meditations*. That is, they too are to meditate. Descartes begins his first meditation by pointing out that he came to realize as a student that he accepted many things as true which were actually false. He has thus decided to make a clean sweep of all his past opinions and to begin from the very foundation to establish a secure structure of knowledge. He does not have the time to review each of his opinions singly, one by one, so he adopts as a procedure an examination of the *basis* for his opinion, and withholds his assent from whatever is not plainly certain and indubitable as he withholds his assent from what is plainly false. So to discover *any* reason for doubting something justifies his rejection of it as though it were false.

He says that up to this point in his life he has accepted as true above all what he has received from sense experience, but he now realizes that his senses have misled him sometimes. How then can he rely on them? Perhaps they are unreliable only when objects are distant or minute. If we could specify the situations in which they are reliable, perhaps we could rely on our senses even though what we perceive is not always the case. Descartes dismisses this possiblity, for he believes that he is presently in a situation in which the conditions for sense perception are optimum. Yet he cannot be sure on the basis of his senses that he is indeed sitting by the fire, holding a paper in his hands, and so on. This is not because he thinks that perhaps he is a lunatic with a deranged mind. It is rather because he has had the same sense impressions while he is asleep as when he is awake. He has had dreams in which he was sitting by a fire as now, while actually he was asleep in bed. It does not help to move around deliberately and to think that nothing so distinct as that happens in dreams, for one realizes that one has been deceived by such thoughts before while asleep. There are then no certain sensible signs that enable us to distinguish being awake from being asleep.

He then reconsiders this conclusion. Perhaps I am asleep; it may be that I am wrong to think that I have hands and a body. Such experiences must have some basis in real physical objects. Painters, however much they invent new creatures such as sirens and satyrs, always have some basis in reality for these fictions. There must be something physical outside of dreams, something extended and a place for them to exist, even if I am dreaming. Thus the fields of physics, astronomy, and medicine which rely on composite bodies may be dealing with fictions, but arithmetic which simply counts objects of any sort and geometry which treates extended bodies, are sound. Indeed, they can give us truth even if they are dealing with dream objects. Whether I am asleep or awake, two and three make five and a square has four sides. This is impossible to doubt even in dreams.

Mathematics is not immune to doubt after all. If God exists, God could arrange it so that I had sense experience, that is *representations* of sense experience, just as I now think I have, when in fact there is no earth, sky, nor any physical universe at all. In addition, I realize that some people make mistakes in things they think they know perfectly. May not God likewise make me go wrong when I add two and three, or count the sides of a square? If this seems out of keeping with God's goodness, might there not be an evil demon who does this? If a demon is my source of existence, then indeed my sense experience in no way can give me certainty. There is no contradiction between my having sense experiences and the reality supposedly corresponding to them being different, or indeed there being no reality beyond them at all.

Descartes in this first meditation makes it clear that such suppositions are highly improbable. He is not in a state of actual doubt. The doubt he is talking about is not a psychological state at all. Rather he claims that sense experience does not *entail* the existence of a physical universe. That is, it can be true that we have the sense experiences we have, and it be false that there is a physical universe. There is no logical contradiction in this supposition. Thus, sense experience cannot give us *certainty*. He builds up to this conclusion step by step: from the fact that we sometimes misperceive (in bad conditions), that in dreams we are sometimes deceived, to the hypothesis of an evil demon who deceives us. It is really the possibility of systematic deception by an evil demon that drives the wedge between sense experience and certainty (and also defining "certainty" as only possible with the exclusion of every *logically* possible reason to doubt, for we are not in actual doubt because there is no logical contradiction in the possibility that there is a deceiving evil demon even though there is no actual reason to believe that there is one). What Descartes is after is not to put us into a state of actual doubt but to show us that if we are to get certainty—entailment between grounds and conclusion or between evidence and conclusion—it will have to be on some other basis than sense experience.

John Locke, the founder of empiricism, which bases all knowledge on experience, agrees with Descartes the rationalist on this crucial point. Locke says that sense experience can give us probability only. (He thinks however that this is enough to improve our life on earth and to know our duties.) To go beyond probability, the grounds for a truth claim must be such that they logically entail its truth (so that we have a logical demonstration). That is, it is impossible on *any* supposition for the grounds to be what they are and the truth claim to be false. I may indeed have an experience of seeing a round tower, but that does not entail that the tower is round. It may be so far away that it looks round but is in fact hexagonal. I may indeed have an experience of sitting before a fire, but it does not logically entail that I am, for I may be asleep and dreaming. I may indeed count objects and measure them, but that does not logically entail that there are physical objects since the sense experiences of an external world could exist and there be no such world. There is no logical contradiction between it being true that I have sense experiences of objects and it being false that there are physical objects.

What is the value of such silly thinking? By means of doubting and thus rejecting sense experience as the foundation of knowledge, Descartes is able to proceed to ask himself if there is anything of which he is certain. He then formulates the now famous, "I think, therefore I am." This is true even if there is a demon bent on deceiving me, for to be deceived I must exist. Likewise, if I am always dreaming, still I must exist to dream. To be *thinking* is a ground for a truth which is absolutely certain and immune from doubt because thinking logically entails existence.

With the sure knowledge that he exists, and without reliance on sense experience, Descartes proceeds to investigate his existence. He states that his criteria of truth are clarity and distinctness. This he gets from an examination of his *Cogito, ergo sum* ("I think, or I doubt, therefore I exist"). Armed with these criteria, he proceeds to find that he is aware of himself as a conscious being (a substance) that doubts, understands, asserts, denies, wills, and imagines. Even sensations and perceptions such as seeing, hearing, and feeling are properties of his consciousness, and not of his body since he knows that he exists but he does not know that anything physical exists.

Descartes thus arrives at a knowledge that he is distinct from a body since he can know that he exists and has many powers and yet does not know that there is any physical universe at all. At this point he concludes that mind and body must be *distinct* substances, even though later he will discover that they are conjoined. But to be distinct means that it is possible for the self to continue to exist when that conjunction is broken by death.

By further analysis of the idea of himself, he arrives at a knowledge of the existence of God, using some novel proofs including an independent discovery of an ontological proof similar to Anselm's. When the existence of God is demonstrated, the evil demon hypothesis vanishes. We may have confidence in our sense experiences, for God, who is good, would not deceive us into believing that there is an external world corresponding to our sense experience, as we quite naturally assume. This correspondence between sense experience and physical objects is not perfect. By a careful analysis of our experience of physical objects, Descartes finds that the only properties they have are extension, figure, and the capacity to be in motion. These are *logically inseparable* from the very idea of a body. Thus they constitute the *essence* of bodies or matter.

Thus by freeing us from a reliance on sense experience as a basis for certainty, Descartes is able to establish that we are *essentially* mind, even though we also have bodies, and that matter is *essentially* extension (figure being the consequence of extension and motion and rest its states). If we rely on sense experience, we will never realize that we are essentially mind—a nonextended reality—because in sense experience we appear to be inseparably connected to a body and so take it that it is impossible for us to exist without a body. Likewise, matter appears to our senses to have colors, to be warm or cold, to be of various textures, and the like. By our senses we could never come to realize that matter is *essentially* extension and that these sensible experiences are produced in our minds by its shapes and motions. Matter thus has no inherent forms or final causes in it. It operates mechanically. The three basic ontological realities then are minds, extension, and God. Minds gain knowledge which is certain because it is necessarily true, by means of detachment from reliance on the senses. The mind does not receive its knowledge from outside through the senses but by attending to the ideas or thoughts (ideas are not sensible images) which are innate to the mind. Descartes claims to have reached these and other far-reaching conclusions from his meditations in which he withholds his assent unless the evidence is such as to logically entail the conclusion (or as he puts it, unless he clearly and distinctly sees that it is true). In this relation between evidence and conclusion, Descartes has imitated the relationship between ground and conclusion in mathematics.

The second of the three great rationalists, Spinoza, took this connection—logical necessity—with utter seriousness. In fact he believed that this is the *only* relation between things in reality. There is no such thing as possibility in reality. It is only in relation to us (to our ignorance) that things can be said to be possible. We simply lack knowledge concerning the relevant connections in so much of our experience. Thus Spinoza interprets Aristotle's standard for scientific knowledge—to show why X is so and cannot be otherwise—to mean *logically* cannot be otherwise. One of the values of Spinoza's work is that it stimulated people in the seventeenth and eighteenth centuries to make a distinction between logical necessity, which is a relation between propositions, and physical necessity, which is a relation between sensible things. We will have more to say about this when we examine Hume's work on causality.

Spinoza also accepted Descartes' definition of substance.

According to Descartes, only God fits the definition since God is the only being which does not depend on anything else in order to exist. Descartes called mind and body substance in a secondary sense. That is they depend *only* on God in order to exist. Mind can exist by itself and matter can exist without mind. Spinoza insisted on the meaning of substance in the primary sense, and denied that other senses have application. Spinoza was able to show that since the only relation in reality is that of logical necessity, there can be only one substance and all else is part of it. A substance, since it is utterly independent, cannot be limited by anything. Substance is infinite in every respect. There cannot be two or more substances because they would interfere with each other and thus would not be infinite. In addition, substance cannot create anything which is independent of itself—a genuine reality apart from itself—since the only relation is that of logical necessity. (From this we can see that "creation" in Christianity is a unique relation, for it is not that of logical necessity, nor is it the same as the relation between creatures because no creature is a creator of other creatures in exactly the same sense as God is a Creator of creatures.)

According to Spinoza, substance exists by necessity, and so our world is necessary and all its members are modes of substance. Mind and body are attributes of substance, the only two, out of an infinity of attributes, that we are aware of. Mind and body are *aspects* of one substance, not different beings (or substances) with different and opposite properties (one extended, the other nonextended), as in Descartes. This permits Spinoza to give a novel theory of the relation of the mind and body of a person (who is, nonetheless, a mode of substance). The mind and body are aspects of the same thing, which is itself neither mind or matter. (This is called "double aspect" theory and is closely related to another theory concerning the relation of mind and body, "neutral monism.")

Spinoza was considered by his contemporaries to be a dangerous thinker, and few of them would admit to having read him, except for the purpose of refuting him. He was considered to be an atheist. Actually he treats the universe itself, or nature, as deity. (This was not an improvement as far as his contemporaries were concerned.) He ascribes to nature many of the metaphysical attributes the Scholastics had given to God, for he inherited through Descartes much of the Aristotelian-Scholastic conceptuality, and by the denial of all accidents, possibilities, and freedom, he can argue for a monistic pantheism. It is highly religious in tone, for, as he put it, his work was an intellectual worship of God. Such reverence, which is hard to characterize, is to be found today in some scientists and nonscientists who look upon the intricate workings of nature with a kind of religious awe. Spinoza's work was a metaphysical construct based on reason alone, however, not the result of a sense of awe. Its evidence is rational arguments based on ideas which are internal to the mind but which represent (or are an aspect of) external reality (which is also an aspect of substance).

Leibniz, the third and last of the great seventeenth century rationlists, who was influenced by virtually every current in Western culture and who produced a many-sided philosophical synthesis, is of interest to us primarily for his reformulation of the principle of sufficient reason. Spinoza believed that to explain anything is to show why it is so and why it *logically* cannot be otherwise. Leibniz believes that this identification of the principle of sufficient reason with the principle of contradiction is a mistake. They must be distinguished, for the reason something is connected to something else in reality is not that it *logically* must be connected but that it is *best* for it to be connected. Thus to explain why something is so and not otherwise is not always to show that it *logically* cannot be otherwise but sometimes that it is not best for it to be otherwise. That it cannot be *morally* otherwise is a sufficient reason or a sufficient account of the thing.

The notion of "best" is sometimes used by Leibniz to mean "most efficient," but he also applies it to moral and spiritual matters. Thus Leibniz argues that some propositions are indeed true by *logical* necessity; that is, their truth is based on the principle of contradiction. To deny their truth would involve a logical contradiction. But there are other propositions whose truth is based on the principle of sufficient reason. Their denial does not produce a logical contradiction. They are true because it is best that they be true. All true propositions are true by necessity, but some are true by *logical* necessity whereas others are true by what Leibniz calls *moral* necessity.

This interpretation of the principle of sufficient reason, according to Leibniz, prevents us from falling into Spinoza's monistic pantheism and allows for contingency and freedom.

The principle of sufficient reason enabled Leibniz not only to escape from the logical determinism of Spinoza's system, but also to avoid Descartes' view of freedom as utter indifference between alternatives. According to Leibniz, there is always a sufficient reason for acting one way rather than another. We are never in a position of "indifference" or utter balance between alternatives, which is to say we never act arbitrarily. Thus Leibniz opposes Descartes' "libertarianism" as that view of freedom is called. But he is not a hard determinist, as is Spinoza, because to act rationally or freely is to act as we do because it is *best*, not because it is logically impossible to act otherwise. Leibniz's position is thus between those of Descartes and Spinoza. It is a distinctive type of determinism sometimes called "soft determinism" or "compatibilism."

Not Spinoza's metaphysical monism but the new science of mechanics brought the issue of freedom to the forefront of concern in the seventeenth century. For human beings are corporeal beings in a material universe which is supposed to operate in a deterministic manner by mechanical impact of matter on matter. Descartes' mind-body dualism in which mind is immaterial and unaffected by body seemed to save human freedom. But it has a grave disadvantage. It is inconceivable how an immaterial mind can affect its body, can move it. Descartes nonetheless insisted that we can by thought affect our bodies—for example, raise our hands—and thus exercise our will. Likewise, the external world can affect us indirectly through our bodies. This interaction between mind and body is supposed to leave human freedom intact, for our minds are immaterial (unextended) and so not subject to *material* causality.

Neither Descartes' interactionism, nor the theory of occasionalism, in which there is no *physical* interaction (a thought is the occasion for a corresponding motion of the body, and *vice versa*, thanks to God's action on each occasion) is satisfactory. Leibniz's adaptation of occasionalism, by which God does not intervene on each occasion but preprograms the mind and the body to run parallel with each other (preestablished harmony), has not had much of a following. There has been a bit more interest in Spinoza's double aspect theory of mind and body, but it is Descartes' interactionism, so graphically described as "the ghost in the machine" by Gilbert Ryle (*Concept of Mind,* 1949) which has been by far the most influential theory of the relation of the mind and body. It provoked its direct opposite, behaviorism, which appeared in the late nineteenth century. It is largely the Cartesian conception of mind and matter as distinct substances with polar opposite properties which has made human freedom and the mind-body problem so prominent in modern philosophy.

Although Descartes, Leibniz, and Spinoza are all classified as rationalists, they are very different from each other on important matters. Nonetheless all three believe, as did Plato before them, that the mind has innate ideas, that is, ideas not acquired from sense experience.

John Locke (1632–1704) created empiricism, a new approach in epistemology by his denial of innate ideas. He tried in his celebrated work, *An Essay Concerning Human Understanding* (1690), to trace all ideas back to their origin in experience. He called this the "plain historical method."

The word "idea" is a troublesome one. It is used very widely in the seventeenth and eighteenth centuries. It comes from one of the Greek words Plato used for his Forms (which is why Plato's Forms are often called "Ideas" in English and the city Plato designs in *The Republic* is called the "ideal state"). But the word "ideas" is used by rationalists and empiricists to refer to the *contents* of our minds. Ideas are what we attend to; they are the objects of thoughts. They can thus include the sensation of heat, the sight of a horse, the concept of heat, and the concept of a horse, and so on.

Ideas gain something of a quasi-autonomous reality, apart from sense objects, partly because of the notion that they are innate and partly because of the representative theory of perception. According to the representative theory of perception, which we saw in operation in Descartes, we may have perceptions of sense objects when there are in fact no such objects. We are never *directly* aware of external objects in sense perception but of *representatives* of them which we call "ideas."

Locke shared with Descartes the belief that what we are directly aware of is ideas, and that some of them represent objects external to us. He also accepted Descartes' view that not everything in our ideas of external objects represents things actually present in external objects. In addition, he accepted Descartes' view of knowledge and certainty. We have knowledge only when something is self-evident to us (we intuit its truth), or by discursive reasoning we proceed from what is self-evident, step by step (the connections between each step being self-evident) to a conclusion. Such knowledge Locke thought to be much less common than Descartes believed since for Locke all our ideas have their origin in experience. Ideas which originate in sense experience give us neither the "real essence" of material objects (as Aristotle believed was possible) nor first principles by which we may demonstrate that a generalization, discovered by sense experience, holds universally.

Locke was convinced, however, that we could achieve *probability* on the basis of sense experience, and indeed great probability over a wide range of matters in the scientific study of nature, in ethics, in politics, and in religion. Certainty was not to be achieved beyond a very narrow range of things, but to demand it where it is not available and to lapse into doubt or even scepticism as some Cartesians did, was self-defeating. Locke was convinced that the empirical methods of his friend the chemist, Robert Boyle, who relied on experimentation—indeed sheer trial and error much of the time—was the only appropriate way to proceed. The real constitution of material things is so small as to be beyond the reach of our senses. Thus we do not know the *real* essence of material things, as both Aristotle and Descartes thought. We must instead rely on observations and make our generalizations on the basis of observations, whose truth is indeed only probable.

Locke's polemic in Book 1 of his *Essay* is thoroughly effective against any view of innate ideas understood as consciously present to our attention and universally endorsed by humankind. On the other hand, Locke claims that if innate ideas are said to be *dispositions,* which become actual ideas only after they are activated by experience, they are not to be distinguished from ideas acquired from experience. Thus there is no reason to call some of our ideas innate and others acquired ideas. Locke claims to rest his case, however, on his ability to trace our chief ideas back to their origin in experience, rather than depending on his polemic against the existence of innate ideas. By showing the origin of our ideas of substance, cause, identity, infinity, and other such crucial philosophical ideas, he believes he has rendered the doctrine of innate ideas superfluous.

Locke does not limit experience to *sense* experience. Experience includes our awareness of our own processes of perceiving and reasoning. (All too often Locke has incorrectly been said to support the doctrine of sensationalism, that is, that the only thing of which we are aware is what we perceive by the senses.) His "plain historical method" marks British philosophy to this day. To determine what we mean, or to determine why we should believe something to be true, so often automatically means to people, especially in the English-speaking world, a search for something in experience, and in particular in sense experience.

This is not wholly due to Locke, but also to the success of modern science, or better yet to an interpretation of the reason for the success of modern science. Its success is attributed to its reliance on sense experience, in contrast to the "a priori" (not based on experience) methods of Plato, Aristotle (because of his belief in essences or substantial forms), and the rationalist philosophers of the seventeenth century. A picture of the rise of science that is widely held is that it occurred when people began to make observations and experiments. In fact, people like Aristotle did make careful observations, and the scientific revolution in physics was not particularly based on experiments, even in Galileo's case, but relied heavily on conceptual effort. The popular picture is not wholly erroneous, but it is not an adequate characterization of the nature of science.

Locke's *Essay*, although not universally approved (it was strongly attacked by Bishop Stillingfleet of Worcester for its denial of innate ideas, for example), was generally received with great acclaim. Descartes' theory of vortices—great swirling pools of fine matter which carried the heavenly bodies around like chips of wood floating on a tub of swirling water—had been utterly discredited by Newton's *Principia Mathematica* three years before the publication of Locke's *Essay*. Descartes' search for indubitable knowledge had provoked self-conscious critical analysis which led many intellectuals to scepticism. Locke's work, with its stress on probability, was a balanced position between scepticism and certainty. In France, the cultural center of Europe, it was compared to Newton's work. As Newton had unveiled the laws of the outer world, Locke was said to have uncovered the laws or workings of the inner world, the mind.

All was not well, however. George Berkeley (1685–1753), while still a very young man, published his *Principles of Human Knowledge* (1710). He pounced on Locke's doctrine of abstract ideas. This was Locke's account of how general words can apply to particulars. Locke believed that general words stand for ideas. His program was to trace everything, including words, back to its origin in experience. The idea for which a general word stands is formed by abstracting from a group of particulars the fashion in which they are alike (leaving out the ways they differ from each other). The resulting idea is an abstract idea. That idea is what a general word means, and it can be applied to particular things because of the resemblance between the particulars and the abstract idea. Berkeley took Locke to mean that an abstract idea is a mental *image*, and then asked his readers to try to form an abstract idea (an image) of a triangle whose sides are of no particular or determinate length, and whose angles are such that it is neither an equilateral triangle, nor an isosceles triangle, nor an obtuse triangle, and so on. As it is impossible to form such an image, he concluded that there is no such thing as an abstract idea.

In its place, Berkeley proposed that what we do in fact is to select some *particular* to represent other particulars similar to it. We then *use* the idea of that particular in a general way, by saying things about it which are also applicable to other particulars similar to it. It is the use to which we put a particular which gives meaning to our general words, not a general or abstract idea for which it stands.

This proposal reflects Berkeley's penchant for what we perceive. He coined the phrase *esse est percipi*, ("to be is to be perceived"). An abstract idea cannot be imaged, therefore there is no such thing. The only exception to his principle is minds. They cannot be perceived, but in order for there to be perception, there must be perceivers.

Berkeley is most famous for his rejection of the existence of matter, or more precisely, of Locke's "material substance." Locke, as we have said, held to a representational theory of perception in which what we are directly aware of is ideas which are representations or copies of external objects. But we must, according to Locke, make a distinction between primary and secondary ideas. Those ideas which *represent* qualities in external objects are primary ideas. Those ideas which do *not* represent qualities in external objects are secondary ideas. They are present only in the perceiver, and so are subjective. Both primary and secondary ideas are caused by the primary qualities of material objects. These for Locke are the tiny, insensible, material particles of which material objects consist.

This distinction is familiar to us from Galileo and Descartes. Locke follows them by emphasizing *quantitative* properties as primary although their lists of primary qualities do not match precisely. Locke offers several arguments for the distinction, but Berkeley demolishes them all. He shows that there is no way to make the distinction. What Locke says of primary ideas in his arguments intended to distinguish them from secondary ideas can be said equally of secondary ideas. In addition, Berkeley argues that ideas are the only thing we can be aware of, and the only things ideas can resemble or be like are other ideas. There can be no material objects which resemble our ideas, thus our ideas are not representatives (or copies) of material objects. Berkeley rejects the existence of a material substance or substratum which is utterly uncharacterizable since *ideas* are the only characteristics we can be aware of. What we are aware of are *sensible* objects, and they are nothing but a collection of sensible ideas. Minds, which have ideas, exist, but there is no need to assert the existence of some unknown and unknowable something called a material substratum or material object underlying our perception of sensible objects.

Berkeley's position in which sensible objects are held to be collections of sensible properties is called "phenomenalism" (from the Greek word for "appearances"). Things for Berkeley are as they appear. Phenomenalism appeals to those who prefer an ontology in which reality is primarily what we are aware of in sense experience. For a phenomenalist, terms in scientific theories which do not refer to anything which can be directly experienced must either be reducible somehow to what we do directly experience or treated as useful fictions which assist us in the discovery of truth about what we sense. Thus, in the twentieth century among logical positivists phenomenalism has required enormous programs of "translation" of scientific vocabulary and also of common language about material objects and minds, as we find in A. J. Ayer (*The Foundations of Empirical Knowledge*, 1940). Berkeley's own device for ensuring the continued existence of sensible objects when we are not perceiving them (for to exist is to be perceived) is to invoke God as one who continuously perceives all things. Phenomenalists who came after him, in their programs of "translation" of all words into a vocabulary of words that refer to what can be sensed, replaced Berkeley's God with a definition of a material object as "a permanent possibility of sensation." Thus even if no one is perceiving a tree, it does not cease to exist because it is a permanent possibility of sensation; that is, given the requisite condition (for example, someone looking in the right direction) a tree will be perceived. Berkeley was not considered an important philosopher until after 1865 when his complete works were issued. By then, familiarity with the ideas of the German idealism of Kant, Fichte, and Hegel had created a more hospitable climate for taking him seriously, especially in England.

A similar fate befell David Hume (1711–76), the last of the classic empiricists. His philosophical works went unnoticed during his lifetime, so much so, that he turned to writing a history of England. It was Kant who first recognized his significance and brought him to the notice of the entire philosophical world with his *Critique of Pure Reason* (1781). Thus we shall first turn to a description of the Enlightenment before we examine Hume and Kant, who although themselves products of it, undermined much of its synthesis and turned the modern world in a new direction.

Newton's *Principia* was the crown of the new science of mechanics. Although it provoked controversy for a generation, it became for the avant-garde the beginning of a new age for humanity. Its general impact was compared to the breaking in of light, lifting the darkness, so that people could see the universe for the first time the way it really is. They saw it as a precise, harmonious, rational mechanism, with laws of motion which applied universally to all matter, from the tiniest particles to the vast heavenly bodies.

This new science of nature became a basis for hope and optimism. It was not only what it had achieved, but what it inspired people to think was yet to be achieved that was important. Locke's *Essay* was interpreted to have spread light to the sphere of the human mind, and vindicated once again the belief that a new beginning for human history had dawned. Just as nature and human understanding could be analysed and their laws grasped, so too could the laws of society and social relations be understood. With such knowledge, social problems could be solved and rational governments be created.

The enemies of enlightenment and progress were superstition, mystery, and tradition which perpetuated them. What impeded progress above all was Christianity. One of the early critics, whom the *philosophes* (or social critics, as they were called in France) used in their propoganda against the Roman Catholic Church, was Pierre Bayle (1647–1706). His *Historical and Critical Dictionary* was perhaps the most widely owned and read book in eighteenth century France. Bayle, although he claimed to be a believing Christian, never tired of claiming that the contents of Christian revelation were irrational: it has the entire race condemned because of the action of one man and woman, they are blamed by a God who foresaw their disobedience and nonetheless created them, it is unable to explain the existence of evil, and the like. He also stressed that Christianity could not be the foundation of morals, nor is it necessary for a person to be a Christian to be moral. He pointed, on the one hand, to the atrocities committed by Christians against each other in war and, on the other hand, to the moral behavior of the people of China who had never heard of Christianity.

This was not lost on the *philosophes*, especially Voltaire. They were not anti-God, but they wanted a rational, enlightened religion. Their conception of "rationality" can be illustrated with Descartes' famous example of a piece of wax (in his *Meditations*). Descartes listed the properties of a piece of wax: shape, color, solidity, smell. Then he heated it and found that its shape changed, its color and smell were gone, and it was now liquid. The only property that remained the same in the two states was extension. This then was the essence of matter. Matter did not have a hidden moving impulse toward a final goal of realization, a mysterious specific form. This ability to penetrate and exhaust the contents of what is examined became the ideal for the *philosophes*. God's nature could be fathomed, just as could matter, and religion could be rationalized. Miracles, mystery, and revelation were all devices used to support the authority of an institution, the church. But God's existence is evident from nature—this is the book of God—and nature's order as discovered by Newton revealed God as rational and good. The proper worship of God consists of a decent and moral life, not craven fear, belief in superstition, and the attendance of church services.

The attack on Christianity as the enemy of enlightenment was a powerful theme in Edward Gibbon's (1737–94) *Decline and Fall of the Roman Empire*. Rome was presented as one of the greatest achievements of humanity. Christianity, which replaced it, was not only greatly inferior to it but also largely responsible for its demise. Now reason and enlightenment were once again lifting humanity free of this incubus. People would build a new world on rational lines, free from prejudice, and superstition.

Bayle, Voltaire, Gibbon, and others were looking at Christianity primarily as a social and cultural phenomenon. It was viewed as a fact, no different from any other physical or social fact. In light of the conviction that reason was able to penetrate to the essence of any phenomenon, the so-called reason of theologians seemed actually obfuscation. Human nature was not to be understood by reading treatises on sin, grace, and salvation. Instead it was to be found by the method of Montesquieu (1689–1755), who engaged in an empirical study of environmental factors, such as climate, to find their effects on the physiological and psychological make-up of people. Only so could a science of politics be created.

Descartes, whose ideal of a clarity free of all possible doubt greatly contributed to this view of reason as an instrument of analysis, actually held to an older Platonic view of reason. Reason was not a mere instrument but had a content which it does not gain from sense experience. That content must be freed of the prejudice of sense experience before it is available. It is only by degrees and prolonged contemplation that we become aware of its contents. Descartes' very title *Meditations* suggests contemplation. In fact his book—divided into six parts, each of which is supposed to form the subject of a full day's meditation—is far from the *philosophes'* procedures for attaining clarity. For them reason goes to work directly, uncovering the basic laws underneath the superficial diversity of nature, mind, and in time, society. The rationality of the universe is obvious, and the powers of reason have been demonstrated by the success of Newton and Locke.

The work of Hume and Kant undermined this optimism. Confidence in reason returned after their critical work, but it was a more sophisticated view of reason. In this chapter we shall consider three aspects of Hume's work which undermined the Enlightenment and which have relevance for Christianity. Then we shall examine Kant in the next chapter.

Hume's greatest work, *A Treatise on Human Nature* (1739), was ignored when it was first published. It attempted, to trace our knowledge back to its sources in experience. Unlike Locke, who believed that we could rely on experience to give us solid probability, Hume found that neither reason nor experience provided such a basis. Hume falls back on instinct and habit. He uncovers not nature's rationality but its assistance in the face of the lack of rationality.

Hume divided all our perceptions into ideas and impressions. They differ in degree of force and vivacity. Impressions are those lively perceptions which occur when we see, hear, feel, love, hate, will, or desire. Our ideas are copies of impressions. To trace our ideas back to experience is to trace them back to the impressions of which they are composed. Whenever we have any suspicion that a philosophical term is being employed without any meaning, we are to trace it back to the impressions from which it supposedly has been derived.

Like Berkeley before him (and perhaps independently) Hume is unable to find any impression of a material substance to which sensible qualities belong. We have no idea of substance, distinct from a collection of particular qualities. But unlike Berkeley, he thinks this is also true of "mind" as an immaterial substance. For when he examines himself, all he finds is particular perceptions of heat or cold, light or shade, love or hatred, pain or pleasure. He never catches himself at any time without a perception and never observes *anything but the perception*. So we too are bundles or collections of perceptions, which succeed each other with an inconceivable rapidity, and which are in a perpetual flux. There is nothing underlying the flux which gives us our identity as one thing over time. Rather there is a stream of perceptions whose interrelations make us selves.

Our ideas of continuing material objects and selves arise because of three principles of association: resemblance, contiguity, and cause and effect. These principles by which we associate impressions do not reveal to us any *necessary* connection between our impressions. We merely happen to find that when various impressions are associated in these three ways, the idea that they are connected arises quite naturally. It is at this point that Hume performs the crucial analysis of necessary connection. He does not deny causality, as is frequently said. His view of causality is that it is a natural association that we make between our ideas. What he denies is that we have an impression of a necessary connection between our impressions or between the ideas formed from our impressions.

His analysis goes like this. In causal sequences we believe that there is some power in a cause which produces an effect. To know such a power would be to know what it is that enables a cause to produce a *particular* effect. We would therefore know both the cause and effect and the relation between them. But in fact we never observe such a power in any particular causal sequence. If we see one billiard ball strike another, and then observe that the one which is struck moves, we have observed a series of impressions in a particular sequence. But we did not observe any power in any of the impressions producing an effect in any other impression. The same is true of our thoughts, whether we are merely thinking (having one thought succeed another thought) or having a thought about moving my arm succeeded by my arm moving. From a *single* sequence of any kind—purely physical, purely mental, or partly mental and partly physical—we never know what will follow what; we just have to watch, for we are aware of no *power* in any of our impressions which produces other impressions. We rely upon *repeated* experience of the same sequence or series of impressions before we can learn what impressions can be expected to come after other impressions.

We may think we perceive a power in those series of impressions in which we encounter resistance from bodies we push or pull since we must exert force. This may mislead us into thinking that there is a force between all causes and effects. But if we think about mental sequences, which involve impressions which are causally related, we never encounter resistance and an exertion of force like we do in pushing or pulling a body. Nor do we usually feel resistance when we will to move an arm. Yet both of these are causal sequences. As we saw with the example of billiard balls, we never perceive any resistance or effort between our various impressions. Rather we project the idea from our need to make an effort when we push or pull an object, thinking that a billiard ball must make an effort too. But our own experience of making an effort in some cases, should not be generalized and said to be present in *all* causal sequences. All we are aware of in those sequences which are causal is a constant conjunction of impressions.

Even in those cases in which we do have an impression of resistance and an impression of making an effort, we do not perceive any power being transferred. We require repeated sequences involving resistance and effort to know what impressions will follow other impressions. What then leads us to think that there is more present in causal sequences than a constant conjunction of impressions?

When we regularly experience A followed by B, we come to *anticipate* or expect B whenever A appears. That feeling of anticipation misleads us into thinking that there is a necessary connection between A and B. But all events are entirely distinct and separate. One follows the other in our experience, but we have no impression of any power between them, no impression of necessary connection between them. If we did, we would know from a *singular* (individual) sequence that B will follow A because we have an impression of power in A that produces B. We require, however, the observation of a sequence *repeated* several times before we expect to observe B after we observe A. This includes those cases in which we encounter resistance when we push or pull an object. It is from experience that we learn what impressions will follow others.

We sometimes expect an impression to follow a particular impression the first time we experience that particular impression. But this can be explained by the similarity to sequences of impressions we have seen many times before. Because the particular impression encountered for the first time resembles the antecedent of a familiar sequence of impressions we have a feeling that it will be followed by a specific type of impression.

Thus all our common sense and scientific laws are based solely upon principles of association and extend no further than our experience. Our scientific laws are not necessary but contingent. The fact that we have observed sequences of a particular kind in the past does not mean we shall observe them in the future. Little could be further from the confidence of the Enlightenment in the power of reason to reach the essence of all things—matter, the mind, human nature, society, religion, God. It was confident that it could find the laws of their natures and explain their working. But Hume's analysis of causality threatened the new science of mechanics, and the great synthesis achieved by Newton. The laws of motion do not show us any necessary connections between things, said Hume. The sequences we have experienced in ordinary life never yield any connections which must hold universally and infallibly. So there is no basis to say any scientific law must hold universally and infallibly. Our knowledge extends no further than our sense impressions.

This part of Hume's work was ignored or dismissed by his contemporaries. Many who bothered with philosophy took refuge in the school of Scottish Common Sense Realism whose main exponent was Thomas Reid (1710–96). Reid believed that Hume's sceptical conclusions were inevitable consequences of Descartes' and Locke's representative theory of perception, according to which all that we are immediately aware of is ideas. Reid argued that we have an immediate awareness of objects (hence his "realism"). Many of his critical remarks on Hume and some of his own analyses of perception and memory are astute, but his attempt to establish that we have certainty on some matters of belief and morals by an appeal to "common sense" is frequently a tour de force.

The Scottish school had considerable influence in America. The question of religious certainty was resolved for many by an appeal to religious experience, especially a conversion experience at revival meetings. This went along with a scorn for learning. Those who sought to give a place to learning and a foundation for Christianity that was not reduced merely to an emotional experience seemed to be cut off from a use of reason by Hume's scepticism. Common Sense Realism they hoped would enable them to counter the scepticism of Hume on the one hand, and to steer a middle course between the religion of sheer reason of the Enlightenment Deists and the emotionalism of the revivalists on the other. What in fact often resulted was a static view of Christian doctrine and morals with no sense of historic development, a defense of biblical inerrancy, and a rationalistic style of apologetics. Some revivalists themselves took up Scottish Common Sense Realism as a bulwark for their biblical pietism.

It took a person of Kant's caliber to recognize the power of Hume's analysis and its far-reaching implications. As Kant put it, "it woke me from my dogmatic slumbers," meaning thereby his previously unexamined assumption of the power of reason to attain knowledge of humankind, nature, and God which went beyond sense experience, and in the case of God, beyond the power of any possible sense experience. Hume roused him to examine the powers of reason to give us knowledge in mathematics, science, and metaphysics (which for him included theology). However, at least two other philosophic matters are of importance for theology in Hume, so we shall consider them before we look at Kant's effort to determine the powers of reason.

In 1748 Hume published a completely rewritten version of his *Treatise*, entitled *An Inquiry Concerning Human Understanding*. It did not fare much better with the public than the *Treatise*. It contains a chapter on miracles, however, based on Hume's interest in historiography—problems with the writing of history—which anticipates the growing historical consciousness of the next century. His comments on miracles are very relevant to Christianity since the Bible recounts miraculous events. Hume does not reject miracles on the basis that they are scientifically impossible, for nature does not have "iron laws" which cannot be violated as far as he is concerned. His challenge differs from that of earlier critics of Christianity, such as John Toland (1670–1721) and Matthew Tindal (1655–1733) who wanted a natural religion based on reason alone. It is instead an argument from the probable reasoning employed by historians who seek to determine what is most likely to have happened in the past.

Hume takes it that in our reasoning as historians all we have to go on is our experiences of today. In our experience nature operates with regularity. Because of the common course of nature, it is always more likely that reports of miracles in the past are not correct than that they are true. Reports of miracles come to us from less enlightened times than our own, and in those eras, the claims that a miracle had occurred originated among the least educated people and from the least developed parts of the country. In addition, people who report miracles usually have a stake in some cause, as did the disciples of Jesus. But even should we get reports of miracles from much nearer our own time, and from witnesses who have no apparent self-interest in the matter, we still should not give credence to the reports. Since human credulity and knavery are well-known to us, whereas interruptions in the common course of nature are not known to us at all, it is always more probable that the reports are incorrect than that they are correct. The argument that the church in its early days needed miracles in order to give its teachings plausibility and to spread quickly, but that once the church was established it no longer needed them, is regarded by Hume as a rationalization. Even should we have an interruption in the expected pattern of nature's operations, we are to seek a new regularity in nature which will account for our upset expectations. It is always more probable that we have not completely understood nature than that a report of a miracle is true.

Hume's argument does not show that miracles are impossible, nor that all the reports of miracles in the Bible are untrue. He only argues that we are never justified by historical reasoning in believing a report of a miracle. Nor should we give miracles any credence in writing history. We must, of course, take into account the fact that some people *believed* in this or that miracle because a belief, even if incorrect, can affect events.

Hume seems to have put forward a sound principle for the writing of history. Miracles are by definition an exception to the common course of events. When we weigh various factors in seeking to determine what is most likely to be the case, the balance falls against miracles, *when one discounts reasons from other domains for belief in the events reported by a religion.* A historian *as a historian* must always give less weight to the miraculous in any account than to natural causes, even should one not be able to specify the natural causes.

Herbert Butterfield has pointed out, on the other hand, that we have achieved this conception of historical writing—"scientific history"—by *methodologically* excluding from the writing of history the assumptions and understanding of people and nature which *divide people* into Christians, Jews, Marxists, and atheists. The ideal of scientific history (which is more of an ideal than an achievement) is that what is to be accepted as history must be equally acceptable to Christians, Jews, Marxists, atheists. The gain is accuracy on some matters. The price is that we exclude from the discipline of history all questions that have to do with the significance and purpose of human life. So to say accurately that "history is concerned to find out what actually happened" must be said with a realization that historical method filters out and excludes many possibilities.

Hume's attack on miracles, which operates with the notion of "scientific history" is a serious threat only to those who wish to base their religion on a historical probability which is acceptable to any historian, regardless of his or her understanding of human nature and regardless of his or her commitment to atheism, Marxism, or the like. It presents problems to biblical scholars, who are simultaneously trying to write "scientific history" and to deal with a document which, whatever it is, is not itself written as scientific history. So two ways of talking about events are used: the way they are said to be according to history, and the way they are said to be "in the eyes of faith."

Hume's other contribution that is of importance to us is his posthumously published *Dialogues Concerning Natural Religion* (1779). By then natural religion or Deism was dead on the Continent, and even in England it was a passing thing, though in America it was still strong among many of the nation's Founding Fathers. Nonetheless, the issue and the way Hume discusses it are still of vital significance. The basic issue was raised by Plato in his dialogue *The Sophist*. Plato tells us that we are faced with a choice between regarding nature either as bringing forth animals, plants, and lifeless substances from self-acting causes without creative intelligence or as so acting because of the design of some intelligence (265c). Hume discusses the question on the basis of what we should say when we rely strictly on reason alone. It is important to see what we can say about nature's order on the basis of reason alone even though Christians believe that the world's order is the result of divine creation.

Hume's *Dialogue* is between three characters who examine the order of nature, its disorder (suffering), and its existence; these and nothing but these are used. They seek to determine what the order, disorder, and the existence of nature enable us to say about the *nature* of God. (All three claim that God's existence is not at issue.) Cleanthes represents Deism, or natural religion (in contrast to revealed religion). He thinks that natural religion is based on experience and not on remote speculative reasoning, which by going beyond the boundaries of experience cannot be relied upon. He therefore has no use for Demea's views, which are supposed to represent orthodoxy, and which describe in Scholastic fashion the attributes and operations which make God different from anything in our experience. Cleanthes himself prefers what is plainly before us all: the marvelous order of nature, which is apparent even to the most casual person. He claims that it is obvious that nature is designed; this thought springs *naturally* to our minds. It is not the result of abstract reasoning, nor has it been taught to us by a group with some self-interest in the belief that there is a God. In other words, it is a natural, not an artificial, reaction.

Philo, who loves controversy, never denies the fact that we *naturally* react to nature's order with the thought that it is designed. But he tries to show that this response tells us nothing about the source of the world's order beyond its *remote* similarity to our own intelligence. Nature's source is unlike us in any other respect, in particular in moral characteristics, and so we cannot use nature's order as the foundation for any religion or moral system. Nature's order tells us nothing useful about the nature of its source. It is simply a fact to be acknowledged that nature's operations are vaguely and remotely mindlike.

Thus Cleanthes, in order to establish a natural religion, must do more than point to nature's order and to our natural tendency to think that it is designed. Accordingly, he formulates an argument, a version of the argument from design or the teleological argument. It is an argument based on an analogy between the world and some object which we know to have been designed. Cleanthes points out that a machine or a house is caused by an intelligent designer. The world is like a great machine or like a house. As the effects (machine, house, world) are similar, their causes must be similar (intelligence).

This argument is not a strong one. Machines and houses are very dissimilar to the world. Machines need lubrication and fuel to run, and houses have walls, windows, and foundations. Philo undermines Cleanthes' argument by suggesting that the world is similar to a vegetable or an animal. We do not know the cause of their order, so we do not know the cause of the world's order. Cleanthes protests that the world is very different from a vegetable or an animal. It receives no nutrition and has no sense organs. Philo immediately agrees. The world is very unlike a vegetable or an animal, but it resembles a vegetable or an animal as much as it resembles a machine or a house, which is to say that it does not resemble any of them very much. The strength of an argument from similar effects to similar causes is directly in proportion to the likeness of the effects. Cleanthes has been forced to admit that the effects are very dissimilar, so he must admit that the causes are very dissimilar.

Philo continues his criticism by pointing out that the only things which we know by experience to be caused by intelligent design are artifacts, such as machines and houses. These are only a small fraction of the entire universe. It is not a wise practice to make inferences concerning the whole from a very small sample. Indeed, arguments from effects to causes are sound only because experience has shown us that when we have constant and repeated association between two things, then they are causally related. But in the case of the entire universe we have no experience of an entire universe being caused by something. We have a singular instance of an ordered world, with no experience of world orders being produced. It is thus not proper to use the causal principle, which has arisen from the experience of repeated sequences of events, to a case of such singularity as the cause of the world's order.

The discussion now turns to another problem inherent in the teleological argument which relies on the principle that if effects are similar, the causes of those effects are similar. Here Demea, the representative of orthodoxy, charges Cleanthes (and thereby natural religion) with anthropomorphism. If the cause of a house or a machine is *human* intelligence, and the world is precisely like a machine or a house, then the intelligence of its cause is precisely like our own. Its intelligence is greater than our own but not different in kind. This does not disturb Cleanthes. He is quite prepared to be anthropomorphic. Few religious people are. Hume is simply pointing out what natural religion is committed to.

There are difficulties for the "orthodox." Philo points out to Demea that according to the line of reason he has employed in his attack on Cleanthes, he is committed to the view that we know nothing of God's nature. Orthodoxy in its flight from anthropomorphism so stresses the vastness of the distance between the nature of creatures and God that it is driven to "mysticism," that is, it is unable to say what God's nature is in any way.

Philo then turns to another line of attack. Let us pretend that the world is significantly like an object of human contrivance, so that the world can be said to have been designed. This does not give us the God we have been accustomed to think of. First, if an effect is finite, we cannot infer that its cause is infinite. The cause whose existence we infer from an effect can be said to be no greater than is needed to account for the effect. The effect we are concerned to account for is the world's order. Since this is a finite effect, we may not infer a God or infinite power as its cause. (This is the same principle that underlies Whitehead's remark that we are not to pay God metaphysical compliments.) Second, we do not know that the world is perfectly designed. The world might have been better made; thus God cannot be said to be perfect in wisdom or intelligence. Third, there may be more than one cause of the world's order. Perhaps it was designed by a committee. Philo soon gets carried away into flights of fantasy about how the world may have attained its order until he is brought abruptly to a halt by Cleanthes. Cleanthes reaffirms his rejection of the use of reason in a speculative way. Our reason is based on and limited to our experience. He is quite willing to admit that the order of the universe does not entail an infinitely powerful or infinitely wise God, nor even establish monotheism. As long as it is admitted that its order naturally leads us to think that it is designed, he is content, and he correctly points out to Philo that he has said nothing which undermines this.

Demea, of course, is not satisfied with Cleanthes' religion. He turns to another kind of argument: a cosmological one, similar to Aquinas' third way. It is actually one formulated by Samuel Clarke, a close friend of Newton's. Clarke's argument, like all cosmological arguments, relies on a version of the principle of sufficient reason, namely that whatever exists must have a reason for its existence. His argument is as follows. It is impossible for the universe to consist of contingent beings only. That is, a contingent being is a being which depends on some other being for its existence. If we have an infinite succession of contingent beings, each dependent on another in the series, we can explain why each one of them exists by reference to another. But if we take the entire chain or succession of contingent beings *together as a whole*, it is clear that this collection itself requires a reason for its existence, just as much as does each individual contingent being within the collection. We may ask, Why does this *particular* succession of contingent beings exist and not another? Indeed, why does it exist at all, rather than nothing? Its reason cannot be chance, nor can it be nothing. It must then be a necessary being, one which carries the reason for its existence in itself.

Hume's replies (in the person of Cleanthes) have become classics, and until the last decade they were thought by most philosophers and Protestant theologians to be conclusive. We will examine the two most important ones. Hume claims that "necessary" cannot be properly used of a being. "Whatever we conceive as existent, we can also conceive as nonexistent. There is no Being, therefore, whose nonexistence implies a contradiction." Thus there can be no necessary being, a being whose nonexistence implies a contradiction.

Hume's Cleanthes claims that this reasoning is conclusive, and he is willing to rest his case on it alone. In recent years, however, it has been pointed out that the sense of necessary Hume is using is that of *logical* necessity. Christianity speaks of God as a necessary being in the sense of one who has no beginning and no end because God is not dependent on anything in order to exist. Nothing could cause God to begin or to end. To say that God has no beginning or end because God does not depend on anything to exist does not show that God actually does exist. It does mean, however, that if God exists, that existence is a necessary existence. This understanding of necessary being does make sense. It is not incoherent. This means that Clarke's cosmological argument cannot be dismissed simply by saying that the argument must be wrong because the very concept of a necessary being is incoherent.

Hume has another major objection, however. Cleanthes claims that the existence of an infinite series of contingent beings actually poses no question. Clarke admits that each particular contingent being's existence can be explained by reference to other contingent beings. The series of contingent being stretches back infinitely. What then is there left to explain? Clarke claims that the infinite series of contingent beings *taken as a whole* needs to have its existence explained, but Cleanthes says that this is absurd. There is a *whole* only by the act of your *mind*. The whole (or the collection of contingent beings) exists because you have by an act of your mind made it a *whole* or a *collection*.

But this response by Hume's Cleanthes is no longer accepted as decisive by the philosophic community. The question Clarke puts is not why the *collection* of contingent beings exists (for indeed the collection as a collection exists because of an act of mind). The question is why the collection has the *members* it has and not other members, or none at all. For even though each member can be explained in terms of another member, why the collection has *these* members and not other members is not thus explained, nor is why it has any members at all. (See William L. Rowe, *The Cosmological Argument*, Princeton, N.J.: Princeton University Press, 1975.)

As I have said, both of Hume's objections to the cosmological argument were thought to have been decisive in non–Roman Catholic circles until the past few years. The fact that they are not decisive creates a new philosophical situation in Western culture, for it means that the *existence* of the world does after all pose a legitimate question. We may not be able to answer it *philosophically*, for the cosmological argument depends on the truth of the principle of suffi- cient reason (whatever exists has a reason for its existence). This principle seems self-evident to many people, but it does not seem self-evident to many philosophers. We do not know whether it is true or false. So a person may legitimately respond to the question, "Why does the world exist?" by saying, "Why should it have to have a reason for its existence? What makes you think that it must?" To reply, "But everything must have a reason for its existence," is sim- ply to be repeating the very principle at issue. No one has yet been able to show why everything must have a reason for its existence in a way that has won the approval of the philosophical community at large. Nonetheless, it must be stressed that we are entering a new situation today, for it is clear that the world's existence does pose a question even if we cannot answer it either by philosophical means or by scientific procedures of investigation. But the question can no longer be pushed aside in Hume's fashion.

The examination and refutation of the cosmological argument in the *Dialogues* is, however, only an interlude. Hume resumes his attack on the teleological argument. He has already shown it to be severely limited in what it tells us about the nature of deity. He now goes on the offensive in Parts 10 and 11 of the *Dialogues* by posing the problem of evil. If our reason to say that there is a *benevolent* intelligence is the order of the universe then our suffering and that of animals is a reason to say that intelligence is not benevolent. If we consider only the positive and negative features of our world as the basis for our judgment, then it is impossible to say that from a mixture of good and bad, one can infer a purely good source. Instead the only thing one can conclude is that it is either good and bad, or that it is simply *indifferent* to the welfare of human beings and ani- mals. Nature itself seems indifferent to human beings and animals; so it is likely that its source is too. We can thus say nothing about the moral attributes of the source of nature's order.

In spite of all his arguments against natural religion, a religion based solely on the order and existence of nature, Hume is unable to shake the *natural* tendency of the human mind to think of intelligent design when we experience the order of the universe. His own philosophy, which rests so heavily on our natural or instinctive responses, forces him to respect it. So in concluding his *Dialogues* he has Philo admit that the cause or causes of nature's order bear some remote likeness to our intelligence. Because he must concede this, he is anxious to stress that nature's order does not allow us to say anything about the moral attributes (or benevolence) of its cause or causes. He can thus claim that nature's order cannot be used as a foundation for any religion or for morals. But even if one concedes that nature's order cannot be *the* foundation for religion or morals, this does not prevent nature's order from being used as *one* strand in a case for the reasonableness of belief in God, as we find in some apologies (see, for example, the work of Basil Mitchell).

Hume's work did not come into prominence immediately, but once Kant took notice of him, he took place alongside Kant as a major representative of a new direction in Western intellectual culture. Natural religion, which had grown up on the foundations of the new mechanistic science of nature, was utterly discredited. That halfway house between Christianity and atheism was utterly swept away. A new beginning would have to be made to find a world view that was intellectually viable. So we shall now turn to Kant's own attempt to form a new synthesis and to those aspects of his philosophy which are of theological significance.

9

Kant and
the Limits of
Knowledge

Kant was thoroughly schooled in the German rationalist tradition of Christian Wolff (1679–1754), a disciple of Leibniz. He knew that for all their stress on reason and on innate principles, both Descartes and Leibniz recognized the value of sense experience. The details of nature required careful observation because one could not go from the first principles of reason to particulars. Descartes himself spent his last years carefully studying the plants of a botanical garden. It was by a combination of reason and experience that detailed and accurate knowledge of nature was to be achieved.

What troubled Kant about Hume's analysis of causality was that it showed that there is no observable necessary connection between our impressions. Kant firmly believed that Newtonian mechanics is true, and that nature's laws are fixed and hold universally. He could find no flaw in Hume's analysis. Since Kant would not for a moment consider abandoning Newtonian science, the cornerstone of the Enlightenment's optimism, he was forced to ask, How is it that our reason has the power to know that there are necessary connections when we do not observe any between our sense impressions? He claimed to be the first person to renounce "dogmatism" in philosophy because he refused to take the powers of reason for granted, and to conduct a critique of reason itself. He describes the nature of this inquiry with great precision in a single question: How are a priori synthetic propositions possible? Let us see what he means by it.

Kant points out that all our knowledge *begins* with experience, but this does not mean that it all *arises* out of experience (B 1). He calls knowledge which is independent of experience "a priori." It is not independent in the sense that we know it before we have any experience at all. Rather it is that *its truth is not established by experience.*

But if all our knowledge *begins* with experience, how can we tell that all of it does not *arise* from experience? How can we *distinguish* what has its source in experience from what does not? The crucial marks or criteria of a priori knowledge are that it is necessary and universal. Experience can teach us that a thing is so but not that it *must* be so. If we have a proposition (a statement) which is *necessary*, then it is an a priori proposition. A posteriori propositions, in contrast, are propositions warranted by experience. They are not true by necessity. They happen to be true, just as, for example, it happens to be true that all the books on my desk are written in English. It is not necessary, however, that this statement be true. I had to tell you that it was true because you could not look for yourself. You do not need either to depend on me or to look to know that it is true that my desk and the books on it are extended (an a priori proposition). You may reply that of course they are extended. This is because what we *mean* by material objects is that they are extended. Kant would agree. The statement is true and necessary because it is an *analytic* statement. An analytic statement is one in which the predicate is in the subject. There is no new knowledge gained from an analytic statement because part of what we mean by the subject (material objects, which is what my desk and books are) is asserted by the predicate (extended). An analytic statement is based on the identity of the subject and the predicate. Its truth depends on the principle of contradiction. (That is, I cannot deny its truth without contradicting myself.)

In contrast to analytic propositions in which the subject is in the predicate, there are synthetic propositions. A synthetic proposition is simply a proposition in which the predicate is *not* in the subject. Because the predicate is not in the subject—part of its meaning—it *adds* to our knowledge of the subject. Another way a synthetic proposition differs from an analytic one is that to know that it is true we must consult something besides the meaning of the words we are using. Something besides the meaning of the words must justify the claim that "all bodies have weight." This is a synthetic proposition because "weight" is not part of the meaning of "body." (And the statement is false because a body in space can be weightless.)

This brings us to the second criterion or mark of a priori knowledge (knowledge which is independent of experience, i.e. not established by experience), namely *universality*. "All bodies have weight" is in the form of a universal statement. That is, it asserts that *all* bodies without exception have the property of weight. Now it is not possible for us to establish the truth of universal statements *by experience*. We may check hundreds, thousands, or millions of bodies, and we still have not checked *all* bodies. If then we have a universal statement which we know to be true (unlike the one about all bodies having weight), then it is not based on experience.

What about the statement, "All the books in my office are written in English, French, or German"? It is universal in form and its truth is established by experience (and can be by anyone who visits my office). Kant says that such statements are not truly or strictly universal, even though they are universal in form. A truly or strictly universal statement is one in which "all x's are y's" and it is not possible to verify it by sense experience because the number of x's is unlimited (unlike the books in my office). We do not know that all crows are black because we have not and cannot check all the crows that have existed, do exist, or will exist to see if they all are black. If we have any knowledge which is truly or strictly universal, then it is a priori. Its truth is not established by sense experience, even though we have experienced many instances of its holding true, and even though we would never have been able to think of the statement at all without experience.

These two marks or criteria enable us to determine which propositions, whose truth we know, are independent of experience. If a proposition is either necessary or (strictly) universal, then it is a priori. We know that experience cannot show us that it *must* be so or that it holds universally. (The two criteria are actually logically equivalent: if one holds, the other holds.)

Do we actually have any a priori knowledge? We have a priori analytic knowledge, for it is, of course, necessary that all bachelors are unmarried males. We do not need to make a sociological survey as evidence for its truth, simply because its necessity and universality are a result of the meaning of the words "bachelor" and "unmarried male." The question is whether we have a priori synthetic knowledge. Are there any propositions in which the predicate *adds* to our knowledge of the subject, and at the same time the proposition is necessary and universal? Kant says yes. There are two main groups: mathematics and physics (which for Kant meant Newtonian mechanics).

In mathematics we have propositions in which the predicate is not in the subject, and everyone agrees that mathematical propositions are necessary and universal. We know, for example, that $7+5=12$, and that the proposition is necessarily true. Someone may object and say that it is necessary because it is an *analytic* proposition. Kant argues that it is not analytic; the predicate is not in the subject. That is, we know what $7+5$ means, and we know what 12 means, but it is not from their meaning that we know that $7+5=12$. This is easy to realize when we deal with larger numbers. We know what $14,763 \times 4,261,124$ means. If it is the subject of an analytic proposition, then we ought to know what it comes to without calculation, for if the numbers being multipled (the subject) mean the same thing as what they equal (the predicate), then by knowing the meaning of one we ought to know the other. The fact that we have to calculate shows that they do not mean the same thing. Thus, mathematical propositions are synthetic.

With physics the situation is the reverse. It is clear that its propositions are synthetic, but are they necessary and universal? Kant, in the introduction to the *Critique* stresses the great success of physics, and on this ground provisionally cites the principles of physics as an instance of a priori synthetic knowledge. In the main part of the *Critique* he claims to demonstrate that the principles of physics are a priori or necessary and universal principles.

Having established that there are two bodies of a priori synthetic knowledge, Kant now formulates the nature of his inquiry as How are a priori synthetic propositions possible in mathematics? How are a priori synthetic propositions possible in science (meaning physics)? Kant does not mean here to ask *whether* they are possible. He claims that in fact we do have such knowledge in these two cases. What his *Critique* seeks to show is *how* pure reason has achieved such knowledge. It is clear that experience cannot warrant knowledge which is necessary and universal. How then did reason confer on mathematics and the principles of physics their characteristics of necessity and universality? This is what a critique of reason is to show: how reason has done this.

SUMMARY OF KANT'S MAJOR TERMS

a priori (lit. from the first)	*a posteriori* (lit. from what comes after)
—not verified by sense experience	—based on or verified by sense experience
—necessary	—contingent
—universal	—may be universal in form but are not strictly or really universal

analytic	*synthetic*
—the predicate is part of the meaning of the subject. So these propositions are a priori (or necessary and universal) because of the meaning of the terms.	—the predicate is *not* part of the meaning of the subject.

There are two types of synthetic propositions:

1. synthetic a posteriori propositions which are verified by sense experience.
2. synthetic a priori propositions which are necessary and universal. They cannot be verified by sense experience. Propositions in mathematics and the principles of physics are synthetic a priori propositions, Kant says. The question of the *Critique of Pure Reason* is *how* are such propositions possible, that is, how are they verified or on what are they based.

The explanation is characterized by Kant as a "Copernican revolution." He points out that Copernicus was able to account for the observable phenomena of the heavens by making a reversal in what we think moves and what is at rest. Instead of the earth being at rest with all else turning around it, it is the earth which is in motion around the sun. So too with knowledge. We can account for the existence of necessary and universal truths by reversing the traditional relationship between the subject (the mind) and object. Instead of the subject changing in order to know objects, it is objects which are affected by the subject in our processes of knowing them. We can know that some things must be true and must hold universally because the necessity and universality are supplied by us, by our faculties of sensing and by the *categories* by which we understand. We see things in space and time because space and time are forms of our sensibility. Space and time are our means of sensing. Whatever we sense, we know it will be spatial and temporal. Geometry is the science of space; therefore the propositions of geometry will be true of all our sensible perceptions. (Kant has no body of knowledge for time comparable to geometry for the faculty of space.)

Kant's view has sometimes been explained by the analogy of seeing things through sunglasses. We see things with a particular color because our glasses are tinted. So too we see things in space and time because it is as if we wear spectacles of space and time, but this is misleading. We ourselves, our bodies, are in space and time, and our consciousness is in space and time. Kant's phenomenalism, that is, the doctrine that all that we are aware of are phenomena or appearances, is radical. It includes *us* in so far as we are aware of ourselves as sensing and thinking beings with bodies. Therefore, it is false to say that for Kant sensible objects are *in us* or *in our minds*. The "us" spoken of is itself an appearance. Whatever underlies us, objects, and space and time themselves is utterly unknowable.

How does Kant carry out this Copernican revolution? How does he argue for it? He uses what he calls a "transcendental method." He uncovers the *necessary conditions* for experience as we know it. He begins with something which we all agree is the case, and shows us what else *must* be true in order for what he begins with to be true.

For example, he takes geometry, which we all agree to be a body of necessary (and synthetic) knowledge. He asks what *must* be true in order for the propositions of geometry to hold true for all space, not only the spaces we have measured but *all* space. He argues that space must be a *form* of our faculty of sensing. If space were an independent reality, we would have to investigate part after part of space empirically to determine whether the propositions of geometry are true of every part of space. In other words, were space independent of our faculty of sensing, our knowledge of its properties would extend no further than those parts of space we have examined. Clearly we know that a line is the shortest distance between two points for every part of space and not just those we have experienced. We know this because space is a form of *our* way of sensing, so that whatever we sense will be spatial and have the properties Euclidean geometry describes.

This is Kant's transcendental method. It shows the necessary conditions for the truth of some proposition, or experience, or even a body of knowledge. Given the truth of geometry, for example, space must be "idealized" (that is, made a form of the subject's way of perceiving). This is the only way to account for the synthetic a priori propositions of geometry. Transcendental arguments enable Kant to explain how we have a priori knowledge not only in geometry but also in science. It is precisely because our faculties for perceiving and understanding actively form *what* we experience. The only way we can perceive is by means of space and time, and the only way we can understand is by processing the data we receive through the senses by the categories of our understanding. The result is that what we experience and know are phenomena (appearances). That is, we experience and know things not as they are (*noumena*), but as they appear to us. How things are in themselves apart from us is utterly unknowable. We affect *whatever* we experience so radically that we can say nothing about objects or ourselves as they or we are in themselves or ourselves. It is precisely what enables us to have a priori knowledge in mathematics and science which prevents us from having it in metaphysics. The human mind which begins with the data of sense experience unconsciously organizes it by use of its categories into objects and events of conscious experience. Our reason, which has begun this process of organizing raw material into objects and events, seeks to complete the organization. From pairs of sensible objects, one causing the other, we seek to move to wider generalizations about the connections between objects. Our reason is never satisfied to discover the cause of x, but presses on to find the cause of its cause, and so on. Likewise, our reason seeks to know what underlies the subject which experiences objects, that is, what underlies our phenomenal selves. This drive to move from one thing to its ground, and from there to what finally has no ground itself, is what takes us from science to metaphysics. The drive inherent in reason for complete understanding of the ground for all sensible objects, and the ground for us as subjects, and finally the ground for both objects and subjects which itself has no ground is the domain of metaphysics. It drives us beyond the bounds of all *possible* experience, to find the ultimate ground for experience.

Metaphysics has three branches: the self (rational psychology), the world (rational cosmology), and God (rational theology). Let us consider the first branch. We naturally think that there must be something which underlies the consciousness we have of ourselves as subjects who experience objects and who can also be aware of our own consciousness. Kant agrees; there must be something. He calls the synthesizing activity (the activity which unifies all the data we take in) which makes possible our consciousness of our experience as our own experience, the "transcendental unity of apperception." Given our experience of ourselves, there must be something which gives this unity to our consciousness of ourselves as subjects. But whatever that synthesizing process which produces our consciousness of ourselves as subjects (the transcendental unity of apperception) is, it cannot itself be experienced. It is the necessary condition of our having experience, and so it cannot itself be experienced (or we would need still something else underlying our experience of it to enable us to experience it). The condition of our having experiences—the transcendental unity of apperception—cannot be experienced. It is beyond all *possible* experience, in contrast to many other things which no one has yet experienced but which are things which can in principle be experienced.

But this transcendental unity of apperception which we must

posit as the ground of our experience does not enable us to infer that we exist as *noumenal* selves. There could be a single subject as the source *both* of our conscious experiences and of that which underlies us and enables us to have conscious experiences. Put in another way, we may say that the consciousness we have of ourselves as subjects does not entail that we are *noumenal* subjects. It is not a necessary condition of experience that there be *a* noumenal subject for each phenomenal subject. There *may* be, but we cannot know that there is, for we can never experience it (for it would be the very condition for experience which we have experienced), nor can we infer it from our experience. We are constantly tempted to affirm the existence of a noumenal ego; it is natural to seek a *final* termination or ground for anything that is dependent or conditioned. That drive is inherent to reason itself. So reason can create the illusion that each of us is a noumenal self. Clearly the experience of ourselves as subjects must have a ground. Our experience of ourselves is dependent on something. It is conditioned, but *what* it depends on is never knowable to us. Nor can we know the source of the unity given to our experience so that we are conscious of ourselves as subjects. So we are tempted to infer it from what we do experience. Since a single ego for all of us producing the experience of each of us as subjects is a possibility, reason cannot infer a noumenal self for each of us. Thus we find an important place where reason is limited in what it can determine. We cannot experience the ground of our experience, and so we are tempted to assert the existence of what is *beyond* all *possible* experience (to assert that we are noumenal subjects). Reason does not have the power to establish that we are noumenal subjects. This branch of metaphysics—rational psychology—is thus impossible.

In the second division, rational cosmology, reason is even more limited. For when reason goes beyond the bounds of all possible experience to find the ground for various questions we ask about sensible objects, it finds itself involved in contradictions. Kant calls them antinomies and states four of them. In each case we can demonstrate by reason that a proposition is true and also demonstrate that its denial is true. In the first antinomy, Kant proves that the world had a beginning and also that it has no beginning; that it is spatially finite and that it is spatially infinite. In the second antinomy, Kant proves that there must be a smallest particle of matter and that there cannot be a smallest particle. In the third, we are forced to assert that there is freedom and also to assert that there is causal determinism. In the fourth we are forced to admit both that there is and that there is not a necessary being. We can see the principle involved in all of the antinomies most easily by an examination of the second one. It goes as follows. Our reason seeks to understand material objects. One way we understand them is in terms of what they are made of, their constituents. So we begin a series of explanations: we explain an object in terms of its constituents; then we explain each constituent in terms of its constituents, and so on. If we are ever to complete our explanation of material objects in terms of their parts, we must insist that there are particles which have no parts. Otherwise we go on and on forever trying to explain material objects and we never come to know what they are made of. If we do get to something which is the smallest part of matter, then we cannot explain *it*; for it itself has no parts, and so we have not got a complete explanation of material objects. We see that to explain material objects in terms of what they are made of we must get to something which accounts for them, but if we do, it is something which cannot itself be explained. Thus we see that there both must be and also cannot be an explanation of material objects in terms of their constituents. In each of the four antinomies we find the same principle at work. Reason seeks to answer questions about material objects—whether taken as a whole (the whole cosmos in terms of time and space) or as particular objects (their constituents, their relation to each other, the kind of beings they are ontologically). Reason cannot answer its own questions. Indeed reason is driven to contradictory conclusions.

Kant's solution is to say that material objects are *phenomena*, not things in themselves. We can study phenomena in science. There we know that our general principles must hold: objects will be spatial (and conform to Euclidean geometry) and temporal; they will be substances which have attributes and are related by necessary connections. These are the forms of our perceptions and understanding. We cannot experience anything which does not conform to them. But the categories of our understanding are wholly *formal*. Kant says that they are *regulative,* not constitutive. That is, they are rules for organizing data supplied by the senses, but they have no content. All content must be supplied by the senses. This he summarizes in his famous remark, "Thoughts without content are empty, intuitions without concepts are blind" (A51/B75). Sensible impressions must be organized. This is done by the understanding. But the concepts—rules or categories—the understanding uses to organize sense impressions have no employment without impressions. They are simply rules to organize data, and without impressions they are empty.

The understanding is supplied with data for its categories to organize by the sensibilities (or senses). We can thus make steady progress in science going step by step in our empirical inquiries concerning material objects. Rational cosmology arises only when reason seeks to go beyond the reach of empirical inquiries, and to ask about the extent of the universe as a whole in space and time, about the ultimate constituents of material objects, whether freedom is possible, and whether there is more than contingent beings. It then seeks to use the categories of the understanding *without* empirical data. This is a mistake since the categories are principles or rules for the organization of data supplied by the senses. When we use the categories of the understanding to tell us the ultimate basis for the empirical objects we study in the sciences, our reason gets itself into contradictions. If we recognize that the categories are to be employed solely to organize experience, then we will see that rational cosmology is impossible. We see that reason is limited and that it has no power to go beyond all possible experience to the ultimate ground of experience.

Kant tells us that he has sought to limit reason to make room for *faith.* Thus in the third division of metaphysics, rational theology, Kant seeks to show that we cannot prove the existence of God. Belief in God is a function of *practical* reason (the domain of moral action). By showing that *pure* reason is limited to organizing the data of sensible experience, Kant bars all reasons for and objections to belief in freedom (which is crucial for morals), immortality, and God which are based on science or sense experience. Pure reason is unable to give us any basis whatsoever for belief in freedom, immortality, and God because it deals with appearances only. On the other hand, precisely because pure reason deals with appearances, it results in common experience and science cannot rule out the possibility of freedom, immortality, and God, nor in any way be used to judge their probability. To limit pure reason to appearances makes metaphysics as a science (or as knowledge) impossible, but it opens up the possibility of a *rational* basis for our metaphysical concerns in *practical* reason.

Let us examine the section on rational theology in which Kant claims to have refuted all possible proofs for God's existence. Kant claims that there can be only three possible proofs of God's existence: from the very concept of God (the ontological argument), from the existence of the world (the cosmological argument), and from the order of the world (the teleological argument). The teleological argument Kant says is not sound, as Hume has shown. Even if it were, its conclusion that there is a designer does not give us a God who is a creator. So we must rely on the cosmological argument for that.

The cosmological argument, however, is unsound. It relies on the principle of causality, one of the categories of the understanding. We may use that principle on beings which are possible objects of experience only since it is a rule of the understanding for organizing the data supplied by our sensibility. If we insist that there must be a first cause in the series of caused beings, we have used a principle of the understanding which is limited to organizing the data supplied by the senses to apply to what is beyond all possible experience (to the ground of experience). To put it another way, the causal principle applies to *each* individual being, but it does not apply to the cosmos as a whole (the collection of all individual beings).

Kant's main objection to the cosmological argument is its dependence on the same principle as the ontological argument relies on. The principle of the ontological argument is that a necessary being is one whose existence is entailed by its essence. God is a necessary being, therefore God exists. If the cosmological argument claims that the concept of a first being *means the same as* the concept of a necessary being, then we do not need the cosmological argument. We can move immediately from the concept of God as a necessary being to God's existence. On the other hand, if the concept of a first cause does not mean the same thing as the concept of a necessary being, then even if the cosmological argument proved the existence of a first cause, it would not be a proof of the existence of God. Thus Kant claims that the ontological argument is the crucial proof of God's existence. The teleological argument at best gives us a designer only, and the cosmological argument at best gives us a first cause only.

The ontological argument, however, is not valid. Kant claims that the ontological argument treats "existence" as a *real* predicate. Even though the term "exists" may be predicated of a subject, it differs from those predicates which *characterize* a subject. Predicates such as "six feet tall," "red," "intelligent" characterize a subject, and so are "real" predicates, but "existence" does not characterize a subject. What it does is to claim that a subject with certain characteristics is *instantiated*. Existence is thus not itself one of the characteristics which is instantiated. To prove that God exists because divine essence includes existence as one of its characteristics is mistakenly to treat existence as if it were a characteristic (or a real predicate).

This criticism was once considered to be a conclusive refutation of the ontological argument. Norman Malcolm in his article "Anselm's Ontological Arguments," *Philosophical Review* (January 1960), has shown that Anselm had in fact *two* ontological arguments. In the first one he did indeed treat existence as a predicate, but he did not do so in his second. In the second ontological argument, the predicate is "necessary existence" and necessary existence is a real predicate. That is, it is a characteristic. At least it is if it is interpreted to mean that God does not have a beginning or an end, and that God is not dependent on anything else to exist.

This nullifies another objection which Kant, following Hume, uses, namely that "necessary" applies to *propositions* and not to beings. A proposition or a statement can be necessary but a being cannot. Therefore the concept of a necessary being, which is used by the ontological argument, is incoherent, says Kant. But, as Malcolm points out, the concept of necessity used in the expression "necessary being" is not that of *logical* necessity, which is indeed a relation between propositions.

Kant has a third objection. The proposition "God exists" is

either analytic or synthetic, that is, either the predicate is in the subject or it is not in the subject. If the predicate is in the subject, the statement is an analytic proposition. An analytic proposition is true only because of the *meaning* of the words. It does not establish the existence of anything. It is a mere tautology (the subject is simply repeated in the predicate). On the other hand, if the predicate is *not* in the subject, you cannot connect the subject to the predicate on the basis of their meaning. The ontological argument does. It proceeds from the meaning of God as a necessary being to the claim that because God is a necessary being, God must exist.

This is not a conclusive objection. For the ontological argument proceeds from a *discernment of the essence of God*, not from a *meaning* assigned to the word "God." On the other hand, it is a moot point whether we can indeed discern the essence of God, as Aquinas pointed out long ago.

We thus reach a standoff. There is a version of the ontological argument which is fallacious because it treats "existence" as a real predicate. There is another version of the ontological argument which is not fallacious. It uses "necessary existence" as a predicate, and this is indeed a real predicate. The sense of "necessity" is not that of *logical* necessity, and that God is a necessary being is not the result of an arbitrarily imposed meaning. But this does not prove that God exists. The second version of the ontological argument succeeds in showing us the *kind* of existence God has. If God exists, that existence is a *necessary* existence because it is an existence which has no beginning or end and which is not dependent. The ontological argument does not show that a being with *that kind* of existence exists. We have no insight into the nature of the necessity of a "necessary being" to see whether it must exist, as Kant puts Aquinas' point. Kant claimed to prove that reason *cannot* prove God's existence. It appears from recent work on the ontological argument that all that can be said is that reason has not yet produced a version of the ontological argument which in fact does prove God's existence. The difference then is between *cannot* and *has* not.

Kant has often been thought to subject the idea of God to the categories of the understanding so that "God" is a concept of human understanding and therefore a *phenomenon*. Kant is careful to distinguish the *categories of the understanding*, which organize the data supplied by the faculty of the sensibility, from the *ideas of pure reason*. The idea of the self, for example, as a continuing permanent reality underlying all our sense experience and as being able to act freely is the idea of a *noumenal* reality. There *may be* a noumenon to match this idea of pure reason, but we are not able to know by experience or by pure reason whether there is or not. The same is true of the idea of God, of a reality which is absolutely unconditioned and which is the ultimate condition of everything else. This is something which *may* exist. It is simply that we are not able to determine by sense experience or by pure reason whether God does or does not exist.

In addition, Kant claims that we may characterize or describe God analogically. He explicitly rejects Hume's argument that we must either speak of God anthropomorphically or say that God is so different from anything else that we cannot attribute to God any characteristic whatsoever. Kant's account of analogical predication is essentially the same as Aquinas', which we described earlier. (See Kant's *Prolegomena to Any Future Metaphysics*, 356–60.)

Once Kant has shown the boundaries within which pure reason can work and beyond which it cannot legitimately go, he presents his ethical theory in the *Critique of Practical Reason* (and in briefer form in his *Foundations of Metaphysics of Morals*). Practical reason is the domain of action. By an analysis of moral obligation Kant gives a basis for *postulating* (as he puts it) freedom, immortality, and the existence of God. Freedom is a necessary condition for obligations; immortality and God's existence are implied by moral obligation even though they are not necessary conditions for moral obligations.

Kant claims that in all previous moral theories obligations are put forward *conditionally*. Obligations are *means* to ends and ultimately to the chief end, our happiness. The form in which previous theories present obligations is thus *hypothetical*: if you want to be happy, then you ought to act in such and such a way. Kant claims that *moral* obligations are thus misrepresented. Moral obligations are *unconditional* or *categorical* in form. We are to do *x* because it is our duty to do *x*, and not because *x* is or may be a means to our happiness. Kant thus excludes every benefit a person might achieve as a basis for acting morally. He removes the gratification of our sensuous nature, approval, and the prospect of rewards from God as motives. One is to obey moral laws simply because they are moral obligations.

Moral obligations imply that human beings are noumenal beings. In order for human beings to be morally obliged they must be free since it is possible to be morally obliged only if one can fulfill obligations. ("Ought implies can.") All phenomena, however, are completely determined by the principle of causality. So human beings *insofar as they are subject to moral obligations* have freedom. Thus as moral agents they must be noumenal beings.

A moral agent is a rational being. That is, human beings, insofar as they act morally, are not determined by their sensuous nature. Kant explains why a human being acts as a rational, rather than as a sensuous being. As rational beings we are the authors of the moral law which we are obliged to obey. We recognize an obligation to act in certain ways because that is the way a rational being would *will* to act. If we were free of all sensuous attractions and the desire to be happy, we would act rationally. Such actions would not come to us in the guise of "obligations" but as rational actions.

Kant puts forward a second metaphysical claim—our immortality—on the basis of practical reason. It is wrong to seek to be moral *in order to be happy*. Our motive ought always to be duty for duty's sake. But it is also clear that a person who is moral *deserves* to be happy. Such a person *ought* to be happy. If the universe or reality is *rational*, then a person who deserves to be happy will be happy. We, of course, have no guarantee that this will happen in this world. In fact, we have good reason to believe that it will not. Thus there must be a power (God) who rewards the moral and punishes the wicked after this earthly life. We do not *know* that we are immortal or that there is a God. Our knowledge is restricted to phenomena. Immortality and God are postulates of practical reason, a matter of rational faith.

In *Religion Within the Limits of Reason Alone* Kant recognizes the radical corruption of the will. The fact that human beings do not obey the moral law can be explained only by the postulation of the will's corruption. Kant at first seems to give a version of the Christian doctrine of original sin. But that doctrine would force him to rely on a Christian doctrine of pardon. He claims that the will, in spite of its radical corruption, must be able to obey the moral law to some extent. A person who shows moral improvement can be pardoned for *past* offenses because his or her moral improvement has made him or her worthy of pardon. He also does not want to admit a Christian doctrine of original sin because we would then have to rely on grace to assist our corrupt will. We would then have an excuse for moral failure by claiming that we have not received grace and we could neglect our duties for the same reason.

Kant insists that the moral law is not based on the divine will. It is utterly autonomous. Furthermore, Jesus Christ is not divine but only a symbol of a perfectly moral person. As a symbol, he can encourage us to believe that we too can obey the moral law perfectly. He is not a savior because nothing can replace our duty to obey the moral law. This view of Jesus is quite common among intellectuals of the Enlightenment.

The stark limitation of our knowledge to phenomena (appearances) as the only way to deal with Hume's scepticism, however, went against the optimism of the Enlightenment. Some means of getting around Kant had to be found. One way was taken by the English-speaking world. It simply accepted contingency, so there was no need to turn to Kant's drastic remedy. Another direction was taken by the Germans. They believed that some way had to be found to reassert the power of reason to give us knowledge of ultimate reality. Philosophy or metaphysics *must* be possible. We are not limited by the boundaries of "critical philosophy" (Kant's name for his own philosophy) within which our only knowledge is a knowledge of the workings of our own minds and of phenomena, with only a few postulates based on moral obligation. For the Germans the only way forward was to engage and struggle with Kant's philosophy. It is that attempt which we shall now trace because of its impact on theology.

10
Hegel and the Restoration of Optimism

Hegel, like Kant, wrestled with the thoughts and problems of his predecessors and offered a new philosophical synthesis. Our concern is not to offer a survey of his system but to present those aspects of it which are of relevance to theology. We begin by asking, What is it that a theologian finds of particular interest in Hegel? It is precisely what enabled Hegel to overcome the severe limitations Kant placed on knowledge, namely history. Plato, Aristotle, Plotinus, Descartes, Kant, and the other philosophers we have examined did not seek the ultimate principles of truth—the unchanging basis of whatever there is—in history. By history Hegel means the process of the growth of knowledge (in the sense of the development of both human consciousness and various disciplines, such as logic and physics) and the development of civilization and its institutions. Plato looked to eternal Forms as the foundation of the realm of becoming; Aristotle looked to the forms present in things; Plotinus to the One from which everything descends and ascends eternally. None looked to history as the manifestation and realization of the ultimate reality. For Hegel history is the progressive self-unfolding and self-realization of the Absolute.

Christians believe that God is the source of the universe, of its principles of operation, and of its purposes and goals. God is a personal being who has made the divine purposes known to the people of ancient Israel and above all in Jesus Christ. Because the domain of the historical is of particular significance to Christianity, there is thus an affinity between Christianity and Hegel. Hegel's range of interest, however, is universal. Christian theologians focus on ancient Israel and Jesus Christ but since they are concerned about the universal significance of these, they are interested in Hegel. Does what Hegel says confirm and support Christianity? Does Hegel deepen Christianity's understanding of its own revelation, as some theologians have felt that Plato and Aristotle do? Or does Christian Hegelianism cause such modifications in the Christian revelation as to subvert it, as others have charged that Christian Platonism or Christian Aristotelianism do? We cannot here, of course, answer such fundamental questions. Instead we shall only present some of the major features of Hegel's philosophy which are of theological significance so that readers can better understand what is involved in these questions.

Hegel believed that Kant had misconceived the nature of logic, the organon or instrument of thought. Reality is a *continuum*, with nothing separate and unrelated. But because of Aristotle, philosophers had all employed a logic which divides what is actually continuous into discrete or separate units. This is perhaps easiest to see in Locke. He treats "ideas" (or the concepts with which we think) as if they are complete units in themselves ("simple ideas") and as if they are connected to other ideas by association to form complex ones. The reality, which simple ideas copy, is made up of discrete particulars. The Enlightenment broke down because it was unable to find *objective connections*, whether in thought or in reality, between discrete particulars. Hume's work was simply an explicit statement of the impossiblity of finding objective connections. The mere contiguity and sequence of ideas and impressions is the only basis for grouping them together into particular objects, and the connection between these objects is once again mere association of discrete particulars.

Kant's attempt to restore objective connections between particulars turns everything we experience into phenomena or appearances, and we are cut off from any knowledge of reality. In fact, the subjects we are aware of as ourselves are themselves phenomena or appearances. What is behind the phenomenal subject is unknown and unknowable. What is behind phenomenal objects–though called things-in-themselves (or noumenal objects)–is unknown and unknowable. We have knowledge of appearances at the price of not being able to say anything about what is behind the appearances. Thus Kant, instead of helping, has driven an even larger wedge between ourselves as knowers and what it is we seek to know. In his attempt to restore objective connections between the things we are aware of, Kant has indeed brought together the subject or knower and the object. But the subject and object are phenomena only, so that we are utterly cut off from any knowledge whatsoever of ourselves and of objects.

Johann Fichte (1762–1814), Hegel's older contemporary, tried to relate the subject and object of knowledge by an Absolute Ego. Kant argued that there is a transcendental activity which takes place unconsciously in order for each individual to cognize objects and to be aware of itself as a conscious subject. Kant calls this unconscious synthesizing process the "transcendental unity of apperception." But he did not say what underlay this producer of phenomenal subject and object. Fichte pounced on this and made the underlying reality a single Absolute Ego. It underlies both phenomenal subject and object and produces them. Thus there are no things-in-themselves behind phenomenal objects, so there are no things-in-themselves which we are forever cut off from knowing. The phenomenal objects we are aware of are the only objects there are. Likewise there is no noumenal self behind the phenomenal self. There is only the Absolute Ego underlying all of us and producing an awareness of ourselves as subjects. Fichte does not really resolve the problem of the relation of subject and object in knowing. He simply reduces the dualism of subject and object to one of the terms of the relation, namely to the subject (the Absolute Ego from which all else arises). We thus still have a dualism of the Absolute Ego (subject) and what is not the Absolute Ego (the "not I" or the object of the Absolute I).

Friedrich Schelling (1775–1854), who was Hegel's close associate for a time, proposed an "absolute identity" as the absolute whose indifference is both subjectivity and objectivity. It is known only as that which is the difference between subjectivity and objectivity. Fichte and Hegel both replied that no difference can arise from absolute identity. Difference can come from identity only when it is already a component of that identity. Thus Hegel himself develops the idea of a unity or identity which is dialectical, that is, an identity which includes within its own unity what is its negation or opposite. (We shall illustrate this with a section from Hegel's work on the relation of a master and a slave, each of whom has internal elements of both dominance and subordination.) Hegel thus posits an Absolute with a dialectical unity in which it, as Spirit (*Geist*), becomes other than itself in history or time, and then rises above the opposition between itself and the other by knowing itself in the other and by developing itself in the other. Thus the final, absolute dialectical unity consists in the act of knowing (in absolute knowledge) in which opposition is included within the Absolute Spirit in its knowing and overcoming of the other. We shall illustrate these summary remarks. At bottom is the conviction that reality is a continuum, so that nothing is ever utterly separate (discrete). Otherwise there would be no hope of ever bridging the gap between things or of connecting things, especially of bridging the gap between the subject and the object so that knowledge is possible.

Hegel believes then that both the empiricists and Kant made the fundamental mistake of treating reality as made up of discrete particulars. Their logic, based on Aristotle, misled them since the terms or categories of thought in logic are abstract. As abstractions the terms of logic are discrete and so they do not properly represent the continuum of reality from which they are drawn. Particular things indeed are different from each other, and logic, whose terms are abstractions from reality, highlights the differences. It presents the identity of a particular thing—its essence—as what makes it what it is and not something else. But their logic does not indicate that a thing's identity includes its relations to that which it is not. Logic thus misleads us because reality is a continuum in which everything *in order to be itself* has as part of its identity its relations to what it is not. Apart from its relations, a thing is not itself. Such a logic in trying to represent relations, represents them "abstractly," that is, it treats each term of the relation discretely, and so terms are related *externally*. Whereas in reality, in contrast to such a logic, things are related *internally*, that is, relations are part of a thing's identity.

Hegel's point can be illustrated by contrasting two ways to conceive of a line. To conceive a line as though it were made up of discrete units leads to paradoxes. If a line is made up of discrete units, however many times we subdivide it, we never reach a part of a line which is so small that we cannot divide it. A line must therefore consist of units with no length at all. Then how can we get a line which has length by putting together units which have no length at all? This and other paradoxes indicate that it is a mistake to conceive of a line as made up of discrete parts, instead of conceiving of it as a continuum not made up of discrete parts.

Hegel seeks to present to our thought all reality as a continuum. This means to present it "concretely." Reality cannot be captured in the abstractions of logic as hitherto conceived; we need a *new* logic which recognizes that in any affirmation something is left out, and in any denial something positive is ignored. Only by presenting the way something is both different from and like other things can we adequately express what it is. Fully to say what something is involves saying what are its relations to all else. Particular assertions are only partly true, and they are also partly false since they lack completeness. "Concreteness" for Hegel then is not a particular which we can see and touch; concreteness is to conceive of a particular in its relations to other things and ideally in relation to all else.

The continuity of reality also requires that *time* be taken seriously in the domain of philosophy or truth, for reality is a continuum both spatially and temporally. To grasp reality we must not approach it with categories of thought considered abstractly, as in Kant; we must see logic and the categories of thought in the historical process. We must recognize that in the historical process the ultimate reality, the Absolute, is realizing itself. Reality is in the process of becoming fuller, more articulated. Hegel views the entire cosmos and its history as the Absolute coming into greater actualization and greater articulation in multiplicity in an orderly, rationally understandable way. Hegel's view is similar to Plotinus' but with two important differences. First, in Plotinus the descent from unity to multiplicity and the ascent from multiplicity to unity are not historical movements. We do not see all the past, present, and future as directed toward greater and greater realization of reality itself. For

Plotinus, the One is ever complete and realized; it simply radiates its fullness always, so there is no temporal or historical dimension to ultimate reality. Our time and history are of no significance for the One itself. Second, in Plotinus as we move from the One, we have less and less unity (or more and more multiplicity), and so we are further and further from true being or reality. In Hegel it is the opposite. It is as we get more and more concrete articulation in time and space in the course of history that we get a greater and greater realization of the Absolute itself.

Hegel presents his mature system as having three major aspects: logic, nature, and Spirit (*Geist*, which also means "mind"). Logic treats and relates all concepts under the notion of Absolute Idea. It contains all the concepts and their inner relations. It is they and they are it, so to speak. Logic taken as a whole (as Absolute Idea) is concretely realized and present in the unfolding reality of nature. To understand nature involves a study of the rise and development of all the specialized disciplines that investigate nature, and a study of the relations between the specialized disciplines. The third division, Spirit, includes both logic and nature, deepening and enriching the accounts to be found in each of them. As we ourselves are spirits, the account of Spirit includes every layer of our consciousness and all our relations to what we are not (the objects of our consciousness). It shows how subject and object, which are not absolutely identical, nonetheless have an affinity which is progressively realized. Finite spirits and Infinite Spirit have an implicit unity-in-difference that is progressively becoming explicit.

This is but a suggestion of the immense detail in Hegel's system, for it includes a study of the relations between all finite spirits in society, in the state, and in their cultural achievements in art and religion. Since all is connected and all exhibits a progressive manifestation of the Absolute, what we find is that logic, nature, and history are like the manifestation of a mind unfolding and realizing itself. Logic, nature, and history exhibit an orderly progression which is similar to our own thinking. Logic, nature, and history exhibit relations within themselves and to each other that are like the movement of a mind. We thus find that human beings are not in an alien universe after all. We have an affinity with the rest of reality. The mechanistic science of the scientific revolution established a conception of nature in which human beings, because they act purposively, are alien. Hegel restores a picture of nature as having inner teleological movement, so that human beings are at home there. He reestablishes the older Greek concept, which we first described in our study of Plato's *Timaeus*, of a series of purposive orders: Forms (for Hegel the domain of logic), nature, society, the individual.

Hegel not only revives a premechanistic cosmos, but he also restores the Enlightenment's faith in our ability to know nature, both physical and human, and restores confidence in our ability to improve the physical environment in which we live and also the social order. He gives a picture of all nature and history as a progressive unfolding and realization of an inner *telos* of which our knowledge in various academic and scientific disciplines, our social and political institutions, and our own human self-realization are all a part. He even includes periods of apparent decline as part of an inevitable progress. Every reversal makes a contribution to an even greater realization of that *telos* inherent in reality itself.

We shall now look at two parts of Hegel's system in detail so as to gain a better understanding of it. Both are in the domain of Spirit. The first deals with the early development of finite spirit. It treats a part of Hegel which is relevant to political theology today, namely Hegel's analysis of oppression in the relation of a master and a slave. The second deals with the opposite end of the development of Spirit, the realization of our identity with Absolute Spirit. We shall consider it in relation to Hegel's study of the Christian doctrine of the incarnation. It is this aspect of Hegel's work which D. F. Strauss (1808–74) and Ludwig Feuerbach (1804–72) used in their attempts to undermine Christianity. In this way we can briefly present those things in Hegel's philosophy which are of particular significance for understanding theology today.

The first selection from Hegel's system is taken from his *Phänomenologie des Geistes* (1807). The usual translation of the word *Geist* as "mind" is too narrow in its connotation, but on the other hand "spirit" is such a vague word in English. Hegel called his work a phenomenology of *Geist* because it traces the development of spirit or mind through various stages in which it apprehends itself as phenomenon (in Kant's sense). Spirit or mind is able to so progress in its development that it comes to be aware of itself as it is *in itself* (as noumenon in Kant's sense) when there ceases to be any opposition to it (no opposition between subject and its object). Kant's boundary within which our reason is secure but which it is unable to transcend is thus (allegedly) overcome.

In the master-slave relation, one person regards the other as a subordinate. Not only are they not on the same plane, but they are not the same type of entity. One is a subject; the other literally is an object. The slave is to fulfill the master's will, so the slave is like an extension of the master's body, which moves and acts at the master's whim and command.

Hegel is concerned to characterize the self-consciousness that is operating in the master-slave relationship. To grasp this we need to look at the plan of his book. He operates with the idea that consciousness exists and develops in stages containing various layers and contradictions. His *Phenomenology* is a sort of biography of the growth of mind, similar to a *Bildungsroman*, a genre of novel concerned with the educative development of the main character. The master-slave analysis is but one small section describing the development of consciousness, a part or aspect of *Geist* or spirit. Hegel begins at the level of sense experience, where a *subject* is aware of *objects*. There is a dualism of knower and known. They are alien or opposed to one another. This opposition is overcome when consciousness comes to the insight that the object is not completely separate from the subject but has an affinity to the perceiver; for when the object is perceived, it is the perceiver's object. It is not just "object," but "his or her object." Dualism is overcome by duality, a duality of (1) a subject and (2) the objects of the subject's perception. The object is known or incorporated into the self as its object.

We see here Hegel's conviction that reality is a continuum. A subject and an object are indeed different. But they are not *wholly* unrelated or wholly *alien* to each other, for the object known is the object-of-the-subject; that is, it is the *subject's* object. This is in microcosm Hegel's method. He begins with things which seem to have an identity in themselves and to be different or to be "opposed." Then he shows that there is an "identity-in-difference," so that they are not wholly alien to each other but are *internally* related. Something of one of them is part of the identity of the other, and vice versa, so that what seemed utterly different and opposed is no longer utterly different and opposed. It would thus be partly true, and partly false to say that an object is an object and a subject a subject, and that they are utterly different. For part of the identity of an object is that it is a *subject's* object, and part of the subject's identity is the object of which the subject is aware. Now let us continue with the analysis of self-consciousness which we just began.

The self not only is a subject aware of objects that are not itself, but there is a dualism *within* the self. That is, not only are we a subject aware of external objects, but we as a self are both subject and object, for we make ourselves the object of our own consciousness. We have self as subject and self as object. This dualism is overcome by a kind of identity of subject and object whereby what I am is "a self aware of an object that is myself." The object is me as my object. There is a kind of identity in which there is a duality: a single "subject-object." That awareness or consciousness exists.

In this movement we can see increasing richness in the content of consciousness; layer is added to layer; what went before is included in what has been realized so far. The past is not a past that is wholly finished and gone. The past continues to be present in each and every state of the realization of consciousness. An infant first has to perceive objects and to come to be aware that there is a distinction between objects and consciousness of objects. A philosopher with a developed consciousness may by abstraction attend to that infant layer of consciousness. One may mistake a layer of consciousness when abstracted for consciousness itself. One then creates the philosophical problem of our knowledge of an external world, for there is a difference between objects and consciousness of objects. A gap thus appears between the subject (who is conscious of objects) and the external world of objects. This can be seen to be a mistake and corrected when one sees that there is no such thing as "objects" without "awareness of objects." Subject and object are correlate terms, not terms which are utterly alien; so that one term could exist and *be itself* (or be what it is) without the other. Thus the philosophical problem of the external world arises when a layer of consciousness is abstracted and treated as though it were consciousness itself, rather than a stage in the progressive development of consciousness.

We have reached the stage of development of consciousness in which we have a subject aware of objects as its objects, and aware of itself as a subject that is a "subject-object." This brings us to the part of the *Phenomenology* in which the self-consciousness present in the master-slave relation is treated. Hegel claims that to become aware and conscious of oneself to a new degree—to have recognition of one's reality as a subject at a higher level than just as (1) the perceiver of objects and (2) the perceiver of oneself as a subject-object—one must have something else respond to one's *will*, to do what one commands. In this way a person comes to a higher level of self-recognition or self-realization.

Now a person can do this vis-à-vis nature; one can seek to make nature do as one wills. One can also do this in relation to other people because people are indeed objects. But unlike nature, people are a duality of "subject-object." A person can receive a different kind of recognition from others because one can recognize that one is being commanded and the other person can see that he or she is recognized as one who commands. This allows one to come to consciousness of oneself in new ways.

Since we are all subjects, conflict is inevitable. Each can have his or her self recognized and so reach a new level of self-awareness only if his or her will is obeyed. Each person can come to a new level of self-realization only at the expense of the other person. The most extreme form of resolution of this conflict is the master-slave relation. One person dominates, and dominates the other completely. Hegel begins with this extreme resolution—or situation of maximal opposition—and after analyzing its dynamics, shows how movement occurs away from this extreme form of opposition to other relationships of opposition, which though more satisfactory, still have an instability. This drives us forward through other forms of opposition and partial resolution until consciousness reaches its complete realization as Absolute Spirit. This is the condition of absolute knowledge in which Spirit recognizes itself in all that is other, and so all opposition or alienation is overcome.

The master-slave relation, the most extreme form of opposition, between subjects, is, from the point of view of the master, the optimum resolution of the opposition, for the master's will is obeyed and so the master's self is recognized by another. The master's self finds its realization in that recognition. Why then does the process continue? It continues because the resolution of opposition is inherently unstable. Let us see how.

The more the master can subordinate another to his or her will, the more the uniqueness of the master's self is asserted, and the more the master's self-consciousness as a subject is enhanced. But the very *existence* of another subject threatens the master's uniqueness and subjectivity. The master must seek to efface the slave as a subject. One way to do this is to make the product of the slave's work or effort the master's possession. This denies the slave's subjectivity, denies the slave's essential likeness to the master. This overcomes the slave's otherness because the slave's labor is commanded and the product of the slave's labor is the property of the master. The master presses his or her dominance for all it is worth, asking to be glorified and paid homage in order to cancel out the otherness of the slave, and thereby to preserve uniqueness. The master maintains uniqueness by stressing his or her *independence* or freedom, that is, by placing the slave in utter subordination in every possible way.

There is an irony in the situation. The master cannot be truly independent or free unless he or she *has something which is not himself or herself*. There must be something to pay deference, something to be subordinated. The status of master can only be maintained by the ownership of slaves. Thus a master does not have perfect independence. The very idea of independence implies its opposite, dependence, and independence *includes* dependence in its very self. (Once again we see Hegel's major idea: there is identity-in-difference, and it is partly true and partly false to say that a master is independent.)

The very need of the master to be recognized and by that recognition to come to a realization as a specific kind of subject implies the existence of other subjects. The existence of other subjects gives lie to the master's uniqueness. The very uniqueness of consciousness realized in masterhood is dependent on a condition which contradicts its truth. This makes the master-slave relation an unstable one.

The master tries to keep this truth hidden, to suppress it, by making control over the slave more and more arbitrary, so that the treatment the slave receives is completely dependent on the master's will. The more arbitrary the control, the more complete the slave's dependence, and hence the greater the master's sense of independence. But clearly this is self-defeating, for this consciousness of independence requires the existence of something to subordinate and something that can recognize the master's dominance.

The relationship is also unstable because the slave's dependence is not one-sided either; it also contains its opposite, independence. For the slave by working becomes more aware of his or her own reality. Goods are produced at the master's command, but the slave thereby develops skills and becomes aware that the master depends on his or her work. Lacking the slave's skill, the master relies on him or her for the products of life.

Each must now think of self in a contradictory way. Each has some power over the other, and each is dependent on the other. But there are these differences. The slave is in constant fear of and danger from the master who has power of life and death. Yet the slave also has a growing confidence because the master depends on his or her work, and a growing sense of worth based on his or her skill. The master grows in anxiety, needing the slave's labor more and more. When the slave becomes conscious of the difference between the dependent self and the independent self, between what is subordinate and what is free, the master-slave relationship is broken psychologically. This happens when the slave finds an area the master cannot control—his or her thoughts—and realizes that these are inalienable.

Although the slave experiences independence or freedom because his or her thoughts are inalienable possessions, the external world denies this independence because legally he or she is a slave. So the slave becomes a Stoic, denying the significance of the external world. The Stoic cuts the self off from the external world by an indifference to it. In this way "opposition" is overcome, but in practice the Stoic is bound or limited. This stance is also an unstable one, for it contains the untruth that one is independent and in no way dependent. The Stoic progresses to the Sceptic. The Sceptic doubts all, or at any rate can doubt all, thereby exhibiting still another kind of mastery over things, another way to overcome opposition.

Such then is the master-slave relation in Hegel's *Phenomenology*. We see in the analysis of this one relationship the principles which animate his system. We also see how valuable his work is for its details. The master-slave relation, for example, greatly illumines features in every relation of subordination and dominance. It can guide one in assessing which relations are destructive and which are not, and also why. The dynamics he presents can be used to study the marriage relation, the relation of teacher to pupil, parent and child, employer and employee, pastor and parishioner, counselor and client, as well as the relationship between Jesus and his disciples, the relationship of Jesus to God, and the relationship of God to us. Hegel can thus be of value even without an acceptance of his entire philosophy. One need not believe history is the self-realization of Absolute Spirit to find parts of his philosophy useful for illumining certain areas of life.

Now let us look at the other end of Hegel's system. Instead of beginning with the development of consciousness from finite minds, we shall begin with Absolute Mind. We shall regard all things as manifestations of Absolute Mind and see how this affects Christianity. The presentation is based on Hegel's *Lectures on the Philosophy of Religion* in which he describes the rise of religion from its earliest primitive forms to the highest of all religions which, according to Hegel, is Christianity. Hegel interprets Christianity in terms of his system. He says that the truth has different expressions in each of the three domains of Absolute Spirit: art, religion, philosophy. Artistic expressions communicate more on the level of feeling; religion expresses the truth in sensible representations; philosophy expresses the truth conceptually or in the form of reason. No denigration is intended in this ranking, Hegel claims, because every kind of expression is needed. It is merely a matter of different kinds of expression which are ranked according to the "knowability" of the ultimate truth.

Let us now look at Hegel's remarks on the nature of Christianity and particularly his view of Christ within the framework of his philosophy. For Hegel the basic problem in religion and in philosophy, in personal life and in reflection, is reconciliation. In the Christian religion we are familiar with the need for reconciliation; we consider reconciliation primarily as a transaction between a *holy* God on the one hand and a *sinful* creature on the other. For Hegel the opposition between God and creature is that of infinite and finite. This is the rift which must be healed.

Human beings are in the state of evil because they are finite; their finitude itself is evil. This does not mean, however, that all of nature is evil because nature itself cannot directly establish fellowship with God as human beings can. Human beings, because they are thinking beings with the capacity for fellowship with God, are in the condition of evil simply by existing. They are in part natural beings with bodies, desires, and impulses. If they were nothing but natural beings, they would be innocent. Since it is their potential nature to have fellowship with God, their natural existence in itself is to be regarded as evil. We may say then that in Hegel finitude is evil. By coming to self-consciousness and recognizing ourselves as independent beings we enter a state of evil but we also enter a state in which our destiny is fellowship with God. We remain in the state of evil until this destiny is fulfilled.

Let us now turn to a description of the other side of the opposition, the Infinite. Hegel insists that whatever is real must become concrete and manifest in the world. To speak of things merely as ideas is to speak of abstractions. Unless the ideas take sensible form in time and space they are utterly unreal (Kant's noumenal realm of things-in-themselves). This is true of God as well. To be real God must become manifest, must become revealed, must become knowable. Now God has, among other things, freedom, absolute freedom. To show this, to make it actual and real, God must grant a free and independent existence to something. God must make something that is other than divinity. This other, by being independent and free, expresses or realizes the absolute freedom that is in God. This independent "other" is the world. On the other hand, it must be stressed that this independently existing thing is the realization of *God's own nature* as one who has absolute freedom. This other which God has established is *God's* own, *God's* other. This means that God must reconcile this other to the divine; God must overcome the independent existence of the other, its separateness is actually the realization of the divine nature. What are in opposition, God and the independent world, must be reconciled and restored to unity.

We can now see from another perspective why finitude is evil. Finitude is evil not because it is limited but because it is only a stage in the realization in time and space of the nature of God. The finite is evil when it is seen as a stage which must "pass away" (be raised up and take its place within a more completely realized reality). The finite must come to an awareness that it is not truly independent but that it is united to the Infinite as a stage in the life history of the Infinite. The finite is evil not in itself but only in contrast to the final stage of a process.

In this framework of thought the fall, to use Christian language, is necessary. Humanity can only exist in a fallen state. This is unavoidable. The finite must exist in independence; independent existence for human beings is evil. Yet the finite must come to exist in order for the nature of God to realize itself in the concrete, in time and space. The fall is a necessary stage in the life of God.

The fall is not only necessary, it is also the source of a greater good. Without finitude, God in all the richness of divine diversity remains unrealized. God remains merely potential, not actual. By the fall God's richness becomes actual. The rich diversity which comes about with the actualization of a finite world separate from God, is, in the final stage, reconciled. All separate existence is gathered together into a single unity. There was unity at the beginning but it was so to speak, an empty unity, a bare unity. In the final stage the unity that is realized is rich and diverse. For it contains the entire universe with its immense variety, all held together in a bond, with human beings conscious of their essential unity with the divine.

The process of reconciliation, then, is a process in which human beings become conscious of their unity with the Infinite. They come to see that all existence, including themselves, is God realizing divine selfhood in the concrete. Through this awareness in human beings, God comes to a new self-awareness. When this consciousness comes about in human beings, the finite ceases to exist as finite; the finite becomes conscious of its identity with the Infinite. It is the reconciliation of the finite and the Infinite.

In all this Hegel has laid an "objective" basis, as it is called in theology (an ontological ground), for the reconciling work performed by Christ and experienced by people in the Christian church. He is explicit that people come to an *experience* of reconciliation in many ways and need not be aware of the objective basis. Briefly, the objective basis for the reconciliation we experience is that we are in reality one with God, who is not essentially different from us, not totally alien. There is a continuity between us and God. If we were completely different from God, there would be no possibility of fellowship. We can be reconciled only with something which is essentially like us. Our reconciliation then is possible only because our separation is a stage in the very life of God, only because we are essentially spirit as God is spirit.

The person and work of Christ are to be understood in this objective context. Hegel says that the incarnation is a necessary event in the life process of God. It had to happen because divine and human natures are not alien. This is a basic truth of God's nature, and, as we have already stressed, whatever is true of God's nature *must* become concrete in the world of time and space. Thus, since divine and human natures are not alien, there must be in the world at some time in its process an instance of a God-human. The truth that the Infinite and the finite are identical requires an instance of a God-human, a concrete instance of the union of the Infinite and finite natures. The incarnation or the person of Christ thus shows that finite nature is compatible with divine nature. It shows that the finite is capable of reconciliation with the Infinite.

Hegel's interest in Christ is primarily in his person, in him as the God-human. As God-human he is a major step in the historical process whereby opposition between Infinite and finite spirit is being overcome. In this emphasis on the person of Christ Hegel differs markedly from Enlightenment thinkers such as Kant. To them Christ was solely an ethical teacher and an example of the moral life. Even in these respects he was expendable since the basis of morals is reason, not a moral teacher or an exemplar of virtue. Hegel's endorsement of the incarnation reversed a trend in modern philosophy.

Hegel interprets the work of Christ (his life, death, and resurrection) from the perspective that he is the God-human. In the life of Christ we see the divine identifying itself with the human to the fullest extent by living a human life. His death shows an identification with humanity to the ultimate degree, for death is the crucial mark of humanity. Christ thus endures death to show the total identification of the divine with the human. Thus the incarnation (the person of Christ) and his life and death (the work of Christ) bring out the full extent of the bond and essential unity of the Infinite and the finite.

Christ's death has another aspect which becomes apparent only with the resurrection. The resurrection shows that the finite is destroyed in the death of the God-human, that is, all the natural aspirations and personal ends of the individual existing in independence for himself or herself are given up. All selfish goals are destroyed. This is made evident in the resurrection. All that is human and finite are seen to be inappropriate to Christ; the divine side is shown to be the true nature of Christ and our true nature as well. Personal goals, independent existence, finitude, these do not belong to human beings *essentially*. They are to be "given up" or "taken up" into the higher truth about ourselves.

Thus we can say that Christ's death is not merely the death of an individual. Christ dies for all, and all die in Christ. This is not evident from just looking at the particular events by themselves. When seen in isolation, they are merely the acts of an individual. However, when they are understood in the light of the objective truth (Hegel's system), these bare events are seen to be a moment in the divine life of God. The Infinite God becomes God-human in time and space, dies, and rises to show that the finite does not truly exist in independence but is identical with the Infinite, a stage in its life. The finite, of course, remains, but it is transformed by being unveiled as a stage in the life of the Infinite itself.

The incarnate one who dies does not merely *illustrate* the eternal truth of the underlying unity. Jesus Christ is not an accident of history. The incarnate death and resurrection had to occur. The events are a realization of part of God's nature, for whatever God is must appear in concrete form in time and space. They must take place in order to bring about in human consciousness the highest degree of awareness of the unity that exists between God and humankind.

One of the fascinating things about Hegel's proposal is that it seems to state a way in which the particular events in Palestine that surround Jesus Christ have universal significance. It shows how historical events have *ontological* significance. One problem with the attempt to make a historical event a truth which holds universally is the tendency to reduce the event to the status of merely unveiling what has always been the case. Hegel, however, by insisting that a truth to be a truth must become an event in time and space, seems to provide a basis for the Christian claim that Christ, in his person and work, has established a new ontological situation and is the basis of reconciliation between God and humanity. Since God and humanity are one, according to Hegel, this truth must become actual by the historic existence of a God-human.

However, the incarnate one does not *create* the possibility of reconciliation between God and humanity. The basis for reconciliation has always existed because God and humanity have an underlying unity. It is this point which both Soren Kierkegaard (see especially his *Philosophical Fragments*) and Karl Barth attack because for them it is of decisive significance. For both of them God is "wholly other," there is an "infinite qualitative difference" between God and creatures. By God's grace alone (a free and loving action), fellowship between God and human beings is possible. The intermediary that establishes the possibility of fellowship is the Word of God which became incarnate.

One may also ask whether within the terms of Hegel's own system there really can be only one instance in history of the divine becoming a particular individual. This question was first raised by D. F. Strauss in his *Life of Jesus* (1835), one of the most important critical studies of the life of Christ. Strauss was a "left-wing Hegelian"; that is, he endorsed Hegel's philosophy but claimed that it was incompatible with Christianity, in spite of Hegel's claims to the contrary. (Right-wing Hegelians saw a complete congruity between Hegel's philosophy and Christianity.) Strauss argued that if there is an identity between the Infinite and the finite, as Hegel claimed, then it cannot be said that God became a particular person. Since *all* human beings are divine in nature, even if only implicitly, an explicit unity *in the race* rather than in an individual would be a higher manifestation of this unity. It is impossible for a single person to partake of or to exhibit the divine-human unity uniquely.

It is not clear, however, that Hegel wanted to maintain that there truly is an instance and only one instance of a God-human in time. There are passages which seem to indicate that the idea of the divine-human unity became attached to a particular individual whose life expressed the truth of the divine-human unity most adequately. This particular life differs only in degree from other lives which express the same idea imperfectly. In addition, there is a passage in which Hegel seems to say that it is necessary for people to *believe* in one and only one instance of a God-human, even though all human beings are in fact of the same ontological status. Christ's ontological status is not really superior to others, but it is only believed to be superior. This belief is something that necessarily arose. The passage reads,

> This substantial unity is Man's potential nature; but while this implicit nature exists for Man, it is above and beyond immediate consciousness, ordinary consciousness and knowledge; ...
> This explains why this unity must appear for others in the form of an individual man marked off from or excluding the rest of men, not as representing all individual men, but as One from whom they are shut off, ...(*Lectures on the Philosophy of Religion*, trans. from the 2d Ger. ed. by E. B. Speirs and J. Burdon Sanderson, London: Kegan Paul, Trench, Trübner, & Co., Ltd., 1815, 3:73).

This passage contains the germ of the main thesis of another influential left-wing Hegelian, Ludwig Feuerbach. He claims that the essential nature of humanity—our identity with the Infinite—is not part of our immediate consciousness. This leads us to think of it as uniquely realized in one person only. We are thus excluded or cut off from our own essential nature. What is implicit in us, our potential, thus does not become realized. Christianity—belief in the uniqueness of Christ as the God-human—thus becomes a form of alienation from our own nature.

In his book *The Essence of Christianity* (1841) Feuerbach breaks with Hegel. He rejects the theory that history is the process of the

Absolute finding itself in the "other." Religion is not the representation in sensible form of this philosophic truth. Religion is instead the projection of the attributes of human nature into an imaginary being (God). Human characteristics which we admire, such as power, kindness, moral purity, and intelligence, are attributed to deity. This is true of every religion. Examine a people's deity or deities and you can determine which human characteristics that people values.

Feuerbach explains the psychological mechanism of projection by postulating in human beings an inner drive to perfect themselves. We become aware of our present shortcomings because we have an unconscious ideal of a perfected human nature. Because we are less than we aspire to be, we take the ideal standard (our essence) and project it onto deity. God is then said to have the perfections we ought to have. Now we can excuse our failures on the ground that only deity is perfect, whereas we are mortal and imperfect creatures. We appeal to deity to perfect us by grace, and so we become passive instead of actively seeking to improve ourselves.

Feuerbach thus believes that religion keeps us estranged from our own true selves. The task of philosophy is to restore humanity to itself by liberating us from religious illusions. He therefore rejects the Hegelian Absolute as a fiction, rejects Hegel's philosophy because it is a mere imitation of religion, and views it as perpetuating our alienation. In our century Karl Barth endorses Feuerbach's critique of religion and in particular of nineteenth century theology as indeed human projection (as "anthropology"). Unlike "religion" and nineteenth century theology, which begin "from below" with a study of human consciousness and the human condition and mount upward, Christianity and Christian theology begin with the divine revelation which comes "from above." Thus, Barth claims that Christianity is not a projection.

Hegel himself claims that there is a compatibility between his philosophy and Christianity. This profession and the inherent tendencies in his philosophy that are contrary to Christianity lay at the base of the split among his followers into a left-wing and a right-wing. They were first split by Strauss' *Life of Jesus*. Strauss not only points out that Hegelianism and the orthodox doctrine of the incarnation are incompatible, but he also argues that the New Testament narratives have very little historical truth. They thus cannot be regarded as symbolically equivalent to a philosophical statement of the truth. They are myths, that is, mere expressions of the aspirations of the original Christian community. Strauss sought to dissociate Hegelianism and Christianity completely.

Feuerbach's repudiation of Hegel's positive evaluation of religion, and specifically of Christianity, was even more radical, for he came to reject Hegel's interpretation of reality as a manifestation of the Absolute. This rejection formed the basis of Karl Marx's claim that it was necessary "to turn Hegel on his head." Marx decided that what moves history is not the Absolute Idea realizing itself in time but economic forces. Marx retains Hegel's dialectical logic but sees history as the manifestation of the class struggle. Marx completed the left-wing revisions made in Hegel by attacking Hegel's political views.

Hegel believed that all human relations find their culmination in the state. The state is the climax of the manifestation of the Absolute Idea in social relations. But Marx objected. The state's origin is not "from above," so to speak. It develops from human social relations. These relations have their basis in economic relations, as people wrestle with nature to gain their livelihood. Alienation of consciousness thus does not begin in the dialectic of the outward movement of the Absolute Idea to a natural world (nature). Rather alienation is caused by the estrangement of human beings from the product of their work. Human labor alone gives value to nature, but the worker is paid a wage instead of the full value of the product of his or her labor. The surplus value is kept as profit by the owner of the means of production. Thus the worker is exploited. A socialist society, by eliminating economic exploitation, will allow people to be properly related to their work, and thus humanly related to the material or natural world.

By the middle of the nineteenth century, right-wing Hegelianism had disappeared. The left-wing had the field to itself. It had in effect repudiated Hegel. His philosophy in its own integrity was no longer significantly represented by any thinker. This was partly because of the developments of left-wing Hegelianism described above, but also because rapid developments in the physical sciences in the nineteenth century discredited Hegel's philosophy of nature, the second of the three major divisions of his system (logic, nature, spirit). Hegel's philosophy was not dead, however. It indirectly stimulated British idealism (ca. 1865–ca. 1920) and also was revived in various forms in many European countries and in America.

11

The Search for Meaning in Contemporary Philosophy: *Existentialism, Phenomenology, Analytic Philosophy, Hermeneutics*

Once again our concern is with what in philosophy matters for theology. This chapter is not a complete survey of twentieth century philosophy. Theology at the start of the century and for several decades did not develop in response to contemporary philosophical movements. Among Roman Catholics the nineteenth century revival of Thomas Aquinas came to flower. Its most notable and influential philosophers, Jacques Maritain (1882–1973) and Etienne Gilson (1884–1978) achieved international reputations. One of its pioneers, Maurice de Wulf (1867–1947), argued that many ideas of Scholasticism must simply be abandoned, especially in cosmology and physics, but that many of the constitutive principles or basic concepts are fruitful today. Since I have followed Gilson's interpretation of Aquinas, there is no need for our purposes to say more about neo-Thomism.

Among Protestants the dominant theologian, Karl Barth, made a decisive break with the liberal optimism of the nineteenth century. In the first two volumes of his *Church Dogmatics* he referred to Soren Kierkegaard (1813–55) as one who had above all stood against the reduction of theology to anthropology, or to the highest dimensions of the human spirit. Until then Kierkegaard had had a negligible influence on theology. It is for this reason that we have reserved treatment of Kierkegaard for this chapter even though he died in 1855.

Kierkegaard objected to Hegel's claim that his philosophy was a philosophical expression of Christianity. He attacked both Hegel and those church leaders who accepted Hegel's claim. Kierkegaard protested that Christians had forgotten what Christianity is; otherwise people would not have been deceived by Hegel's claim. In his description of what it is to become a Christian, Kierkegaard developed an original analysis of human existence which significantly influenced the twentieth century movement known an existentialism which in turn has influenced theology.

Hegel's basic convictions that there is a continuity between all things and that reason has the power to uncover that continuity provoked Kierkegaard to say that Hegel had forgotten what it is to be an *existing* human being. The marvelous progress that Hegel was able to exhibit in every aspect of culture did not relieve every existing person from beginning as a "primitive" in two vital respects. In the domains of ethics and religion there is no accumulation by the race which an existing individual inherits as his or her own simply by becoming educated in the achievements of the human race. Ethics and religion are not part of an individual's own "subjectivity" (or person) unless they are acquired or appropriated by an individual for him- or herself.

Ethics and religion cannot be appropriated "objectively" as, for example, we acquire a knowledge of Newtonian physics by use of our reason. We attend to a demonstration of the laws of motion and so grasp their truth. Ethical and religious claims have to do with the kind of *subject* a person is to *become*, not with a demonstration about objects (or even truths *about* subjects). An existing human being must decide or choose to *become* an ethical or a religious person. One is not "immediately" ethical or religious; there is no transition to these by means of information and demonstrations. Were it possible for a theory or a philosophy to tell an individual what he or she is—to determine completely the *kind* of person he or she is—then that person would cease to be an individual, that is a person who is responsible for what he or she becomes or does not become. If we did not have this freedom, we would no longer be responsible for what we are. Thus, in Kierkegaard, choice or decision becomes highlighted as the most important feature of human existence.

Given Hegel's claim to absolute knowledge, a transition to Christianity involves no essential change in a person. Human beings have an *implicit* identity with the Infinite. That relation simply needs to become *explicit*. Becoming a Christian simply means that one now knows consciously what one did not know consciously before. There is no *action* (decision) required either by the individual or by God to establish a bond, a relationship. In becoming a Christian what is achieved is simply a conscious knowledge of a unity or bond that has always been there.

Kierkegaard insists that in Christianity there is a radical difference between God and human beings, such that our relationship to God requires divine action as well as human action. The obstacle between ourselves and God is not ignorance only, as in Hegel, but sin. Sin can be overcome only by divine action. God's action in Jesus Christ overcomes the barrier of sin and opens to us the possibility of reconciliation. To be reconciled is not merely to know of this possibility, but to actualize it for ourselves by our response of faith. It is to have faith in what cannot be known since reconciliation is possible by a unique and free act by God. That such an act has taken place cannot be known or verified by what we can learn of the dialectical movement of history.

We can, of course, be told about God's act. Such "direct communication," however, can at best only put a person in the position to recognize that Christianity may possibly be true. However much we can find to support that possibility, by philosophical or historical study, it never relieves us of the need to respond by faith, by our own decisive choice. We still must take responsibility for becoming a Christian.

To become a Christian thus requires one to turn "from speculation" and to take responsibility for one's own self vis à vis ethical claims and Christianity. Each person must venture in faith, which from the standpoint of "objective thinking" is acting without sufficient reason. But actually a person who has faith *has* reasons for acting. Kierkegaard describes what *motivates* or moves a person to choose to recognize the validity of ethical obligations and to respond with faith to the Christian gospel. From the standpoint of the question, How does one become a Christian? there are only two choices in a person's life that matter. First, there is the choice between recognizing the reality of good and evil or not recognizing them. This is not a choice *between* good and evil; it is a choice whether to recognize that good *and* evil have significance for one's own life, or to exclude both good and evil as factors in one's life. No theory *about* ethics can save a person from having to make this decision. A person is motivated to recognize or enter the domain of the ethical because of boredom and despair or because life lacks significance for other reasons. Only the reality of ethical obligation gives significance to what a person cares about and does. Otherwise what a person cares about and does are mere personal preferences. That I like vanilla ice cream is a personal preference and so is insignificant. So too is anything else that I care about when the reality of ethical obligation is not recognized. The second choice is to become religious. (Kierkegaard treats Christianity as religion A, and other religions as religion B, but this complication need not concern us here.) The difficulties an individual encounters in trying to fulfill ethical obligations may motivate him or her to become religious. In time one becomes burdened by guilt or weary of the effort to be moral. Reasons such as these may move a person to turn to Christianity. Such reasons mean that the "leap of faith" is not utterly arbitrary and irrational, as Kierkegaard has frequently been understood to claim. Such reasons do not establish the reality of ethical obligations nor the truth of Christianity, but they do give an individual reasons for becoming an ethical person or for becoming a Christian.

Barth was deeply impressed with Kierkegaard's stress that God is "wholly other" and freely establishes the basis of a relationship between God and human beings, in contrast to Hegel's stress on the implicit unity between God and human beings. Barth also insists that there are no concepts or categories available to our reason which enable us to gain knowledge of God's existence or nature. He thus repudiates not only the philosophical idealism of Hegel, but also Aquinas' natural theology. Barth focuses on the action of God in self-revelation as the sole and sufficient basis of theology. The Word of God is the primary act of God's revelation: the Word of God which becomes incarnate as Jesus Christ. (Scripture is a witness to the Word of God and the Word is known and made present in proclamation and sacraments.) The revelation of God is "self-authenticating," that is, we have no extrinsic criteria by which to judge its authenticity. Barth's views are largely a revitalized Protestantism, comparable to the revitalization of medieval Scholasticism by nineteenth and twentieth century neo-Thomism. It has far more traces of modern philosophical terminology than does neo-Thomism, however, because Barth, even though he repudiates Hegel's philosophy, uses many words associated with Hegelianism.

Kierkegaard is a major source of twentieth century existentialism, but it would be inaccurate to call Kierkegaard an existentialist. He himself was concerned to understand how to become and be a Christian, whereas existentialism is concerned with what it is to be a human being. This observation can mislead if it suggests that to be an existentialist is to hold a set of doctrines. The label "existentialism" refers to *themes* which occur in a number of writers, who in other respects differ from Kierkegaard and from each other as well. Two of those themes we have already mentioned: the irreducibility and primacy of the individual, and a stress on choice. Kierkegaard and the existentialists also focus on extreme situations in which the normal and familiar ways of understanding and dealing with life break down. God's command to Abraham to sacrifice his son meant to Kierkegaard that Abraham did not have any ethical system or any theology to justify the killing of his son. By citing such extreme situations Kierkegaard and the existentialists seek to reveal to us our own individuality and to have us take responsibility for our own actions and the kind of people we are without the support of philosophy, science, or religion. The individual thus is to face the universe with no rational scheme with which to master or control it.

Existentialism by its penchant for extreme situations calls attention to the contingency in nature and in social relations. William of Ockham, who rejected Aristotelian essences in things, and David Hume, who could find no necessary connection between things, had also described contingency. The existentialists, however, describe how human beings *experience* contingency without the comfort of Ockham's God (who makes nature behave in a regular way by divine will) and without the complacency of Hume, who believed that we had no option *in practice* but to depend on our instincts. Jean-Paul Sartre's (1905–80) neurotic and estranged character, Roquetain, in *Nausée* is the best known example of the human experience of contingency in existentialist literature.

Kierkegaard himself firmly believed in God. His stress on the limitations of reason does not arise from wrestling with the philosophical problem of the connections between things in nature or the limitations of reason in science. It is rather Hegel's excessive claim to be able to comprehend the ethical and religious life by reason which aroused him. His portrayal of life as full of boredom, anxiety, and dread comes from an understanding of life without God by a person who believed in God. He described how one comes to faith and how one lives in faith. He also described quite ordinary people in common situations (for example, the judge in *Either/Or*) and not just people in extreme situations. Often his explicitly Christian books, such as *Works of Love*, are ignored by philosophers.

Sartrian existentialism gives an analysis of human life in which there is no God—not just what it is like for a person to be without faith. Sartre also believes that there are no values except those projected by human beings and that these have no support from an alleged supernatural being, physical nature, or human nature. Thus "absurdity" means different things for the two writers. For Kierkegaard there is no way to account for the breach (sin) between us and God; no way to account for our alienation from God; no way to account for how the eternal can become what God is not—human. So philosophy and science, which seek unchanging first principles, cannot comprehend as a "first principle" an agent who can become what God was not, human, so that by God's ontological change, our ontological status in relation to the divine has changed. The possibility of reconciliation is created by divine action. Kierkegaard seeks to expose the ways Christianity has been so tamed and altered by Hegel and by the social acceptability of Christian institutions that the "absurdity" of the gospel and hence its offense is smoothed out and made imperceptible. Thus with such accounts as the near-sacrifice of Isaac by Abraham, Kierkegaard shows the fear and trembling with which we must approach God, instead of sentimentalizing God's care as always providing a way out for us in times of trouble. God's actions cannot be rationalized or comprehended by any principles of reason, whether a priori, as in Kant, or a priori as unfolding in logic, nature, and spirit, as in Hegel. The only responses to God's actions (should a person actually see what is involved in Christian claims) is either faith or offense at their absurdity.

For Sartre the absurdity is wholly within human beings. We crave fullness and completeness. But we are free, and hence we are never able to be like objects, which are *en soi* ("in themselves" or complete). Objects simply are what they are. Human beings are not objects but subjects. Subjects "exist," so they never "are" anything. That is, they never attain a completeness because by their freedom they can always change. Because of their inescapable freedom, people are never completely what they appear to be in their social roles, either to others or to themselves. We have no essence to be completed or fulfilled. We have then contradictory features: the desire to be complete (*en soi*) and the inability ever to become complete. Our freedom condemns the passion for completeness to futility. Yet we can never give up that passion. So human beings are absurd.

It takes courage to tear the veil off society and our social roles, and experience the resulting contingency. Contingency makes us dizzy because we cannot get our bearings from any fixed point outside us or inside us to give us our identity. The only options are a frank recognition that we cannot make sense of the universe and ourselves, or *mauvaise foi* ("bad faith" or self-deception). To see this absurdity clearly and not to deceive ourselves with the comfort we can derive from hiding our contingency with "objective science," social roles, or religion is to live authentically. We then recognize that the things we value and care for are actually our own projects and yet we personally take full responsibility for their validity by holding to them passionately and with integrity. In this, Sartre seems to imply, human beings have their dignity.

Even though Sartre utterly rejects Hegel's rational system, he is heavily indebted to Hegel's *Phenomenology of Mind*, especially for the theme of "negation." Negation, in Hegel, is the way the dialectic of mind moves to newer forms of consciousness. This has affinities to Sartre's stress on freedom (it negates every identity we achieve). Sartre was not significantly influenced by Kierkegaard directly, but by themes from Kierkegaard which he found in the work of Martin Heidegger, to whom we now turn.

Heidegger (1889–1976) was associated for several years with Edmund Husserl (1859–1938), and served as one of the editors of the series entitled *Jahrbuch für Philosophie und phänomenologishe Forschung.* His own major work, *Being and Time* (1927) appeared in the series. Heidegger's philosophy is very different from Husserl's, so much so that if Husserl is taken as the standard for what pure phenomenology is—and that is frequently done—then Heidegger is not a phenomenologist. Husserl above all sought to bring to light what is implicit in the acts we perform in everyday life. Heidegger tries to open the way back to what has become completely unfamiliar to us, to lead us back into the *ground* of metaphysics, to Being (*Sein*). We cannot recover Being by reflecting on the familiar world. Being is so forgotten that the contexts in which we talk about our world renders any use of the word "Being" empty and meaningless.

We can get a glimpse of the novelty of Heidegger's thought by considering his remarks on Leibniz's question, Why is there something, rather than nothing? which appeared in an introduction to a later work, *What Is Metaphysics?* Heidegger regards Leibniz's question as a metaphysical one, concerned with the first cause *among beings.* He is critical of this because such a supreme being is still a being, even if the highest and the cause of all the others. Heidegger himself is concerned with the attempt to recall the truth of Being, which is concealed in beings. He says his question differs from Leibniz's. His question is, Why is there something, rather than Nothing? "Nothing" is capitalized, he tells us, to make it clear that the focus of his concern is not *beings* but Nothing. Being is so forgotten that we can only hope to gain the slightest echo of its absence from our thinking by speaking of Nothing. Everywhere beings take precedence and lay claim to every "is," while that which is not a being is understood as Nothing. Yet it is Being Itself and remains forgotten. Heidegger quite deliberately distorts language in order to get us to see how much our present thinking and language act to conceal Being. Instead of being an empty word—a nothing—Being is the richest and the most important of all realities.

In *Being and Time* Heidegger claims that he has taken first steps toward the recovery of the "question of Being." He does this by a study of the way human beings exist. He refers to our being as *Dasein*. Literally it means "being there." In German philosophy it means "existence." Heidegger takes it literally, however, and says that human existence is "being there." We differ from rocks, trees, and animals because we can question our identity, we have an openness to being. Other things simply "are"; we "exist." Thus in *Being and Time* Heidegger examines human existence, not for its own sake—and hence not as an existentialist of the Sartrean variety—but as the being which can raise the question of its own being and thus by this openness to being give us access to Being Itself. *Being and Time* is thus a preparatory study. Heidegger's interest is not in human beings as such. It is simply that we are already concretely involved by our very existence with the question of Being because we need to *become* something. This inescapable involvement Heidegger calls the "existentell question." By contrast, an explicit theoretical study, such as his own, into the structure of being deals with the "existential question." But even in the theoretical study we are not spectators. What we are as existing beings *shows* itself to us, once we strip away concealments and distortions. To engage in theoretic study calls for an involvement. An existential analysis shows the distinctive characteristics that mark us off from other kinds of beings. Among them are (1) to exist is to be "on the way," never to be complete, but to be constituted by possibilities (the possible ways of existing are called the "existentialia"), (2) to exist is to choose to be oneself—hence to be always incomplete—or to lose oneself by submerging oneself in the conventions of society. Our affective states—fear, joy, boredom, and anxiety, especially the anxiety over our finitude which comes to us above all with our constant, though suppressed, awareness of death—are crucial "existentialia" (ways to exist). The word "thrownness" captures the brute facticity of our existence, for where we come from and go remain hidden.

In this anxiety over finitude we see material Sartre draws upon and we can recognize Kierkegaardian themes. One should also note that according to Reinhold Niebuhr anxiety over our finitude is the very nature of original sin (see his *Nature and Destiny of Man*). Thus Heidegger's *Being and Time*, although intended as a preliminary study in ontology, was easily appropriated by Christian theologians. The most important and influential use of it was by Rudolf Bultmann (1884–1976).

Bultmann had an international reputation as a New Testament scholar apart from his involvement with Heidegger's philosophy. Bultmann claimed that the gospel is distorted because it is presented in terms of a prescientific cosmology. That cosmology is a three-tiered universe with life on earth placed between a divine realm above and an evil one below, with interventions into our earthly life from both realms. Such a cosmology is utterly untenable in the modern world where we live with a scientific cosmology. Intellectually honest people are often repelled by this mythology and thus never encounter the gospel itself and face its scandal. The Bible must be demythologized so that the gospel itself may be made accessible to modern people.

Bultmann did not reach these views from a study of Heidegger, but he endorsed Heidegger's *Being and Time* as giving an analysis of the human condition which is in full accord with a demythologized Christianity. Bultmann thus adopts much of Heidegger's language and analysis of *Dasein*. He too says that each of us encounters the limits of human existence, especially death, and each of us must either face our finitude authentically or live inauthentically. It is possible to live inauthentically in the very name of Christianity, "objectifying" the gospel into historical events in which supernatural beings from above and below enter into our world. But there is no more room in history than there is in nature for such an entrance. Newtonian "gaps," so to speak, do not appear in history any more than they do in physical nature. Supernatural beings and actions cannot be slipped into the chain of natural causes and effects to act as explanations. His proposal is to demythologize the gospel. The gospel is about ways of existing, either authentically or inauthentically. The gospel's only significant difference from Heidegger's analysis of the human condition is that, according to it, we do not have within ourselves the power to make the transition from inauthentic to authentic existence.

Bultmann's work added fuel to the discussion of relating faith to history which had arisen in the nineteenth century. Because of

Bultmann the problem took a particular form. One does not want, on the one hand, to loose all ties to history, as a thoroughly existentialist analysis tends to do. On the other hand, one does not want to "objectify" the gospel, to limit it to truths which can be appropriated for oneself by a knowledge of what historical study can verify. Something between sheer facticity and fiction is sought. This is one of the reasons for the appeal of "narrative theology" and the revival of tradition. Narrative theology sees "story"—its function in communities and its structure—as the way to understand the Bible.

In spite of his influence on theology, Heidegger himself never moved in a Christian direction. He continued in the direction of his search for Being, looking not to the human condition, but to language, especially to the nineteenth century German poet, Hölderlin, and to the pre-Socratic philosophers for access to the "voice of Being." He himself spoke less and less and instead practiced listening and waiting.

Paul Tillich's work bears many marks of existentialism, and indeed it has some major affinities to Heidegger. The very title of one of his most influential books, *The Courage to Be*, suggests the recognition of the threat of finitude and meaninglessness—existentialist themes. But in addition, Tillich (1886–1965) considered "the question of Being" as the fundamental question of both philosophy and theology, and he explored it by a study of the structure of the being of human beings. Tillich has a far more rational structure to being and Being (or the "ground of being," as he frequently referred to Being) than does Heidegger. This is largely because of a kind of Neoplatonism in Tillich. For the same reason his view of "symbols" as mediating Being differs from Heidegger's twisting and distorting of language as a way of getting access to Being.

Three other existentialists should be mentioned. First is Martin Buber (1878–1965), a Jewish philosopher who focused on the "I-Thou" relation. He singled out dialogue as the prime reality, in contrast to the solitary self. This deeply influenced Protestantism, especially in developing a new approach to revelation. The revelation of God is no longer seen to be primarily propositions or statements. God is said to be one who is always a subject in relation to us. God is not an object of knowledge, but one who is known only in encounter.

Gabriel Marcel (1889–1973) also stresses engagement and participation. A system of thought is available only to detached observation, and human thought has a tendency to withdraw from the immediacy of participation. Thus there is always a tendency to treat the presence met (whether a person or God) as an object confronting an autonomous subject. This is actually to turn oneself into an object. Marcel is most responsible for the development of the notion of mystery, which is contrasted to problems. We seek solutions for problems. When a solution is found, the problem disappears. But in the case of encountering a mystery, there is no "solution." Instead one participates in a mystery. The more one is open to a mystery, the more one learns through participation in it, and the more its depths are revealed. A mystery is never finished with and left behind. Our society has lost a sense of mystery and hence has lost a sense of the depths of life, of good and evil, in short of being, because it tends to treat everything as a problem. Marcel's major philosophical works are *Metaphysical Journal* (1913–23, 1927), *Being and Having* (1935), and *The Mystery of Being* (2 vols., 1951). His favorite medium of communication, however, is his plays, and his main preoccupation is with genuine communication in concrete situations. Love, hope, fidelity are his major themes, and his positive attitude toward life in the world marks him off from other philosophers in this century, especially from other existentialists.

Karl Jaspers (1883–1969) like Buber and Marcel, rejects philosophy as a body of thought or knowledge. For him limit situations—such as death, suffering, conflict, failure, and guilt—lead us to the place where we can hear the voice of transcendence and where faith becomes operative. For him, myths, religion, and philosophy are "ciphers" which can in rare moments give access to what is beyond. They are "commentators" on the original ciphers—nature, history, and personal experience.

For nearly half of the twentieth century existentialism was the only contemporary philosophical current with which theology had any vital contact. Phenomenology touched it only indirectly through the quite idiosyncratic phenomenologies of Heidegger and Sartre. The dominant philosophical movements in the twentieth century as far as universities are concerned are phenomenology and analytic philosophy, not existentialism. Both phenomenology and analytic philosophy grew out of the problems of philosophy, especially as cast by Hume, Kant, and Hegel, not from the issues of human existence. No wonder Tillich lamented the "theological circle" in which theologians read each other but are ignored by the rest of the intellectual world. Since the Second World War, however, both phenomenology and analytic philosophy have had an influence on Christian theology, so we shall now examine them.

Phenomenology is associated above all with Edmund Husserl. It was developed in many different ways, as we have suggested by distinguishing Heidegger's work from that of Husserl. The word "phenomenology" is used very loosely. For example, frequently a study is said to be phenomenological merely because it claims to be purely descriptive, without the issue of truth or falsity being raised. This is very common in anthropology and in the history of religions. Accordingly I shall limit myself to describing some of Husserl's own work and indicate the places where it is relevant to Christianity.

Husserl, like others near the end of the nineteenth century, was concerned with the ontological status of logic and mathematics. Kant, after a period of eclipse, had a revival. His classification of propositions caused a problem. Kant held that mathematical propositions are synthetic a priori. But what if, as was the case in Husserl's day, the possibility of a priori synthetic propositions is rejected? What then becomes of mathematics and logic? Since they apply to everday experience and to science, it seems implausible to say that mathematics consists only of analytic propositions (ones which are true only because of the meaning of their terms), and thus the result of arbitrary definitions. But if they are synthetic (not true merely because of the meaning of their terms), what is their basis or foundation? John Stuart Mill (1806–73), Britian's leading empiricist of the nineteenth century, tried to show that they are empirical generalizations. Logic deals with correct thinking, so it has to do with the mind. Accordingly, logic and mathematics are a branch of psychology.

Husserl's *Philosophy of Arithmetic* (1891) was a psychological account of arithmetic. He completely reversed himself because of the work of Gottlob Frege (1848–1925), who was also a powerful influence on Bertrand Russell and the analytic tradition. Husserl carefully and thoroughly refutes "psychologism," as this form of reductionism is called, in his *Logical Investigations* (vol. 1, 1900). This not only became the first rallying point for the phenomenological movement, but is also important for understanding the nature of phenomenology to this day.

Phenomenology is a nonempirical science. This does not mean that phenomenology deals with analytic truths (propositions which are true only because of the meaning of their terms). Phenomenology yields new information. Yet it does not do so in the way that empirical or factual sciences do. Hence it is a nonempirical science. Phenomenology gives us access to *pure phenomena*. It is crucial to understand what this means. "Phenomena" does not mean what it did to Kant: mere appearances in contrast to unknowable things-in-themselves. Phenomena do indeed appear to us in "immediate experience," but this is not the raw data of sense impressions or of our stream of consciousness. Anything is a phenomenon *if considered in a particular way*. To explain what that way is will explain to a considerable extent what phenomenology is. We can see how phenomenology differs from empirical science by comparing it with psychology. Pure phenomena are to be distinguished from the data of psychology because psychology is limited to factual material and merely factual connections. Empirical generalizations are all that is possible. Phenomenology, by considering objects or the contents of awareness and the acts of awareness in a particular way, can intuit the essences and grasp *essential* connections between those essences. Phenomenology examines the same things as other disciplines, but by considering them in a particular way, enables us to intuit what is essential, not merely what is contingent or empirical.

We can begin our account of how we consider objects in a certain way by describing the intentionality of consciousness. This one insight—the intentionality of consciousness—is shared by Husserl, Heidegger, and Sartre. It is interpreted differently by each, and not everyone who speaks of the intentionality of consciousness interprets it in the direction of idealism, as does Husserl. What follows applies to Husserl, but the basic idea of intentionality of consciousness can be grasped from his view.

All consciousness points toward an object: when we are conscious, we are conscious *of* something. There is no such thing as mere consciousness. So we see something, hear something, imagine something, remember something, and the like. This is not sufficient for us to speak of the intentionality of consciousness. There are several other characteristics. First there is the way intention "objectivates." The sense data of experience must be distinguished from objects. We are aware of many sense data: whiteness, roundness, heaviness, largeness. The stream of our consciousness gives us many such *sensa*. These sensa are related, so that what we are aware of is, for example, a box. But a box is not itself a sensa. A box is an object. Thus a box can be opened, carried, painted. Sensa, such as whiteness, roundness, heaviness, largeness, cannot be opened, carried, or painted. A perception of a box is given to us *through* sensa, but a box "transcends" sensa. The referent of our consciousness—a box (for that is what we are aware of)—is thus not a simple relation. There is a complex structure in which sensa are raw material, so to speak, and are integrated into the total object, a box. We are conscious of a box because all the sensa refer to an object, a box, and are not isolated nuggets of awareness. They come to us as qualities *of* a box. The intentionality of consciousness connects an object to its "horizon." The front of a box, for example, refers ("intends") the sides, bottom, rear, and inside of the box. What we perceive (the front) gives us legitimate expectations of future experiences (perceiving sides, bottom, rear, and inside).

Intentionality is also responsible for the identity of an object. We could only have a stream of white sensa, for example, and none of them would be the color *of the box* unless the intentionality of consciousness identifies all these white sensa as the color of the box. Likewise the various perspectives from which we see an object are integrated into an identical object. Because of the intentionality of consciousness, they are the way a box appears from different perspectives. Thus they all refer to the box. Intentionality also identifies an object in another sense. Because of intentionality, a box (or any other object) has an identity in the sense that it is the same box whether I perceive it, think about it, remember it, or even doubt its existence.

Sometime after the publication of *Logical Investigations*, Husserl characterized intention as *constituting the intentional object*. Hence the intentional object is not a preexistent referent to which an intentional act refers as already given, but something which originates in the act. This is definitely some kind of idealism. Phenomenology as such, however, is not committed to idealism. One may instead speak of objects as *constituting themselves* in our consciousness. Then an analysis of constituting acts only explores how a phenomenon establishes itself in our consciousness, without making it a product of a transcendental ego.

The concept of the intentionality of consciousness (whether specifically that of Husserl or not) means that there is no split between subject and object. Rather objects are objects *of* consciousness and consciousness is always consciousness *of* objects. There is no Kantian noumena or things-in-themselves unrelated to any awareness. The account we have given so far is of the activity of the synthesis of sense data. Intentionality is not restricted solely to the content of consciousness, or specifically to material objects such as boxes, nor to the activity of perception. Intentionality has parallel aspects: the intentional *act* (called *noesis*) and the intentional *content* (called *noema*). Phenomenology is concerned with an analysis both of the act of cogitating (perception, imagination, image consciousness, memory, etc.) and with *what* we are aware of.

Now that we have given an account of the intentionality of consciousness, we can more easily explain what it means to speak of phenomena made accessible by the particular way any act or object is considered. Here I shall rely on an account of phenomenology given by Herbert Spiegelberg in his valuable book *The Phenomenological Movement* (The Hague: Martinus Nijhoff, 1960, pp. 653ff.). Spiegelberg seeks to describe the essential method employed by phenomenology and not specifically that of Husserl. He does this by giving a series of steps or stages of analysis, each of which presupposes what precedes it. Only the first few steps are vital for our purposes.

The first step of a phenomenological analysis is to enlarge and deepen the range of our immediate experience. The battle cry of the phenomenological movement—"to the things themselves"—was sounded by Husserl in his phenomenological manifesto, "Philosophy as a Rigorous Science" (1910). This is not as easy as it sounds. It is something, moreover, which a person must do for him- or herself; phenomenology is something to be done. First there is a purgative stage in which people must free themselves from hardened beliefs and theories. This is similar to Descartes' attempt to be free of preconceptions and prejudgments, so as to attend to whatever comes before consciousness and to allow things previously unheeded to be noticed. For phenomenologists, among the obstructions to "immediate experience" is an acceptance of the simplified abstractions of science and its limited vocabulary as the full picture of reality. Closely related to this is the restriction of all data to *sense* data, a refusal of access to any other possible data.

This purgation puts one in a position to intuit phenomena. "Intuition" does not mean having an inspired idea; literally it means "looking at" (*Anschauung*). It is much more difficult than it sounds. Spiegelberg's example of a phenomenological analysis of "force" is a helpful way to see the difficulty:

> By "force" I shall understand here the referent of such phrases as "using force," e.g., in forcing a door, or in sentences such as "a stone hit me with considerable force," or "the car struck the tree with great force." ... it is particularly important to keep out some adjacent meanings introduced partly in connection with physics and especially with dynamics. Thus "force" as used here must not be confused with "power," in so far as "power" stands for something merely potential, a capacity or ability to do something....
>
> To a phenomenological approach, the question of whether or not physics can get along without the concept of force is irrelevant. The only question is whether it is a phenomenon in our actual experience. This is what Hume seems to be denying when, for understandable reasons, he questions the experience of necessary connection. When at the same time, however, he denies the experience of force it may well be that, in addition to rashly identifying the two, he was also subject to what I called the sense-organ prejudice: since there is no separate sense organ for forces as there is for touch qualities, he concluded that forces could not possibly be perceived.... (*The Phenomenological Movement*, pp. 660-2)

This is only a short part of the first step of a description of intuiting a phenomenon, in this case "force." Even so we see that it is no simple matter because it requires us to free ourselves from associations of the term from physics and from a particular philosophical view (that of David Hume).

Spiegelberg also points out that phenomenology is not primarily concerned with the linguistic expressions with which we began the analysis ("forcing open a door," etc.). This is merely preparatory to the study of the phenomenon referred to by the linguistic expressions. It is indeed a return "to the things themselves." Phenomenological analysis, as mentioned earlier, pays attention to the parallel aspects of the intentional act (*noesis*) and the intended content (*noema*). To say that phenomenology "merely describes" is thus a rather uninformed comment. Phenomenology indeed describes but not merely what lies before unskilled observation; and what it yields is a much richer account of that of which we are "immediately aware."

In the second stage essences and the essential relations between essences are intuited. This part of a phenomenological investigation is no less demanding than the first step in which the range of immediate awareness is extended. The phenomenology of general essences, called *Wesenschau* or eidetic intuition, has aroused the charge of Platonic realism. It is true that Husserl is committed to universals as irreducible entities. But the general essence has no superior or even equal reality to that of particular entities. For Husserl, to apprehend the general essence we have to look at the particulars *as examples* or as instances of the general essence. (This is called the "eidetic reduction": the move from particular to universal essence.) By looking at the particular green cabbage we can see it as an instance of a certain shade of green; we can also see it as exemplifying greenness and even color as such. Thus intuiting a particular opens the way to an apprehension of general essences. In his example of force, Spiegelberg began with the case of forcing a door or being struck by a stone, but each of these particular forces are instances or examples of force as such.

The third step is the apprehension of essential relations. Here Husserl uses what he calls "free imaginative variation." It involves the attempt to drop certain components completely or to replace them by others in our examination of essences. We can then tell if, for example, the length of a side is essential to a triangle, and we can tell whether two or more associated essences are essentially necessary to each other; essentially compatible; or essentially incompatible. What we learn here are not analytic truths since we are dealing with what words refer to, not with words themselves. Nor are these essential insights simply empirical inductions because the particulars are examined as *examples* of essences. Empirical induction could never yield the generality and necessity of eidetic intuition. The insights are obtained by a nonsensuous intuition.

What must be noted here is that phenomenology is dealing with the phenomena made available to us by considering matters in a certain way. This is frequently characterized as the result of "the phenomenological reduction" whereby there is a suspension of our judgment as to the existence or nonexistence of the content of our consciousness. Husserl often described it metaphorically, as the mathematical operation of "bracketing." Bracketing the issue of existence enables us to focus on the content, the "what" of our awareness. This is said to be what makes phenomena available to us. As Spiegelberg insists, if this is all that Husserl meant—a mere suspension of belief in existence or nonexistence—phenomena are not ipso facto available. Phenomenology involves much more, as we have attempted to illustrate by reproducing Spiegelberg's remarks about force and how we come to intuit force as a *phenomenon*. This is not to *deny* the phenomenological reduction, but it is to say that the description of it as a mere bracketing of the issue of existence and nonexistence is inadequate.

A bridge from phenomenology to recent hermeneutics (a movement we shall examine shortly) can be detected from the example of force. The phenomenological exploration of force should have affected our understanding of the *meaning* of the word and the phenomenon. Such a consequence is quite common in phenomenology: an analysis affects our understanding of the meaning of our concepts. It is then only another step, albeit a giant one (and in a direction away from phenomenology as Husserl understood it) to Heidegger's search for *concealed* meanings. What is intuited in a phenomenological analysis is used as a *clue* to hidden meanings.

Husserl claimed that phenomenology is a "presuppositionless" inquiry, seeking to give a foundation to all our disciplines. It does not frame theories but describes phenomena as they present themselves. Are we able to look at things without presuppositions? It is an ideal to be achieved, and part of the development of phenomenology as a method is the continuous attempt to practice presuppositional analysis. The very method itself is in the process of being achieved, clarified, and more properly described as it is being practiced. Thus Husserl himself constantly described himself as "a beginner." Indeed, much of his own writings and those of other phenomenologists have been on the improvement and clarification of the method itself, rather than its use in attending to the concepts and assumptions of various fields of study.

Max Scheler (1874–1928), an early associate of Husserl, used his own kind of phenomenology to analyze spiritual experience, especially in his major work, *On the Eternal in Man* (1921). For Scheler, the eternal in the human is our permanent possibility for religious experience, and it supposedly shows that we are more than natural beings. This work shows that phenomenology does not necessarily "just describe," for its descriptions result in the truth-claims made by Scheler.

The analysis of specifically Christian consciousness and its structure is also being attempted at the present time, but its consequences have not yet been widely felt. This attempt has been stimulated in part by Husserl's notion of *Lebenswelt* or the world of lived experience. It was virtually unknown during Husserl's lifetime, but it has since become one of the most influential ideas to emerge from his literary remains. According to Husserl, the life-world is not immediately accessible to the average person, especially as his or her understanding is formed by a scientific interpretation of the world. A suspension or reduction of the scientific outlook is necessary in order to see the prescientific life-world and its structure. This prescientific world forms an all-inclusive horizon, part of the frame of reference of the various phenomena of consciousness and of all disciplines. Husserl himself believed that science had developed its matrix of concepts and methods by a process of selection. Its forgetfulness of this selectivity is responsible for the intensifying crisis in recent science both internally in relation to its own foundations and externally in its relation to human values and aspirations. In his view, the only way to overcome this crisis is to realize that science had been drawn from a fuller world.

In general we may say that phenomenology has had an appeal to Protestant theologians who have felt caught between the neo-orthodoxy of Barth and the reduction of religion to the subjectivity of feelings in the wake of Schleiermacher. Phenomenology offers them the possibility of a conception of the religious consciousness which does not get drawn into subjectivity and which can also deal with a much greater range of religious phenomena than could Schleiermacher. Roman Catholics, who, like Husserl, oppose psychologism in logic and who hold to essences or forms, often find phenomenology congenial. Husserl's own idealism is not an insuperable barrier because phenomenology is not necessarily connected to it. The openness of phenomenology and its resistance to materialistic and naturalistic reductionism has led to a tolerant attitude toward religion. In this it contrasts sharply to analytic philosophy, which in one of its two major branches is explicitly antireligious. This branch is known as logical positivism, and we shall now turn to an account of it.

Logical positivism developed between the First and Second World Wars, mostly in Vienna, as a reaction to philosophical idealism. It regarded all statements as either analytic or synthetic and proceeded to claim that all synthetic statements are empirical. This created problems for the subject of philosophy itself, for are its statements empirical statements (statements based on sense observation)? Philosophy does not have a subject matter as does physics or history. Logical positivism thus claimed that philosophy is concerned only with logic. By this it meant not only formal logic but the foundations of the sciences. Many logical positivists sought to show how all the terms used in science can be reduced to sense observation statements. Or if they are not themselves reducible directly to sense observation, then they are an essential part of a theory which entails some statements which can be verified or falsified by sense observations. They thought that scientific language could thus be given a foundation in experience but that the language of metaphysics and theology (which was considered to be a particular kind of metaphysics) could not. Accordingly their language was said to be meaningless. In addition, the language of morals and aesthetics was thought to be reducible to the role of evincing emotions, so that even though it had meaning, the language of values did not make truth-claims. Facts and values were thus rigorously distinct. The classic statement in English of logical positivism is A. J. Ayer's *Language, Truth, and Logic* (1936).

The intended victim of logical positivism was metaphysics, not theology or Christianity specifically. The attack on Christianity itself did not come until 1949 when in a very brief but widely known paper, Anthony Flew applied the falsification principle to the belief in God as the designer of nature and to the belief that God loves us. According to the falsification principle, an utterance is meaningless unless some sense observation statement could in principle falsify it. If the state of affairs is compatible with both the existence and non-existence of God and of God's love, the words "God" and "God's love" are vacuous or empirically meaningless. (However much they might mean emotionally). Sentences in which these words occur are not truth-claims, that is, sentences which might be true or false. To be truth-claims they must *exclude* some state of affairs; if they are compatible with all states of affairs, then they assert nothing.

The observable order of the world is equally agreed upon by both atheist and theist. However, the propriety of an inference from its order to a designer is disputed. Flew presses the point that the observable state of affairs—the order of nature—is the same whether one says there is a designer or not. Nothing is added or taken away from the observable order itself by saying that there is or is not a designer. Thus the notion of a designer is vacuous since it does not add or take away anything from the observable state of affairs itself. Likewise Flew argues that "God loves us" is vacuous because God's love is compatible with extensive and horrible suffering. Contradictions between "God is love" and various instances of suffering are avoided by continual qualification of what is meant by "God" and "love." Flew charges that the words die a "death by a thousand qualifications," that is, they gradually become emptied of all empirical meaning because they do not exclude any observable state of affairs (any specifiable suffering). Obviously Flew has raised questions that arise apart from the philosophical position of logical positivism. These questions in the form in which Flew cast them became the way they were discussed for nearly three decades in philosophy of religion in English-speaking countries.

The logical positivists believed that they had the support of Ludwig Wittgenstein (1889–1951). Wittgenstein, an Austrian, spent most of his working life in England. In the earlier part of his career, he was deeply influenced by Bertrand Russell's work on the foundations of mathematics and logic. Russell (1872–1970), like Husserl, opposed psychologism, and in collaboration with Alfred North Whitehead, attempted to demonstrate that all mathematics rests on logic. To achieve this reduction Russell employed a truth-functional logic. In a truth-functional logic, the truth or falsity of a whole (for example, "It is raining, and it is Friday") is completely determined by the truth of each of its parts ("It is raining"; "It is Friday") considered *separately*. The truth of the whole is a function of its parts. This suggested to Russell a view of reality which he called "logical atomism." According to this view, the basic reality is atoms of sense observation, each of which is certain and indubitable. They form the basis of all our knowledge. We can determine the truth or falsity of any claim by reducing a complex statement or statements to their basic or atomic parts, and then match each part with an "atomic fact" (by sense observation). The truth of the complex statement or statements is determined wholly by the truth-value of each part. This accorded well with the views of logical positivism. (A. J. Ayer's *Foundations of Empirical Knowledge*, 1940, is in the vein of logical atomism.)

In the *Tractatus Logico-Philosophicus* (1922) Wittgenstein dealt with language. He tried to show what can and cannot be said meaningfully by specifying the form of a proposition within the limits of a truth-functional logic. This very much restricted what we can say meaningfully. Not only are the concerns of metaphysics and theology unstatable, but so too are the concerns of ethics and aesthetics. Wittgenstein, however, was misunderstood by the logical positivists, who saw in him an ally. For Wittgenstein himself actually believed that there was more than could be said, and he believed that what could *not* be said was far more important than what could be said.

After the *Tractatus*, Wittgenstein slowly revised his views. When his *Philosophical Investigations* was published posthumously in 1953, it became common to speak of the "early" and the "late" Wittgenstein. In the *Philosophical Investigations* he tried to show that language has *many* functions, and that these are not reducible to a single one, as he had thought in the *Tractatus*, which so greatly restricted what we can say meaningfully. Three of his expressions have had a particularly large role in religious and nonreligious circles: language games, meaning as use, and forms of life. Wittgenstein compares various functions of language to different kinds of games: board games, ball games, card games, and the like. Each game has its own specific rules as to what is permitted and not permitted, its own understanding of what it is to win or lose, and the like. So too does language. Instead of describing language as such, as he had tried to do in the *Tractatus*, he said we must look at the way people actually use language to determine what can and cannot be said and to understand what is meant.

Wittgenstein sought to break the hold of a false picture or view of meaning: that the meaning of a word is what it stands for or what it refers to. In this false picture, words are treated as if they are *names* of things, either outside us in the sensible world or inside us as mental images or states of consciousness. But all words are not names nor is the meaning to be found by finding something for them to refer to. Rather, to determine the meaning of a word we are, in many cases, to look at the ways it is used.

To gain some idea, though only a limited one, of this elusive notion of "use," consider this analogy. We can point to a chess piece (a physical object) and tell a person "This is the Queen." We can then show the various moves the Queen is allowed to make. The *uses* to which the Queen can be put show the meaning of the word "Queen." The meaning is not simply the name of the piece. Thus we see that words have uses or perform functions. To determine what words mean is largely (though not exclusively) to look at their uses.

We can get a deeper idea and also some understanding of the philosophical value of Wittgenstein's idea of "meaning as use" by considering sense data. In philosophy one theory concerning what we mean by "material objects" is that they are a collection of sense qualities and nothing more than this. (The position is called "phenomenalism," not to be confused with phenomenology.) This means that we can, in principle, rewrite all sentences in which material object words (e.g., "table," "chair") occur into logically equivalent statements which use only sense data words ("white," "long," "round"). For the statement "That is a white house" we may substitute "I am having the following sense experience: a whiteish, rectangular expanse." Material object language is supposed to be merely a convenient way of talking, whereas what we are really aware of is sense date.

A Wittgensteinian response would be to ask of a sense datum such as "a whitish expanse" whether it can get dirty. A white house can, but what would it be for a "whitish expanse" to get dirty? A white sense datum is simply itself, namely white; a dingy white expanse is *another* sense datum. Thus a sense datum does not get dirty. Nor can it be cleaned or painted. A white house can. The "logic" or "grammar," as it is put, of material object language ("house") and of sense data are different. Thus we cannot make the same moves (as in a game) with both of them. We cannot by substituting material object language for sense data language, get logically equivalent statements. Phenomenalism is attacked and defended in linguistic philosophy, as this branch of analytic philosophy is called, in terms of the things we can and cannot say in our ordinary talk, or in ordinary language. We cannot say of a sense datum that it is dirty but we can say that of many material objects. This shows, it is claimed, that a translation from material object language to sense data language is impossible, and thus that material objects are not reducible to sense data. (This point is the same as that made by Husserl concerning the difference between "objects" and sense data or sense qualities, but they have made it by considerations of language.)

The notions of "language game" and "meaning as use" are closely connected to the notion of "form of life." Wittgenstein is not as explicit here as one would like so that controversy surrounds this expression even more than the other two we have explained. But roughly it means that a person who can understand and use language can do so only because he or she participates (at least to some degree) in a form of life. Wittgenstein asks rhetorically, Is it because dogs are too honest that they do not lie? This is to point to a form of life quite distinct from our human life to indicate that "honest" and "lying" have no role or function or use in the kind of life a dog leads. Likewise, within human life, there are many forms, and the meaning or use of some words are to be understood by a knowledge or understanding of a form of life. Religious language, for example, has its place in a form of life to which particular individuals may or may not have access. Wittgenstein says he has some idea of what it means to say that God is a judge, but none whatsoever for saying God is a creator. This does not license him to say "a creator" is a meaningless notion, as it might have done with his earlier views of language. Rather it indicates to him that he does not have a sufficient understanding of religious language because of a lack of understanding of a form of life.

Wittgenstein was particularly concerned with the confusions which result from a misuse of language. When words are taken from their place in a form of life (when language "goes on a holiday," i.e., is not doing its proper work) or when a person does not have a sufficient mastery of the use of particular words, confusions result. For example, a person might ask, "Where is 6:30?" because of a misunderstanding of the "logic" or "grammar" of the expression "6:30." (It is not the sort of thing which has a place. This correction is a grammatical point, as Wittgenstein would say.) Philosophy was viewed by Wittgenstein as a way to clear up confusions or to prevent them by means of the grammar or logic of words. Philosophy thus should not seek to resolve problems by giving new answers for inadequate ones. For example, consider the mind-body problem. One way to deal with it is to show that Descartes' "interactionism" is utterly inadequate, and then to try to find another answer for the relation between the mind and body, such as that of Spinoza's double aspect theory or Leibniz's preestablished harmony. Wittgenstein proposed that instead of giving another philosophic theory, we reexamine the language used to describe our thought, perceptions, actions, and bodies so as to enable us to see that Descartes poses a pseudo-problem. It is not that we need a better answer than Descartes'; it is rather for philosophy to enable one to see that a problem (if a philosophical one) is a pseudo one. Wittgenstein compared philosophy to psychological therapy: what one needs is not an answer but a cure.

We may conclude our presentation of phenomenology and analytic philosophy by indicating some ways in which phenomenology and linguistic philosophy converge. Phenomenology, with its stress on the intentionality of consciousness, and linguistic philosophy, with its stress on language games, use, and forms of life, are both concerned with meaning. They both have begun to interest theologians because they suggest new ways to understand the meaning of theological and biblical language. Each approach encourages a person to attend more carefully to discourse, the relations of people to discourse, and to kinds of discourse (e.g., narrative, liturgy, parable). Husserl was famous for telling people to "look to the things" and to describe them. Likewise Wittgenstein used to say, "Don't think, look." Both are admonitions to break free of some theory or preconception which distorts and to attend carefully to what is actually before one, in an intentional act or object, or in the use of a word, respectively. Neither offers a system of thought on which one may base Christian doctrines as one may on Platonic, Aristotelian, Kantian, Hegelian, or process thought. One should also not be misled into thinking that there is *a* phenomenological method or *a* linguistic method. There are many different ways in which people in each movement practice phenomenology and linguistic philosophy. Differences are often significant. In addition, the methods are not easily learned; they are skills. To learn such skills requires considerable practice, usually under the supervision of someone who is very good at the practice already. That phenomenology and linguistic philosophy are skills rather than doctrines to be learned as indicated by the fact that people in both movements talk about "doing phenomenology" and "doing philosophy" instead of learning *about* phenomenology or linguistic philosophy. That they are skills very hard to learn is indicated by the fact that there are very few people who can perform easily in both ways, or even appreciate both methods. To me perhaps the greatest value of both approaches is an attitude of expectancy, an attitude in which a person allows a phenomenon or a reality spoken of to emerge and to exhibit itself, so to speak. The attitude is similar to the appreciation of creative art in which one attends and allows an object to reveal itself. This is true even though both Husserl and Wittgenstein achieve this result by rigorous thinking and analysis. In neither does one find philosophy practiced as though it were merely the manipulation and arrangement of matters already well understood.

It should be mentioned that the iconoclasm of logical positivism may have misled people into thinking that linguistic philosophy is not as open to religion as is phenomenology. A first-hand acquaintance would show that it is cultural secularism rather than anything inherent in the practice of linguistic philosophy which accounts for the coolness toward Christianity on the part of many of its leading practitioners.

The most recent philosophical development of theological interest, hermeneutics, actually has its source in a theologian, Friedrich Schleiermacher (1768–1834). Wilhelm Dilthey (1833–1911) is credited with having recognized a new discipline in Schleiermacher and with not only reviving it but significantly reshaping it. In this century, hermeneutics has developed considerably under the stimulus of Bultmann's demythologizing project. It has also been heavily influenced by Heidegger's work, especially as developed by his disciple Hans Georg Gadamer, and there is a significant stream which flows from Marcel through Paul Ricoeur. Excellent surveys of hermeneutics and its role in both biblical and theological reflection are available. Our concern is the modest one of treating a few crucial philosophical concepts in the discipline.

The discipline of hermeneutics—or the problems and principles of interpretation—has its roots in the rise of historical consciousness. Dilthey is responsible for insisting that the methods and explanations in the natural sciences are unsuited for gaining historical understanding. Historical understanding is not a matter of explaining events and processes in terms of general laws. Rather history concerns human life, and only because we are human beings ourselves can we project ourselves into the experiences of others. History is understood only *through* ourselves. In addition, we also understand ourselves through history. We enlarge our own present experience through our understanding of the past.

Dilthey tried to mark the distinction between the natural sciences (*Naturwissenschaften*) and the human sciences (*Geisteswissen-schaften*) by his stress on "lived experience." He used the word *Erlebnis* (experience) in a new way to convey the notion that human experience is embedded in the stream of life, and we can view and understand the human sciences only through participation in that stream. Human experience has a connectedness—a reference beyond what is thought of as the subjective data of mere introspection. The participation of a human being in lived experience—which both makes history accessible to us and which also makes us, through history, accessible to ourselves—is absent from the natural sciences. They treat the human subject and its objects in isolation from each other, so that the matrix of concepts in the natural sciences are "objective." But the human disciplines are embedded in human life and cannot be properly understood by such "objective" concepts, or in isolation from lived experience. They rely upon an involvement with life which precedes the split or division between subject and object.

At one point in his career Dilthey was interested in Husserl's work because Husserl seemed to be breaking new ground in showing a way to avoid the tyranny of those disciplines whose concepts were formed by isolating subjects from objects. Indeed Husserl's doctrine of the intentionality of consciousness does seek to overcome the subject-object dilemma. This dilemma can be characterized as follows. On the one hand, there are three options. We may treat the self (subject) as known but the existence of its objects as doubtful, as in Descartes. We may have objects constituted by the self so that the existence of objects independent of the subject is denied, as in Berkeley. Or we may reduce what we are aware of to mere appearances and have objects as "things-in-themselves" and utterly unknowable, as in Kant. On the other hand, we may begin with objects as bundles of sense qualities as real, as in Hume, and reduce the self to a bundle of sense qualities. If we emphasize the subject, objects tend to be lost (doubtful, denied, or unknowable); if we make objects fundamental, the subject tends to be lost (to be reduced to sense qualities). This impasse is broken, supposedly, by Husserl's intentionality of consciousness, in which objects do not exist with a subject, but equally there is no subject without objects. Dilthey himself never appropriated Husserl's work, but various forms of the intentionality of consciousness became the foundation of hermeneutics as practiced from the perspective of phenomenology, a perspective which has dominated the discipline. Dilthey himself was aware that his insight into the indispensibility of participation in life for historical understanding and for human disciplines needed stronger philosophical support than he himself had provided.

Another aspect, not confined to Dilthey but greatly emphasized by him, is a temporal or historical dimension to all understanding. From our study of history we have become conscious that the character of all human experience, concepts, and institutions are conditioned by time, place, and circumstance. This is nicely captured by a term used by Husserl and adopted in hermeneutics, "horizon." All of us live within a horizon, and we perceive and understand within the limits of that horizon.

This brings us to the "hermeneutical question," as it is called, the question of how to understand or to interpret texts from periods and cultures that are not our own. Just as we exist within a horizon, so too does a particular text have its own horizon. We thus have the world of the text and the world of the interpreter. Hermeneutics is the study of the principles of how we bring them together so that understanding is possible. Such an understanding is said to involve a "fusion of horizons," a phrase coined by Gadamer.

This fusion involves what is called the "hermeneutical circle." It has two aspects. First, our horizon provides us with a "preunderstanding." It affects the way we regard and understand a text. It is from within our own presuppositions that we treat it. This can be thought of as a bad thing, as if we must be stripped of all presuppositions and understand a text from its own point of view to achieve "objectivity." There are indeed many serious problems connected with a subjective reading, in the perverse sense of subjective. Those influenced by various forms of the doctrine of the intentionality of consciousness stress that there is no such thing as a pure object or pure understanding. Such a "realist" conception—of an object knowable apart from any involvement of a subject—is a fiction. Rather it is precisely because we have a horizon (preunderstanding) that we are able to interpret and to seek to understand a text at all. This is not to say that this solves our difficulty. It is actually a way to state the hermeneutical problem, namely, how do we move from our horizon toward a fusion of our world with that of the world of the text? This is achieved, in part, (it is claimed) by putting *our* questions to the text, and then in turn being affected by the text itself, so that our own self-understanding (horizon) is reshaped by the text. A constant back and forth between our world and the world of the text moves us closer and closer to a "fusion of horizons."

It is in this context that tradition and narrative theology have received support from hermeneutics, and in turn have contributed to hermeneutics. Our preunderstanding or our horizon by which we are able to understand a text at all, is affected by our participation in various traditions. All of us see from, understand from, interpret from some tradition or other which has formed and continues to form us. This tradition gives us access to other horizons and in particular to the past and is not something to be shed. Narrative theology is a particular form by which some traditions are passed on and by which some people participate in them. The structure and functions of stories, or narratives, are examined as a way to approach the Bible and to interpret it. There are, of course, important questions to be considered about how we may criticize our own tradition and reshape it, but this does not mean that we ever perceive or understand apart from some matrix of culture.

The second aspect of the fusion of horizons has to do with a principle that runs from Hegel right through Gadamer: the parts must be viewed in terms of the whole. Not only does this principle hold in trying to understand a word in terms of a sentence, a sentence in terms of the larger context of a paragraph, and so on, but of an entire text in terms of a culture, and of a culture itself within an ever widening circle. The principle suggests that short of "absolute knowledge," in Hegel's sense, a text is never exhausted, but it is capable of shedding new meaning and significance beyond the interpretation of any period. It also means that the meaning of a text is not identical with the intention or self-consciousness of its author but may have and take on meaning beyond the author's intention or awareness.

Heidegger is largely responsible for turning the discipline of hermeneutics in the particular direction of opening it up to transcendent dimensions. His analysis of human existence or *Dasein* can be viewed as part of his attack on the split between subject and object. His analysis is an attempt to present the world given *with Dasein*, prior to the split into subject and object, and prior to conceptualization. To this extent *Dasein* is comparable to Dilthey's notion of lived experience in which "truth" is not something one sticks onto propositions or to naked objects but is accessible only to one grounded in human existence. For Heidegger, however, "objectifying" tendencies cut us off from truth that is unavailable not only to the natural sciences but also to the human sciences, including philosophy as generally practiced. *Dasein* gives us access to Being or at least is a way into Being.

Gadamer drew upon Heidegger's reflections, and his own creative work has greatly shaped current hermeneutical discussion. One major shift from Heidegger is that Gadamer starts his analysis with the self in community and within a tradition, rather than the solitary self of *Dasein*. In Gadamer's major work *Truth and Method* (1960), he develops an analogy between play and art. When we play a game, we are absorbed in the play. The game creates a world into which we enter and take part. It is the game's reality, not the thoughts of the players, which give the play reality. Likewise, a work of art is not to be reduced to an "aesthetic experience." A work of art has its true being in the fact that it becomes an experience that changes the person who experiences it. What remains and endures is not the subjects who have experiences but the work of art itself. Both play and art draw a person into their areas and fill a person with their reality. A picture, for example, creates an *ontological* event in which truth is disclosed in the present.

A text operates in a similar fashion. Its language, as we seek to understand it, draws us into its world (its horizon). As in the case of a picture, disclosure takes place, so that understanding is an ontological event (a change in our being). Eventful language is grounded in Being rather than in merely human thought, however. For both Heidegger and Gadamer, neither language nor art can be reduced to what can be contained in an individual consciousness.

Gadamer's work has clear implications for biblical interpretation. Bultmann had posed the problem of biblical hermenuetics as the gap between the world of the text, in which there are supernatural interventions in the natural world, and our own horizon, in which such thinking is (allegedly) mythical. The issue of how "acts of God" in the biblical accounts are to be interpreted is thus critical, and indeed this question is still very much with us in biblical interpretation. The discussion has been influenced by the view of understanding a work of art and the world of a text as ontological events, permitting the introduction of a transcendent dimension into the question of the fusion of our horizon with that of the biblical horizon. It has led to the concept of divine disclosure through the biblical text as a "word-event" in the work of Ernst Fuchs and Gerhard Ebeling. The text's disclosures to human understanding are moments with an ontological dimension, as eventful language is grounded in Being rather than in merely human subjective states. (This approach is often referred to as the "new hermeneutics" because disclosures and changes in our self-understanding are not subjective or reducible to human consciousness only, as seems to be the case in Schleiermacher and Bultmann.)

Our study began with a stress on the mystery of God as the foundation of all Christian theology. It is perhaps fitting that we conclude it by mentioning the title of a recent book in hermeneutics, that of Eberhard Jüngel, *God as the Mystery of the World*. Its very title suggests that perhaps theology has not completely forgotten that it must forever wrestle with the mystery of God, recognizing that God is beyond the powers of our intellect and yet if we recognize this, we may find that the intellect is illumined with understanding.

Suggested Reading

Armstrong, A. H., ed. *The Cambridge History of Later Greek and Early Medieval Philosophy*. Cambridge, England: Cambridge University Press, 1967. Covers philosophy from Aristotle to about A.D. 1000 and includes Arabic and Jewish thought.

Armstrong, A. H., and R. A. Marcus. *Christian Faith and Greek Philosophy*. London: Darton, Longman & Todd, 1960; New York: Sheed and Ward, 1964. Compares Christianity and Greek philosophy on ten topics, each author contributing five essays. Brief but rich.

Armstrong, A. H. *Plotinian and Christian Studies*. London: Varicrum, 1979. A collection of previously published articles on diverse topics. Although Armstrong's Roman Catholic convictions are clear, he shows great sympathy for Plotinus.

Burtt, E. A. *The Metaphysical Foundations of Modern Physical Science*, 2d ed. rev. Atlantic Highlands, N.J.: Humanities Press, 1967. First published in 1924, but in spite of the growth of scholarship, it remains sound and irreplaceable on the shift from an Aristotelian physics to a mechanistic one and the implications of that shift.

Butterfield, Herbert. *The Origins of Modern Science, 1300–1800*, rev. New York: Free Press, 1965. Not as technical as Burtt but a splendid study.

Cochrane, Charles Norris. *Christianity and Classical Culture: A Study of Thought and Action from Augustus to Augustine*, rev. New York: Oxford University Press, 1957. Emphasizes the Latin or Western church.

Copleston, Frederick C. *History of Philosophy*, 10 vols. Ramsey, N.J.: Paulist Press, first published 1946–66. Well-written, balanced account.

Edwards, Paul, ed. *The Encyclopedia of Philosophy*, 4 vols. New York: Macmillan Publishing Company, 1972. Useful to compare its articles to the *New Catholic Encyclopedia* because the emphasis is frequently different.

Evans-Pritchard, E. E. *Theories of Primitive Religion*. Oxford: at the Clarendon Press, 1965. A major anthropologist unmasks naturalistic or atheistic accounts of religion as unscientific.

Foster, Michael B. "Christian Theology and Modern Science of Nature," two parts. *Mind* 44, 45 (1935, 1936). Foundational studies which helped change the view of Christianity as opposed to the rise of modern science.

Foster shows the positive, indeed indispensable contribution of Christianity to the rise of our science.

Foster, Michael B. *Mystery and Philosophy.* Westport, Conn.: Greenwood Press, 1980. Reissue of the 1956 original. An uncompromising contrast of Christianity and analytic philosophy, with a brilliant presentation of the nature of mystery in Greek and Christian thought. The finest single response to analytic philosophy. Brief.

Gilson, Étienne H. *History of Christian Philosophy in the Middle Ages.* New York: Random House, 1955.

Hartshorne, Charles. *The Divine Relativity: A Social Conception of God.* New Haven, Conn.: Yale University Press, 1948. A classical statement of process philosophy.

Jones, William T. *A History of Western Philosophy*, 5 vols. New York: Harcourt, Brace and World, Inc., 1969–75. Very lively, with good selections from the philosophers covered, but not always reliable on Christian theologians.

Kenny, Anthony, Norman Kretzmann, Jan Pinborg. *The Cambridge History of Later Medieval Philosophy: From the Rediscovery of Aristotle to the Disintegration of Scholasticism, 1100–1600.* Cambridge, England: Cambridge University Press, 1982. Companion volume of Armstrong's Cambridge history. Consists of a collection of essays on virtually every aspect of philosophy in the period covered by more than forty contributors.

MacIntyre, Alasdair. *After Virtue.* Notre Dame, Ind.: University of Notre Dame, 1981. A major study of classical and modern ethical theories, analyzing the present breakdown in ethical philosophy.

New Catholic Encyclopedia, 15 vols. New York: McGraw-Hill, 1967. Suppl. vol. 16, 17. Washington, D.C.: Publishers Guild, Inc., in association with McGraw-Hill, 1974, 1979. An invaluable reference work.

Palmer, R. E. *Hermeneutics: Interpretation Theory in Schleiermacher, Dilthey, Heidegger, and Gadamer.* Evanston, Ill.: Northwestern University Press, 1969. This book and that by Thiselton supplement each other nicely.

Passerin d'Entreves, A. *Natural Law: An Introduction to Legal Philosophy*, 2d ed., rev. Atlantic Highlands, N.J.: Humanities Press, 1964. Brief and authoritative.

Passmore, John. *A Hundred Years of Philosophy*, 2d ed. London: Duckworth and Co., 1966. Rev. ed. New York: Basic Books, 1966, 1967.

Sokolowski, Robert. *The God of Faith and Reason: Foundations of Christian Theology.* Notre Dame, Ind.: University of Notre Dame, 1982. An example of the value of a phenomenological approach in theology, without the jargon of phenomenology.

Spiegelberg, Herbert. *The Phenomenological Movement: A Historical Introduction*, 3d ed. The Hague: Martinus Nijhoff, 1982.

Thiselton, Anthony C. *The Two Horizons: New Testament Hermeneutics and Philosophical Description with Special Reference to Heidegger, Bultmann, Gadamer, and Wittgenstein,* Exeter: Paternoster Press, 1980. Grand Rapids, Mich.: Wm. B. Eerdmans Publishing Company, 1980.

Tice, Terrence N. and Thomas P. Slavens. *Research Guide to Philosophy* Chicago: American Library Association, 1983. Gives a brief survey of every historical period and sixteen subdivisions of philosophy, with a statement of the present state of scholarship and bibliography. Emphasis is on philosophy since the eighteenth century.

Waismann, Friedrich. *The Principles of Linguistic Philosophy.* Edited by Rom. Hare. New York: St. Martin's Press, 1965. Comprehensive and beautifully written.

Warnock, G. J. *English Philosophy since 1900.* London: Oxford University Press, 1958. Short, elementary, instructive, well-written.

Weinberg, Julius R. *A Short History of Medieval Philosophy.* Princeton, N.J.: Princeton University Press, 1964.

Index